SURFACE AND DEPTH

MICHAEL T. GILMORE

SURFACE AND *Depth*

The Quest for Legibility in American Culture

OXFORD
UNIVERSITY PRESS

2003

OXFORD
UNIVERSITY PRESS

Oxford   New York

Auckland   Bangkok   Buenos Aires   Cape Town   Chennai
Dar es Salaam   Delhi   Hong Kong   Istanbul   Karachi   Kolkata
Kuala Lumpur   Madrid   Melbourne   Mexico City   Mumbai   Nairobi
São Paulo   Shanghai   Taipei   Tokyo   Toronto

Copyright © 2003 by Oxford University Press, Inc.

Published by Oxford University Press, Inc.
198 Madison Avenue, New York, New York 10016

www.oup.com

Oxford is a registered trademark of Oxford University Press

Library of Congress Cataloging-in-Publication Data
Gilmore, Michael T.
Surface and depth : the quest for legibility in American culture /
Michael T. Gilmore
   p. cm.
Includes bibliographical references and index.
ISBN 0-19-515776-1
1. American prose literature.—History and criticism.
2. Social problems in literature. 3. National Characteristics,
American, in literature. 4. American fiction—History and criticism.
5. Literature and society—United States. 6. United States—In literature.
7. United States—Civilization. I. Title.
PS366.S62 G55 2002
818'.08—dc21   2002002636

9 8 7 6 5 4 3 2 1

Printed in the United States of America
on acid-free paper

ACKNOWLEDGMENTS

In writing this book, I have benefited enormously from the generosity of friends and colleagues. I was invited to deliver various pieces of the manuscript as public lectures, and the occasions spurred me to clarify my thinking, as well as exposing me to the incisive comments (and objections) of audience members. At a very early stage in the project, I presented my ideas to the American Studies faculty at Brandeis; thanks to Joyce Antler for inviting me. I also wish to thank Lawrence Buell, who asked me to speak before the History of American Civilization colloquium at Harvard; Millicent Bell, Teresa A. Goddu, and Leland S. Person, guiding spirits behind the sesquicentennial anniversary conference on *The Scarlet Letter*, where I first tried out my reading of Hawthorne's novel; Cindy Weinstein, my wonderful host at the California Institute of Technology (whose senior thesis on Melville, I am proud to say, I directed twenty years ago); Martin Jay and Catherine Gallagher, who arranged a lecture at Berkeley; Winfried and Birgitta Fluck, with whom I stayed when I spoke at the John F. Kennedy Institute for North American Studies at the Free University of Berlin, and who introduced me to the city's remarkable cultural life; and my former colleague Anne Janowitz, whose guest I was at Queen Mary College at the University of London.

My friend Philip Fisher read the manuscript in its entirety and offered invaluable suggestions and support. Steven J. Whitfield and John Burt, friends and colleagues at Brandeis, also read the whole book and gave me the benefit of their encyclopedic knowledge of American culture. Other readers provided detailed critiques of individual chapters, and it is a pleasure to acknowledge the help of Grant Rice, Michael McKeon, Lewis Wurgaft, and Eugene Goodheart. I had stimulating exchanges with Malcolm Slavin and Steven Varga-Golovscenko about psychoanalysis; with Martin Bruckner about the American landscape; with Andrew Matthews about environmental legibility; with Mary Childers about the ineffable, or that which resists articulation; with Sacvan Bercovitch about Americans and Freud (Saki is my source for the statistic in the prologue about the concentration of analysts in Newton, Massachusetts); with James Obelkevich about American and European attitudes toward sexuality; with James M. O'Toole, about the Catholic confessional; and with Janna Malamud-Smith about privacy, publicity, and the ordeal of starting a new book. I was fortunate to have Elissa Morris as an editor at Oxford University Press. She was a model of promptness and consideration, and she obtained trenchant readings of the manuscript from Marjorie Perloff and Richard Gray.

My greatest debt, as always, is to my family. My daughters, Emma and Rosa, treated my dinnertime lectures with teenage irreverence and prevented me from taking myself too seriously. Deborah Valenze, my wife, continues to be my best and wisest reader. She was always willing to take time from her own work to look at mine, and the book is immeasurably better for her advice. For this, and for a thousand other things, I am more grateful than I can say.

"Hidden in Plain Sight: *The Scarlet Letter* and American Legibility" originally appeared in *Studies in American Fiction* 29 (spring 2001), 121–28; "Freud and Film Redux" was first published under the title "Renovation and Privacy at the Fin-de-Siècle" as Working Paper No. 126/2001 by the John F. Kennedy-Institut für Nordamenikastudien.

CONTENTS

INTRODUCTION

This project had its genesis in a puzzling historical convergence. I had written a book on the cinema as a quintessential American art form and had noticed, as many people have, that the motion pictures originated at the same time Sigmund Freud devised psychoanalysis, in the 1890s. A technology of visual surfaces arose contemporaneously with a technique for sounding the human depths. Further reflection added a detail of special interest to me as a student of American culture: the two inventions had been welcomed in the United States as nowhere else. Not that they had been pioneered here (though an argument can be made for the movies), or developed important innovations on these shores, or found their most subtle practitioners among Americans. But it was precisely the circumstance of their eager and relatively uncritical adoption—the acceptance of *both* of them—by Americans that piqued my curiosity. After all, they would appear to have little or nothing in common. Freud himself regarded the effortlessly ingested cinematic image as the antipode of his demanding intellectual discipline. The joint compatibility of film and the talking cure with the United States was the catalyst that led to *Surface and Depth*.

To solve the puzzle, I felt it necessary to look back from the 1890s to the nation's past. I thought it might be possible to locate a disposition or cultural dynamic, something that antedated the movies and psychoanalysis and was capable of illuminating American receptivity to them (and that presumably abides to this day). What I kept finding, as I reviewed documentary staples from the nation's settlement and founding, was an impulse that I am calling the demand for legibility. It seemed undeniable to me that American culture had been preoccupied from its beginnings with the wish, the requirement, to know and to make accessible. I saw this imperative at work in early religious writings dedicated to the formation of a translucent Bible Commonwealth; in blueprints for ideal cities and for the organization of the landscape; and in political manifestoes that established a written moment of origin for the polity and mandated public oversight of governmental decision making.

The three illustrations I have just mentioned can be related to a single historical circumstance: the absence of a feudal tradition. As a result of its tardy birth, the New World did not have to be dragged into modernity, and it would be possible, in a general way, to describe the subject of this book as America's precedence as the first modern society, a culture that has always been "enlightened" and entrepreneurial. Two theorists of the modern, Karl Marx and Hans Blumenberg, offer implicit support for this view. Both regard the transition from the medieval past as a process of disenchantment. Marx, in *The Communist Manifesto* (1848), speaks of capitalism as an economic system without illusions. The bourgeoisie, he writes in a famous sentence, "has played a most revolutionary part" in stripping away the naturalized "ties" with which the feudal order veiled competition between the classes. As the cash nexus displaced mystifying hierarchies, man was "at last compelled to face with sober senses, his real conditions of life, and his relations with his kind."[1]

Blumenberg reaches a similar conclusion about "the legitimacy of the modern age" (the title of his 1966 book). The spirit of inquiry that swept Europe in the Renaissance claimed as one of its first casualties traditionalism's deference to "the forbidden and the reserved." According to Blumenberg, the optical revolution of the telescope and the microscope inaugurated a new era in humanity's relationship to nature, and untrammeled curiosity, a delight in seeing and learning everything, emerged as the defining disposition of the modern.[2]

I might have followed Blumenberg and denominated my subject "American Visibility." The phenomenon itself has been remarked on by specialists in various disciplines and given a myriad of names. Availability, publicity, transparency, and "the paranoid style" are some familiar ones. Although at times I employ all these categories, and others, too, I decided to foreground the concept of legibility because it conveyed the idea of putting into language or writing. (Blumenberg is also the author of a book titled *Die Lesbarkeit der Welt* [1981], as yet untranslated, which can be rendered as *The Readability of the World.*) The first dictionary definition of "legible" is "capable of being read, esp. with ease," and this dictate seemed to encompass the disparate domains I was examining. Americans did not simply seek to canvass the surfaces and depths; they strove to give tangible, enunciated form to that ambition. They wanted to hear narratives about the operations of the Holy Spirit; to order the continent into lines and squares; and to afford citizens the opportunity to peruse a public enumeration of their rights and of the state's powers and limitations. They dreamed of a readerly, writerly world (to crib and conflate two terms from Roland Barthes). But they also craved ocular mastery over the physical environment, as exemplified, in a later day, by the moving pictures, and "legible" had the advantage of communicating this expectation as well. The second meaning given in the dictionary is "capable of being discerned or distinguished." In the American desideratum, visibility was to complement and facilitate ease of understanding, and a recurrent concern in this book is with the relationship between images and words as ways of knowing.

Yet ironies attend the choice of "legibility." They cluster around the uses of literature and other modes of mediated representation to cushion intrusiveness. Writing or print need not function this way, any more than speech has to be a medium of perfect candor. On the contrary, textuality's distancing can incite exhibitionism. Still, that distancing can also provide a sanctuary from exposure that in some ways is analogous to the quarantined confessionalism of the analyst's couch. So legibility, as used in this study, carries a third, seemingly contradictory, connotation: it can act as a brake on its own rush toward making known.

It should be emphasized that while *Surface and Depth* begins by considering a series of writings, and moves on to works of both high and popular art, it is not a return to some version of myths and symbols. Its subject is not the circulation of aesthetic tropes. The documents dealt with in chapter I initiated and gave shape to aspects of American religion, the American landscape, and American politics. These speeches, pamphlets, and public papers sponsored institutions and practices that have proven remarkably durable, in some cases spanning the virtual entirety of the culture's life. What interests me is the intersection of these discourses and historical realities with the forging of a national literature. Has legibility been an obsession of this country's writing? Have American authors over the centuries affirmed the drive for revelation or regarded it with skepticism?

I suggest that literary forms have been both complicit and at odds with the appetite to know. Popular genres, especially those concocted in the United States, have been apt to reinscribe the transparency ethos. The Western, to take a venerable example, exalts ocular dominion over nature. Cooper endows his famous Leatherstocking, Natty Bumppo, with a preternatural (or, more dramatically, cinematic) ability to vanquish space. The "private eye," hero of the urban detective story, possesses a comparable clairvoyance in psychology. For Poe's C. Auguste Dupin, insight into the human interior is a precondition for survival in the increasingly opaque modern metropolis.

Elite literature follows a more ambiguous course. Works such as Melville's *Moby-Dick*, or Hawthorne's *The Scarlet Letter*, or the fiction of Henry James and Edith Wharton, or Fitzgerald's *The Great Gatsby* have tended at once to embrace the knowledge wish and to check the urge to "strike through the mask." High art has sought to comprehend the white whale, to discover the secret of Hester's lover, to punish the Bellegardes by disclosing the family secret in *The American,* and to get to the bottom of the enigmatic figure of Gatsby. At the same time it has accepted the frustration of its quest and relinquished the possibility of knowledge or revenge or certainty.

I am only too aware of the fact that I am swimming against the disciplinary tide. With some notable exceptions, the idea of a common or shared American culture has held a distant second place in recent scholarship. The emphasis has been on difference. This focus is a salutary corrective to the grand synthetic overviews of an earlier generation. It has recuperated groups and perspectives marginalized or rendered imperceptible by the master narratives. Gender, race, and, to a much lesser degree, class have gained a new and welcome prominence in the American studies of the last two or three decades. As will become apparent, I have learned a great deal from these works and could not have conceived this book without them. But attention to the margins should not, in my opinion, preclude awareness of the center or abort attempts to understand the dominant structures and values that have shaped American experience.

Belief in openness has spawned one set of influential themes. As a concept or phenomenon, publicity is closer in spirit to Alexis de Tocqueville's "equality" than to the later overviews of, say, R. W. B. Lewis (*The American Adam* [1955]) or Leo Marx (*The Machine in the Garden* [1964]). It represents a societal commitment that has manifested itself across a continuum of physical sites, discourses, and activities. And like Tocqueville's equality, the imposition of legibility has been a catalyst for strife. Indeed, this is one of its defining characteristics: it has never been anything else than a contested terrain. The demand to ferret out the hidden has occluded in the very act of illuminating. American visibility, that is, has necessitated and produced American *in*visibility from the beginning. It will surprise nobody that the primary area of struggle has been race.

A second aspect of this study that qualifies as unfashionable is its claim of historical durability. *Surface and Depth* is diachronic rather than synchronic, and it is more attuned to continuities than to radical breaks. Though I hope I have benefited from Foucaultian and New Historicist scholarship, I cannot describe my work as deriving from those models. I depart from them not solely in my emphasis on persistence over time but also, as I have indicated, in my sense of the literary as multifaceted and sedimented in its engagement with an ideological bias. Rather than positing an unbroken field of discursive interchange, I argue for different responses to legibility by different authors and even by different subgenres. A certain cultural unevenness, or relative distance from consensual attitudes, seems as inescapable in the nation's past as it is in the present. We are all conscious of its workings in the books we read, the films we watch, and the cable television channels we stop at and surf past (though we may disagree in our assessments). Which is not to say, of course, that one cannot relish the popular without being thoroughly disaffected from the polity, or enjoy problematic works of art without otherwise embracing the doxa.

Moreover, I dissent from the antagonism with which Foucault and his followers have written of visibility. In a celebrated move, the French theorist demonized Jeremy Bentham's panopticon as an emblem of carceral society. This reading is a disservice to the English reformer. Bentham was no friend of monopolies of either power or knowledge. In contrast to a conservative like Walter Bagehot, who defended "mystery" as integral to the English constitution, Bentham favored opening government to popular scrutiny. He was the author of a famous essay, "Of Publicity," in which he advocated unfettered access to information as fatal to the designs of tyrants.[3]

I am quite prepared to admit, however, that the panopticon's institutionalizing of total scrutability, as a figure for the social order, can be as destructive of democratic procedures as obscurantism. Even when information flows are reciprocal and not a unilateral privilege of power, they can lead to excessive violations of individual rights. Panopticonism has been carried to ruinous lengths in American outbursts of political and religious paranoia. I touch on a number of these episodes, and their prevalence raises questions about the damages of legibility *as* legibility. The knowledge compulsion, that is, can do harm not just because of what it omits or suppresses, as in racial ostracism, but as a result of what it forces into the public forum. The sun's rays are not always wholesome, and they have shriveled the sphere of what is off limits in this country. Americans have turned to the law in an effort to mitigate the damage. Indeed, the arrogance of American publicity has been directly responsible for the prescience of the United States in formulating statutory protections for privacy. If modernity can be defined as the tacit made explicit, the United States is doubly a bellwether in its approach to private life: it has rendered into the manifest domains of legislation and law court that which, in other societies, has tended to be unstated and customary.[4]

Legal interest in secure zones of autonomy coincided with the emergence of the cinema and with Freud's conceiving of his mental therapy. The fin de siècle was the crucial moment for all three. I explore how this conjunction at once revitalized and complicated the American passion for legibility. Film and analysis decisively enlarged visual and introspective mastery, but they did so in cordoned-off or impersonal settings that enshrouded revelation in privacy. The proper relation of the public and the private, the accessible and the insulated, a theme constantly being negotiated in canonical literature, entered the lexicon of common culture. (The cinema's spectators formed an anonymous "crowd," said Vachel Lindsay, not the harmonious community of live theater.)[5] I weigh enthusiasm for the two innovations against the historical crosscurrents of massive immigration, urbanization, and the renewed push for openness signaled by Woodrow Wilson's election to the presidency.

As I noted at the outset of this introduction, my wonder at the American welcome to Freudianism and the movies germinated *Surface and Depth*. But the book is not an interpretation of either film or analytic theory. It attends to the two developments as structures of (circumscribed) revelation, but I am not concerned with particular films, which may defy clarity in story line, lighting, and denouement; nor with actual therapeutic practice, which must inevitably encounter disappointment and the limits of what can be known; nor with the agnosticism, or rather the pessimism, of Freud's later theorizing. The Freud who fascinated Americans was not the dark Freud of the death instinct and untreatable trauma. He was Freud the heroic healer and exposer of secrets, the all-wise physician who regularly likened his decryptions to the crime solving of the detective. (As he put it himself in his case study of Dora, "He that has eyes to see and ears to hear may convince himself that no mortal can keep a secret. If his lips are silent, he chatters with his finger-tips; betrayal oozes out of him at every pore.")[6] This supremely confident strain in psychoanalysis has as much weight as the skeptical side, and to dwell on either dimension without acknowledging the other is to miss the capaciousness of Freud's thought. If America's love affair with therapy has overstressed the legible, the French variant, epitomized by Jacques Lacan, has inflated the element of unreadability.[7]

My main subjects are *mentalité* and literature. By training and inclination I am most comfortable with literary texts, and after the historical review in the first chapter, I concentrate my attention on fiction and nonfiction in the American tradition. Except for chapter 5, Hollywood and psychoanalysis figure less as direct objects of inquiry than as a background presence or leitmotiv. In one context, they might appear as a kind of proleptic analogue to a literary strategy; in another, as influences and incentives; in a third, as a rival mode of dissecting motivation (which is how that much-abused precursor of psychoanalysis, phrenology, was widely viewed by writers in the nineteenth century). Where the two systems have perhaps been most compromised by the larger society's dynamic of disclosure and occlusion has been in their repetition of what fails to get seen. Both the cinema and the therapeutic profession have an inglorious history in the United States of racial exclusivity or ostracism.

American banishing of opacity has, in sum, met its undoing in the color line. The culture itself *created* the illegibility of race by denying nonwhites the right to be visible. The pattern stretches from the attempted extermination of the Indians; through the excision of Jefferson's draft attack on slavery from the Declaration of Independence; to the ghettoizing of blacks under segregation. And nothing has been more indisputably "exceptional" in the American narrative than the longevity of prohibitions against interracial mixture. Sullying the purity of white bloodlines with the additive of negritude was forbidden in many parts of the country for almost three hundred years.[8] How are we to explain the extremity and persistence of these discriminatory practices? Any possible answer must take account of the connection between equality and racial prejudice.

The absence of birth hierarchy among whites—initially a fact and then a dictate of law—distinguished the American settlements from other colonial societies. While internal divisions were kept to a minimum, and the privileged members bathed in light, boundary lines were drawn tightly around the community of equals and those outside its borders condemned to darkness. (It is not a coincidence, though it is not a sufficient cause either, that on the most literal level the unseen were people of dark pigment, the color of blindness or obstructed vision.) The linkage between parity and exclusion is touched on at several points throughout this study, briefly at the end of my remarks on Puritan sectarianism and again, more copiously, in my juxtaposition of Tocqueville and Gustave de Beaumont. The two Frenchmen's accounts of the Jacksonian United States, written at the same time and based on the same journey, together exemplify the inseparability of egalitarianism, the pedigree of race, and the enforced disappearance of racial outsiders.[9]

In literature, white reluctance to see otherness has been thematized in Melville's and Twain's disfigurements of the detective story, "Benito Cereno" and *Pudd'nhead Wilson,* mysteries of race where nothing gets irradiated; and in Ellison's *Invisible Man,* as well as in Philip Roth's meditation on Ellison's classic in *The Human Stain.* The corollary to erasure has been the security found by blacks behind the color line and in the blockage that has marked their dealings with whites, as indicated, for example, by Frederick Douglass's credo, "Trust no man." So we arrive at another irony: canonical art's attraction to obscurity has been most perfectly realized not in high literary culture itself (though Ellison's novel clearly belongs in that category) but in the writings of the "dispossessed," in the African-American tradition's refusal of the war on the illegible.

A few concluding words must be said about the heterodoxy, or perhaps heterogeneity, of the book's method. *Surface and Depth* contains a set of readings of literary texts, some quite detailed, others more concise. Many critics have noticed the prevalence of a concern with knowing in individual American classics, and I do not pretend to originality in every aspect of my interpretations. My aim is to demonstrate the existence of a thematic tradition and to enrich understanding of that tradition by connecting it to a larger imperative. Thus in addition to textual analysis, this study brings together a multiplicity of historical and cultural materials. My choices have been broad and protean, and they include examples that seldom appear in conjunction with each other: Winthrop's "Model of Christian Charity" and the antebellum infatuation with phrenology; prophecy's obsession with dates and numbers and the testing of schoolchildren to measure intelligence; an analysis of the cinema as exemplifying the mind's laws and a call for reformation of the political system. At first glance, readers may find this profusion bewildering. I have been willing to take the risk because I believe that that the data assembled from many sources in chapter 1 (and, to a lesser degree, in chapter 5) cumulatively build a strong case for my thesis. The very multifariousness of the evidence demonstrates the diffusion and the persistence of the commitment to publicity.

Even so, there are institutions and cultural habits that plainly do not fit my model. One area where Americans have arguably trailed in openness is sexual representation, or more bluntly pornography, which has a history of suppression in this country going back to Anthony Comstock in the nineteenth century. (Though Whitman is as sexually explicit as any major European poet; Americans popularized the empirical study of sexual behavior with Alfred Kinsey and Masters and Johnson; and the federal government has now entered the business of pornography by publishing the Starr Report.)[10] American history reveals as well as the inevitable ebbings of legibility, periods when the principle has been dormant or when it has served as a kind of cover for deception and dishonesty. It would be folly to pretend that such backslidings from openness do not exist. In chapter 5 I investigate one case from the early twentieth century, Progressivism's campaign to revive the accessibility seemingly obliterated by the dislocations of industrialism. My point is that the trends discussed in this study have been an overweening force in the nation's life, with rededication to the familiar ideal following almost every setback. Counterexamples, of which I focus on two—privacy as a refuge from cognitive imperialism, and race as the limit of American knowing—may qualify the reach of the legible. They do not refute the reality of its cultural importance.

SURFACE AND DEPTH

Freud's Night Out

It is a familiar story, lavish of portents and ironies. The year is 1909. The founder of psychoanalysis is invited to Clark University in Worcester, Massachusetts, to lecture on his discovery and to receive his first and only honorary degree. This precocious academic accolade presages the curious cultural trajectory of Freud's dark and "Jewish science." In the sophisticated Old World, his ideas languish. An Englishman here, a Frenchman there, a handful of Swiss: other than Jews, the converts are few. The very different reception in the United States astonishes everyone, perhaps the progenitor most of all. The land of pragmatism, optimism, egalitarianism, and mass entertainment becomes the twentieth century's "fortress psychoanalysis," the redoubt of a rarefied technology of mind that filters down into popular culture in bastardized forms while never losing its elite prestige.

So goes the narrative—minus a highly suggestive incident that occurred during the very first moments of Freud's American sojourn. This particular event seldom finds its way into the canonical retellings. (Though it does get mentioned in E. L. Doctorow's *Ragtime* [1975].) Not that the omission surprises: the detail is so apparently trivial, so peripheral to the larger matters at hand, that without the eyewitness report of Ernest Jones, it would almost certainly have disappeared from history. After arriving in New York, according to Jones, Freud's party (which included his disciples Carl Jung and Sandor Ferenczi) spent several days exploring the city as tourists. They paid visits to Columbia University, Central Park, Coney Island, and the Metropolitan Museum. One night the group assembled to dine at "Hammerstein's Roof Garden, afterwards going on to see one of the primitive films of those days with plenty of wild chasing. Ferenczi in his boyish way was very excited about it, but Freud was only quietly amused; it was the first film they had seen."[1]

One would not wish to assign too much meaning to this anecdote, sketchy as it is. Still, the intersection on American soil of the cinematic medium and the pioneer of inward exploration has a certain rightness, a felicity that highlights one of the defining conjunctions of our time. Even as he introduced Americans to psychoanalysis, which was to naturalize itself as the age's signature intellectual discourse, Freud was introduced to the movies in the homeland from which this demotic art form spread outward to conquer the globe. High and low, specialized and popular, met briefly on a September evening in New York, and the United States was never again the same, never less than the cutting edge of the twin modalities of the modern. By 1915, when D. W. Griffith released *The Birth of a Nation*, the classical Hollywood style was already embarked on its triumphant march to international filmic hegemony. Within a decade of Freud's Worcester visit, the United States was far outstripping not just his native Austria but the whole of Europe in acceptance and institutionalization of the new therapy. And by the date of the master's death, in 1939, the psychoanalytic center of gravity had shifted definitively across the Atlantic, borne westward with a generation of Jewish practitioners in flight from the Nazis.

Among the many questions prompted by this confluence is the inevitable "why?" Why did the two phenomena, cinema and the therapy of self-revelation, take almost simultaneous root in the United States? What made them so congenial to Americans that they assumed, for much of the twentieth century, an undeniably American accent (overlaying a German one, in the case of psychoanalysis)? How has Hollywood, USA, managed to coexist so comfortably with Newton, Massachusetts, USA, a suburb of Boston with a population of eighty-two thousand that is home to an astonishing 2 percent of the planet's total number of psychoanalysts?

CHAPTER I

Three Foundational Documents
and Their Indelibility

L egibility has been braided into the American ethos from its origins—indeed, before its origins.[1] The continent loomed like Moby Dick before European eyes: a vast, blank, white slate, from one perspective a great mystery but a mystery upon which the colonial imagination was determined to write order and coherence. The New World's alleged emptiness stoked the urge to know it. "That inscrutable thing is chiefly what I hate," roared Ahab in a statement that can be taken as the American credo. The harpoon-pen in its many avatars has always sought to fill the void (or, if one prefers, the tabula rasa) with luminous and sometimes lethal script.

Originary documents affirming the banishment of inscrutability stretch from the settlement of Boston to the founding of the nation. Three of abiding interest are John Winthrop's "A Model of Christian Charity," a lay sermon delivered to the Puritan emigrants aboard the flagship *Arbella* in 1630; William Penn's plan for the city of Philadelphia, actually a series of projections including a map by the province's surveyor general, Thomas Holme; and the Declaration of Independence, drafted by Thomas Jefferson and given its final shape by the Second Continental Congress in 1776. The Declaration was midwife to two related documents, which I will also consider: the Constitution and *The Federalist Papers*.

On the most obvious level, our three principal texts address religious duties, environmental planning, and politics. But they do not limit themselves to their announced subjects. The writings by Winthrop, Penn, and Jefferson—one a New Englander, the second the father of Pennsylvania, the third a southerner—branch out into all manner of cognate areas, regularly overlapping with each other's concerns, and all set down terms that have persisted in one form or another throughout the country's history. Revisions and transformations, though they have been rife, have not undone the Ahabian imperative.

I will take up the three documents in order of composition. Under each heading are included reflections on some relevant legacies.

"A Model of Christian Charity"

> God Almighty in his most holy and wise providence hath so disposed of the condition of mankind, as in all times some must be rich, some poor, some high and eminent in power and dignity, others mean and in subjection. (p. 82)[2]

It seems on the surface an effort to restore an almost feudal organicism. Winthrop's vision of a structured collectivity with duties and obligations across class lines has a misleadingly regressive air. In actuality, his words are an invitation to the future, or to an oxymoron, an organicism of volition. The American Puritans were the beneficiaries of belatedness. Their movement arose as the premodern civilization of the Middle Ages was breaking up. To this circumstance, the absence of a feudal order in the country's past, the political scientist Louis Hartz long ago attributed the resilience in America of the liberal tradition. But feudalism was not simply a system of social and political hierarchy. It was also a form of religious organization with monasticism at its center. And no group was ever more zealous in proscribing the monastic way of life and making faith a matter of visibility than the settlers of Massachusetts Bay.[3]

England under Henry VIII had dissolved the monastic communities. Reformers criticized the orders for encouraging a sequestered sanctimony. They rejected monks and nuns as a spurious religious elite claiming special access to God. Henceforth, said the reformers, there were to be only Christians, evident to all in their mundane activities, and no more spiritualists of privilege hiding behind closed doors. Or, as Max Weber put it, in his famous account of the "Protestant ethic and the spirit of capitalism," "every Christian had to be a monk all his life."[4]

The monasteries were but the first bastion of secrecy to fall, for the Puritan emigrants sought to suffuse their entire experiment with light. Monkhood in the world entailed responsibilities that were doubly binding on a community of the regenerate. The settlers had entered into a voluntary covenant with God in separating from the mass of Englishmen. They had pledged to love one another and to honor his commandments. This compact, or "commission" (as Winthrop frequently calls it), required overt righteousness to succeed. Although the good works of Catholicism could no longer guarantee heaven, systematic moral conduct remained indispensable as a sign of salvation. It made public that which was in the heart. The Puritan had to submit his or her behavior to the eyes of others, both to manifest personal election and to corroborate the colony's status as a beacon for believers everywhere.

The best-known passage in Winthrop's utterance is that in which he enjoins his listeners to a standard of conspicuous piety: "For we must consider that we shall be as a city upon a hill. The eyes of all people are upon us" (p. 91). The famous line, though a paraphrase of Scripture (Matthew 5:14), may seem odd for a Puritan. Reformers were men and women of the word, not the image. They rejected sacred icons as papist residues, tokens of a creed of outward show. The image spoke to sight, not the understanding, yet Winthrop's phrase summons up a picture and is a call to observation. New England's shining gathering on the heights, visible to all, will inspire "succeeding plantations." The visual is already present among its acknowledged adversaries in a precocious consciousness of publicity. Like the other documents we will investigate, Winthrop's sermon assumes performance before a world audience. But his paraphrase of Matthew addresses the colonists themselves at least as much as those left behind in Europe. Although he omits the conclusion of the biblical verse, "cannot be hid," the Puritan leader never doubts that hiding is impossible in a covenanted settlement. Things unseen by men cannot escape the vigilance of God. Everyone must therefore keep watch on everyone else, because no individual can succumb to sin without all the saints suffering for the lapse. "A Model" is the first warrant for paranoia in American culture.

It was not long before these prescriptions hardened into routine practice. A habit of chronic surveillance denominated "holy watchfulness" became second nature among the early generations of Puritans. All colonists were expected to admonish the comportment of their neighbors, and all were mindful of carrying out their duties in the presence of spectators. Malefactors were punished in public, so that they experienced shame as well as guilt. Ministers corrected errant worshipers by detailing their sins in open congregation. Lawbreakers stood in the pillory or sat in the stocks, and some were branded, either with irons or with cloth letters sewn into their garments. Enforced conformity antedated Tocqueville's tyranny of the majority by two hundred years, with pressure to comply stemming from a similar consciousness of an omnipotent, all-seeing monitor, in this case one's fellow colonists augmented by the Deity whose wrath could devastate the settlement. In scrutinizing each other's smallest actions, the Puritans sought to forestall divine displeasure in the form of plague, Indian wars, and famine.[5]

Winthrop's sermon does not confine supervision to the eyes. His model commonwealth supplements optical policing with verbal judgment. He tells the voyagers that if they fulfill their mission they will be acclaimed around the globe. God "shall make us a praise and glory that men shall say of succeeding plantations, 'the Lord make it like that of New England.'"

But if we falter, Winthrop continues, a storm of verbal disgrace will rain down upon us. We will be "made a story and a by-word through the world," our sins will "open the mouths of enemies to speak evil of the ways of God," and our errand, instead of inspiring hosannas of gratitude, will turn the prayers of "God's worthy servants" into curses (p. 91).

This linguistic refrain, though not so celebrated as the "eyes of all people" line, pervades the *Arbella* speech, and it obviously fits in better with the Protestant exalting of "the Word." Reformers cherished divine communication as the instrument of grace. They believed that men and women experienced conversion by endlessly poring over the Scriptures and by hearing sermons in which God's ministry interpreted his will. These were practices intended, much like the dissolving of the monasteries, to make religious doctrine legible. God's address to his creatures should be accessible to all who could read and write and no longer the mystified expertise of a few. Immediately upon their arrival in Massachusetts, the colonists set up a printing press and founded Harvard College, the first to ensure a supply of Bibles (and other homiletic writings), the second to provide for a learned clergy. The American Puritans also established free schools long before they were adopted elsewhere.

Covenants are agreements requiring both speech and action. They evacuate the boundary between enunciation and behavior, and "A Model" locates this blurring at the commencement of the American venture. As Winthrop insists, the Puritans must make good on their word or promise, put it into praxis, or disaster will befall them. Even the Almighty is held to this standard—or, rather, he holds himself and men to it, in Genesis having demonstrated the necessary performative conjunction by inaugurating the cosmos, and the human saga, through speech. God fulfills his side of the covenant by bringing "us in peace to the place we desire," and we must seal our half of the bargain by "strict performance" of our professions. Anything less, and we proclaim ourselves "a perjured people" (pp. 90–91). Winthrop's ideal New England is to be a social order of such absolute clarity that nothing would separate what men say from what they do.

Another installment on Tocqueville's majoritarian tyranny? Something like this stricture occurred to Nathaniel Hawthorne when, writing in the same era as the Frenchman's visit, he imagined a Puritan commonwealth where the norm was pitiless exposure. Hawthorne was intrigued by his ancestors' disposition to make their deeds, and particularly their misdeeds, a subject of constant scrutiny. In *The Scarlet Letter* (1850), his adulterous heroine, Hester Prynne, has to endure the ignominy of being stared at by the entire community. Her exposure is verbal, too: in the novel's opening scene, the Reverend Mr. Wilson delivers a blistering sermon on her sin that lasts for over an hour. Hester herself is called upon to name her lover before the multitude. She resists this demand for nomination, and her defiant "I will not speak!" violates Puritan protocol as much as does her illicit sexuality. But Hester can find no refuge from publicity. The scarlet letter—a word masquerading as an icon—converts her into "the general symbol at which the preacher and moralist might point, and in which they might vivify and embody their images of woman's frailty and sinful passion."[6]

Behind Winthrop's call for a polity of truthful speech lay decades of revulsion from what the Puritans considered sacramental hypocrisy. Their exasperation was shortly to crystallize into a highly restrictive procedure for full admission to the Massachusetts churches. The first generation of settlers wanted nothing less than to institutionalize election. They fashioned a requirement for church communion that was an ecclesiology of the unattainable, an entry test designed to make the eternal, invisible fellowship of God palpable to men.

"A Model" teems with the language of choice, with the words "commission," "contract," "covenant," and "consent." Although compacts between rulers and the ruled date back to the Middle Ages, the Puritans' decision to remove physically from England gave their plighting a voluntaristic edge incompatible with the ascriptive past. The exiles may have wanted to see themselves as the true "church," successor to the Anglican establishment, but it is evident from Winthrop that they are "knit" together as a sect. They have separated thrice: first, from the homeland where they were born; second, from the parish system to which English birth entitled them; and third, from their inheritance as sons of Adam, "whence it comes that every man is born with this principle in him, to love and seek himself only." They are journeying together as a purified body in which membership "is the fruit of the new birth, and none can have it but the new creature" (p. 87). Every Puritan has professed himself or herself a disciple of Christ, profession being understood not as simple rote repetition, as the lip service it was in Europe, but as the ground of holiness in daily life: "Whatsoever we did or ought to have done when we lived in England, the same must we do, and more, where we go. That which the most in their churches maintain as a truth in profession only, we must bring into familiar and constant practice" (pp. 89–90).

But if the city on a hill is a sect, an exclusive congregation of the regenerate, how do the members perpetuate godliness and guard against pollution? What is to prevent indifferent Christians, with their perfunctory recitation of doctrine, from slipping in? The audacity, or perhaps presumption, of the American novelty lay in its attempted implementation on a universal scale. A conservative churchman like Augustine would have charged the colonists with an itch for forbidden knowledge. Augustine's attacks on "the lust of the eyes" governed orthodox scruples for centuries,[7] and he formulated his theory of the two churches as a check on unbridled curiosity.

According to the great theologian, one church was invisible and pure. It consisted of those predestined for salvation and known with certainty only to the Deity. The other church, visible and imperfect, encompassed all believing Christians, some who had, and some who had not, experienced saving grace. This earthly church could winnow out obvious sinners, but, given human deceit and fallibility, it could do no more than approximate the body of the chosen. To the Puritans, the Church of England was corrupt because it had relinquished the effort to narrow the gulf between this world and the next. As Francis Bacon summarized the church's position, it did not "make windows into men's hearts and sacred thoughts."[8] It admitted all comers, substituting geographic qualifications—the fact, say, that one happened to live in a parish in Exeter—for spiritual ones, and it forced the saints to worship side by side with the damned, at grave peril to their souls.

Flight to the New World gave the exiles the chance they were looking for to consummate their far more selective vision of Christian fellowship. They made their purified assemblage contiguous with the nation, or at least with the political nation. The settlers adopted a provision, formalized in the Cambridge Platform of 1648, whereby all prospective congregants, and thus all would-be citizens, had to testify in open meeting to their having been regenerated. Rebirth and not birth, affirmed in an oral discourse—what might, not unfairly, be termed the first "loyalty oath" in American history— would bring the double boon of entry into church and state. "Thus I was humbled," a confessor might say, "then thus I was called, then thus I have walked, though with many weaknesses since, and such special providences of God I have seen, temptations gone through, and thus the Lord hath delivered me, blessed be his Name &c."[9] The formulaic restraint of this illustration should not blind one to its motive. The narratives aimed to strip away the post-Edenic opacity of worldly affairs. That which could be seen and known nowhere else but in heaven was to be made visible in Massachusetts Bay.

As the Reformers had "outed" monasticism, reconfiguring the cloistered life as a this-worldly discipline transacted in the view of all,[10] so the Americans threw open the doors of the confessional. They replaced a clandestine cataloguing of sins in a darkened box with a "personall & publick *confession*, & declaring of Gods manner of working upon the soul." The Puritan bared his innermost being, not his weekly or monthly trespasses. His examination was corporate because it was supposed to encourage his brethren, and because, as John Cotton put it in condemning the Catholic sacrament, the "wayes of truth seeke no corners."[11]

Despite occasional backslidings and compromises, most notoriously the Half-Way Covenant of the 1660s, the knowability of the invisible has been a hallmark of American sectarianism ever since. Voluntarism, new birth, and public testifying: from Jonathan Edwards in the eighteenth century, through Charles Grandison Finney in the nineteenth and Billy Sunday in the twentieth, to Billy Graham today, these ingredients have been endlessly recycled in a ceremony of unreserve. Some observers have described the scenes of self-exposure, which grew more and more tumultuous over time, as constitutive of a unique American identity. Antebellum outpourings can seem startlingly prophetic of television talk shows like Oprah Winfrey's and Jerry Springer's:

When the churches held conference to receive members [as recounted by an early Baptist history], the congregation would draw up in such crowds, as they would tread upon one another, anxious to hear the experiences of their neighbors and families. And while the candidates were relating their experience, the audience would be in floods of tears, some almost convulsed, while their children, companions, and friends were relating their conversion.[12]

One could continue piling up examples of confessionalism, but two additional witnesses from the present will have to suffice. Randall Balmer, a student of contemporary evangelicalism, has assembled scores of stories of repentance and salvation from camp meetings, chapels, and Bible youth camps. He writes of a people acclimated by their faith to pouring out their hearts. Reticence and deception, including self-deception, are anathema when one's eternal soul hangs in the balance. The Wesleyans, Brethren in Christ, Bible Methodists, and other "saints" interviewed by Balmer threw modesty to the winds. They would apprise him, a total stranger, of the most intimate details of their spiritual odysseys. The Lord "saved me from a life of sin when I was seventeen," recalled one man. "I lied and cheated; I would steal." Another confidant cried as he told Balmer of the self-loathing he felt for having succumbed to homosexual urges in his youth. He was still tormented by fear that his single misstep would deprive him of salvation. The historian Christine Heyrman has documented the same volubility among Promise Keepers in the South. Male evangelicals imbued with that region's patriarchal mystique, the Promise Keepers nonetheless do not hesitate to show emotion in public, to weep, hug each other, and come clean about their deepest guilt.[13]

It need hardly be said that vast changes separate today's born-again Christians from Winthrop's fellow passengers. Historically and doctrinally, they are worlds apart. (As followers of John Calvin, the Puritans felt they could do nothing by their own exertions to win grace. Most present-day Christians believe that responsibility for salvation lies with the individual.) Yet the undeniable differences do not revoke the continuities. The reality of the American experience is that a highly visible piety—the piety of the sect—has remained a constant presence over almost four centuries. It has weathered social and economic upheavals. It has survived wave after wave of immigration bringing a diversity of non-Protestant worshipers to these shores. In the post–Civil War period, for example, sectarian faiths showed resilience in the very cities where millions of Catholic and Jewish newcomers were developing their own religious institutions. Between 1870 and 1920, Protestant churches in the urban centers steadily gained adherents; in England and throughout the Continent, by way of contrast, denominations withered.[14]

This last occurrence highlights the atypicality of the American pattern. The United States is at once the most modern and among the most religious of nations, a coupling approached only by Japan among First World countries. The "secularization" paradigm, according to which faith has waned over the past century (or two or three centuries), may hold good for Europe but flounders before American sectarianism. Certainly the return of evangelical Protestantism to political prominence, chiefly through its association with the Republican Right, has exposed the flimsiness of chronicles of decline.

"Why is there no socialism in the United States?" David Hollinger has suggested replacing the Sombartian chestnut with a more meaningful query, namely, "Why is there so much Christianity in twentieth-century America?"[15] One possible answer, I have been arguing, is that the modern passion for previously proscribed knowledge, for transparency and the externalization of inner states, has always existed within American religion. The irresistible drive for visibility, ordinarily regarded as the handmaiden of the scientific spirit,[16] was incipient within denominational enthusiasm and actualized, however incompletely, in the Puritan emigrants' effort to marry Augustine's two churches. Though backward-looking to secular eyes, evangelical fixtures of belief incubated an enduring American ardor for (self-)revelation.

But of course the compulsion to confess has never been limited to religious rituals (or even to television talk shows). One observes it in the literary cult of truth-telling, an American litany that seems addicted to rhetorical extravagance. The genre is exemplified by Melville's familiar review of *Mosses from an Old Manse*, in which he enthuses over his countryman Hawthorne as Shakespeare's equal—no, the Bard's superior—in "the great Art of Telling the Truth." The last word Melville invariably capitalizes, a bit of flunkeyism he resents showing to the Deity but is happy to confer on courageous speech. (In fairness to Melville, an undercurrent in the essay voices pessimism about the Truth's popular reception.)

Romantic hyperbole, yes, but the romantics were not the only ones to indulge it. The naturalist Frank Norris if anything ratcheted up the emotional temperature in *his* aesthetic manifesto, a dismissal of realism for "going no deeper than it sees." Norris admires the radical truth-telling he associates with "Romance," a species of literature that pierces "straight through the clothes and tissues and wrappings of flesh deep down into the red, living heart of things." This idea of writing is apocalyptic, at least as much as Melville's, and Norris thunders it with religious fervor. Romance, he declares, at once takes "the wide world for range" and sounds "the unplumbed depths of the human heart," shrinking from neither the wretched slums of the modern city nor "the mystery of sex, . . . and the black, unsearched penetralia of the soul of man."[17]

In other writers' hands, this literary credo migrates out of literature to assert its claims over the outer and inner worlds. Emerson takes truth-telling to be the governing principle of the entire cosmos. His astonishing essay "Worship," from *The Conduct of Life* (1860), holds that "sincerity is

the property of all things." Nature and society are inherently moral and dis-
tribute rewards and punishments with the unerring accuracy of the clairvoyant. "You cannot hide any secret," Emerson says, and he adds that the
whole of humanity, and of animate and inanimate matter as well, are a police force relentlessly ferreting out the hidden. "We are all physiognomists
and penetrators of character, and things themselves are detective."[18]

My final instance is Poe, whose disdain for Transcendentalist moon-
shine did not prevent him from regarding confessionalism as a law of the
self. Poe's famous tale "The Imp of the Perverse" (1845) can be read as a
fictional proof of Emerson's thesis. The story is framed, precisely, as a confession, and its subject is the universal compulsion to blurt out self-
indictments. The narrator, having committed a cunning murder, has the
security of knowing he can never be found out by the authorities. But under
the pressure of his imp (a proleptic Freudian unconscious, simultaneously
id and superego), he is driven to play sleuth to himself. He announces his
guilt in an emphatic voice and "with a distinct enunciation" in a crowded
thoroughfare and so consigns himself to prison and the gallows. Detection,
or rather self-detection, is the American Imp of the Perverse.[19]

Authors everywhere claim to be purveyors of truth, but there is something over-the-top about these pronouncements. (Norris's blast sounds like
a recipe for a sigmoidoscopy by Dr. Frankenstein.) One European writer
who certainly thought Americans overdid it was Oscar Wilde, sworn opponent of "the morbid and unhealthy faculty of truth-telling." That the United
States is a disaster, Wilde explains in "The Decay of Lying" (1889), can be attributed "to that country having adopted for its national hero a man, who
according to his own confession, was incapable of telling a lie, and it is not
too much to say that the story of George Washington and the cherry-tree has
done more harm, and in a shorter space of time, than any other moral tale in
the whole of literature." Wilde believes "the only interesting thing about
people" is "the mask that each one of them wears, not the reality behind the
mask," and his essay is a diatribe against the "modern vice" of fact worship.
He singles out Americans because they are, to his thorough disgust, at once
the most up-to-date and the most dogmatically sincere of peoples.[20]

Washingtonianism has colonized no area of American life more thoroughly than the diagnosis of mental behavior. The inevitable illustrations
are phrenology in the nineteenth century and psychoanalysis in the twentieth. Differences aside, the two character-excavating disciplines can be reviewed together because the parallels between them are "uncanny," in
Freud's sense of something once known that has been forgotten or repressed. Phrenology was the premier psychological doctrine of the Victorian age. It previewed Freudian therapy not simply in the ardor of its New
World popularity—unapproached elsewhere—but also in its aims and in a
myriad of colorful particulars.

Phrenological theory, like its contemporary successor, arose in eastern
Europe and was the brainchild of a Viennese physician, in this case Franz

Joseph Gall, who preferred the term "craniology" for his idea. (Johan Gaspar Spurzheim, Gall's disciple and popularizer, coined the better-known "phrenology.") Both psychologies purport to disclose the contents of the mind from what appears on the body: symptoms for Freud, bumps on the skull for the phrenologist. Both claim the status of science, and both have been ridiculed as pseudosciences lacking in verifiable results. Phrenology never gained the formal validation of the medical establishment, but in its heyday, it had its share of academic support. The entire medical faculty of Harvard University turned out for the funeral of Spurzheim, when the Viennese expert died in Boston during a promotional tour. (Spurzheim was accorded the tribute of being the second person buried in Mount Auburn Cemetery.) Americans have hailed both methods of analysis as invaluable additions to humanity's tools of self-improvement.[21]

Phrenology also anticipated Freudianism's appeal to verbal and visual artists. The prominent antebellum sculptor Hiram Powers was an enthusiastic convert, and patrons revered him for his mastery of craniological indices. His statues of Daniel Webster, George Washington, John C. Calhoun, and other statesmen supposedly made the temperaments of those well-known figures visible in their brows and faces. Writers, sensing a rival for judging character, were more satirical, though no less attuned to phrenology's influence. Melville, in a passage from *Moby-Dick* of special relevance here, has his narrator Ishmael remark of the cannibal Queequeg, "His head was phrenologically an excellent one. It may seem ridiculous, but it reminded me of George Washington's head, as seen in the popular busts of him. . . . Queequeg was George Washington cannibalistically developed."[22]

Ordinary citizens joined the craze. Thousands flocked to phrenological firms to have their personalities appraised by trained interpreters. New York's Fowler and Wells, one of the largest outfits, maintained a consulting room and sold handbooks replete with drawings of heads in which every faculty was located and labeled. (Fowler and Wells, also a publisher, numbered Emerson and Whitman among its authors.) For a fee, visitors could have their skulls measured and their bumps categorized. Phrenologists could determine whether one's talents lay in the area of ideality (perhaps a career in the ministry?), or acquisitiveness, or benevolence, or combativeness (which signified not truculence but force and courage). In the melioristic construction adopted by Americans (and not shared by the more pessimistic Gall, in his European skepticism another Freud), one's virtues could be maximized, one's potential deficiencies overcome. Phrenology, and its still more disciplinary partner, physiognomy, caught on in other cultures besides the United States, but seldom with the same voluntaristic resonances. In Europe, the two systems were used to classify and regulate rather than to probe interiority for the purpose of self-knowledge.

Phrenology is not, to be sure, a discursive taxonomy like the talking cure but an uncovering of depth through cranial conformation. The contrast underscores how the American zeal for truth-telling appropriates even the most seemingly mute aspects of identity. Nor is the distinction from a verbal activity quite so firm: the skull is "read," and clients receive the results in a written report. Moreover, the phrenological enterprise strikingly evokes another realm of American experience where the speechless is induced to speak. Its topographical, nonverbal legibility corresponds to the United States terrain west of the Ohio. A glance at one of Fowler and Wells's "Symbolical Phrenological Heads" (see figure 1.1) dramatizes how much the landscape of the mind resembles the landscape of the continent. Familiar icons of antebellum America, the heads are divided into a network of clearly marked spaces. The spaces represent specialized functions and faculties. Each compartment is numbered and illustrated, so that the top half of the skull looks like a grid with sections. The phrenological subject's mental proclivities are as manifest to the eye as the 640-acre holdings of the pioneers.

Psychoanalysis, as an analogue to Protestant confessionalism, would seem vulnerable to objection on structural grounds. Evangelicals testify in

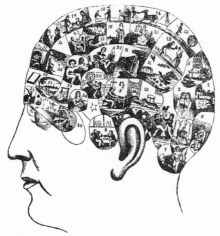

NUMBERING AND DEFINITION OF THE ORGANS.

1. AMATIVENESS, Sexual and connubial love.
2. PHILOPROGENITIVENESS, Parental love.
3. ADHESIVENESS, Friendship—sociability.
A. UNION FOR LIFE, Love of one only.
4. INHABITIVENESS, Love of home.
5. CONTINUITY, One thing at a time.
6. COMBATIVENESS, Resistance—defence.
7. DESTRUCTIVENESS, Executiveness—force.
8. ALIMENTIVENESS, Appetite, hunger.
9. ACQUISITIVENESS, Accumulation.
10. SECRETIVENESS, Policy—management.
11. CAUTIOUSNESS, Prudence, provision.
12. APPROBATIVENESS, Ambition—display.
13. SELF-ESTEEM, Self-respect—dignity.
14. FIRMNESS, Decision—perseverance.
15. CONSCIENTIOUSNESS, Justice—equity.
16. HOPE, Expectation—enterprise.
17. SPIRITUALITY, Intuition—spiritual revery.
18. VENERATION, Devotion—respect.
19. BENEVOLENCE, Kindness—goodness.
20. CONSTRUCTIVNESS, Mechanical ingenuity.
21. IDEALITY, Refinement—taste—purity.
B. SUBLIMITY, Love of grandeur.
22. IMITATION, Copying—patterning.
23. MIRTHFULNESS, Jocoseness—wit—fun.
24. INDIVIDUALITY, Observation.
25. FORM, Recollection of shape.
26. SIZE, Measuring by the eye.
27. WEIGHT, Balancing—climbing.
28. COLOR, Judgment of colors.
29. ORDER, Method—system—arrangement
30. CALCULATION, Mental arithmetic.
31. LOCALITY, Recollection of places.
32. EVENTUALITY, Memory of facts.
33. TIME, Cognizance of duration.
34. TUNE, Music—melody by ear.
35. LANGUAGE, Expression of ideas.
36. CAUSALITY, Applying causes to effects.
37. COMPARISON, inductive reasoning.
C. HUMAN NATURE, perception of motives.
D. AGREEABLENESS, Pleasantness—suavity

FIGURE 1.1

From O. S. Fowler, *Physiology, Animal and Mental: Applied to the Preservation and Restoration of Health and Body, and Power of Mind* (New York: Fowler and Wells, 1853).

public. Therapist and patient convene in a space barred to outsiders. Is not the analytic hour closer to the priest-penitent dyad of Catholicism than it is to any rite authorized by Nonconformity? Michel Foucault was the most forceful proponent of a concordance between the enclosed confessional and the couch. In Foucault's view, Freudianism represented a fulfillment of the confessional's injunction to bare all one's illicit thoughts, those concerning sexual desire in particular.[23]

The best way to meet the structural criticism is to admit its force. Psychoanalysis was a desacralized American *substitute* for the confessional. Freudian treatment offered an opportunity for colloquy in a culture that until the twentieth century had no official place, no institutional setting, for two unrelated people to engage in intimate talk. (Which suggests why a mid-nineteenth-century author like Hawthorne envied Catholics their auricular sacrament.) The verbal cure came along at just the right moment to relieve the double threat to the self created by fin de siècle modernity. It gave refuge from intrusive new technologies that seemed about to overwhelm the private sphere, and at the same time it resurrected the possibility of closeness, of unbosoming, in an age of massive dislocation and anomie. The confessional-like atmosphere of the doctor's consulting room appealed then as a secure precinct for telling all (though in a glasshouse society like the United States, self-disclosure could only be whetted, never contained, by the analytic closet). The confessional box itself, as a religious ordinance, appears to have inhibited rather than facilitated the fashion for openness. Among Catholics, psychotherapy made major inroads only when the practice of confiding one's sins to a priest on a regular basis ceased to be an active part of faith.

Foucault's thesis is seriously flawed. (Terry Eagleton puckishly suggests that Foucault "was never in the box himself.")[24] How could psychoanalysis be the legacy of the confessional if it encountered its stiffest resistance in precisely those countries where Catholicism held sway? This includes Freud's native Austria, where, he complained, churchgoers boycotted his handiwork as a sacrilege. France, Foucault's source for most of his data on the rite, was for most of the twentieth century a bastion of anti-Freudian sentiment. The French did not welcome psychotherapy as liberatory but instead disliked it as an affront to discretion. (And something like discretion continues to characterize French theorizing on the subject. French writers routinely belabor Americans for their "shallow" optimism that the analyst can reach the unconscious depths.)[25]

Where Freud's treatment did best was in cultures that had been convulsed by the Reformation's demand for religious transparency. His early disciples came almost exclusively from nations with Protestant majorities: England, Germany, Switzerland, and the United States. Not a few had ministerial connections, most notably Carl Jung, whose father was a Swiss clergyman. Even in Protestant countries, Catholics commonly showed more disdain than sympathy for Freud's mental science. Far from readying potential patients, the confessional inoculated its users against the consolations of therapeutic interchange.

The American writer Walker Percy is an eloquent case in point. He disputed Foucault's argument even before Foucault conceived it. Scathing critic of twentieth-century culture as "that great shithouse of scientific humanism,"[26] Percy insists on the impassable gulf separating Catholic spoken penance from psychotherapy. The Louisiana novelist, who interned as a psychiatrist before quitting medicine to write, returns time and again in his fiction to the twin seductions of the movies and of Freudianism. In *The Moviegoer*, which won the National Book Award for 1961, the protagonist, Binx Bolling, is an aimless, troubled stockbroker who wastes his life at the cinema; the hero of several later novels, including the futuristic *Love in the Ruins* (1971), is a disillusioned psychiatrist (and sometime mental patient) with the suitably Catholic name of Tom More.

Conversion to Catholicism convinced Percy of the emptiness of secular life. Dr. Tom More, his alter ego, mocks psychotherapy as an updated phrenology, another in the world's concourse of placebos for the spiritually bereft. More endeavors to raise mental diagnosis to some higher, more metaphysical level of relevance. He has patented a machine called an "ontological lapsometer," which measures not one's psychological condition but rather how far one has fallen in the scale of being.

Confession and penance are major themes in *Love in the Ruins*, and the sacraments decisively trump the couch. A long exchange has More's Jewish friend and fellow psychiatrist, Max Gottlieb, pressing him to admit his sexual guilt for maintaining three mistresses. You've gotten it all wrong, More explains. What troubles him is his inability to feel "guilt, contrition, and a purpose of amendment" for what he knows to be a sin. Without that influx of spiritual "life," he cannot be forgiven and begin to heal. More is finally able to confess to a priest, who gently chastises him for failing to "show a bit of ordinary kindness to people" and not "doing what [he] can for our poor unhappy country—things which, please forgive me, sometimes seem more important than dwelling on a few middle-aged daydreams." These words, with their counsel of self-forgetting, for Percy the antithesis of analytic self-immersion, have the desired effect. More feels instantly "scalded" and is able to acknowledge the shame he has fended off for so long.[27]

Percy died in 1990, and Catholics both here and abroad have since moved away from his anti-Freudianism. The trend actually began several decades before his death, and developments within Catholicism itself sparked the change. Perhaps the most important of these was the church's greater push toward public candor. The shift in the analytic center of gravity to Romance-language countries, first to France and then to Argentina, coincided exactly with the reforms of the Second Vatican Council (1962–65). The council reinserted the community back into the penitential process. First, the Vatican incorporated into the private confessional the theme of reconciliation with the church, and second, in 1974, it sought to revive testifying in open congregation, an ancient practice eliminated half a millennium ago with the adoption of the darkened box. Psychoanalysis did not win substantial numbers of adherents among Catholics, in other words, until the church brought the discourse of interiority more into line with the exhibitionism of Protestant sects.[28]

In the United States, although communal penance has apparently not proven popular, the 1960s marked the almost complete abandonment of the privatized sacrament. A constant of American Catholicism for a century and a half quickly declined and then all but disappeared in the aftermath of Vatican II. Worshipers came to see the confessional as mechanical and rushed: the process of enumerating sins followed a set formula, priests asked few questions, and the entire experience lasted an average of only two minutes. As the rite lost prestige, Catholics began to look elsewhere for relief, and more and more turned to psychiatry. Freud's talking method, long an object of suspicion as indiscreet (and overly Jewish), allowed the openness and communication parishioners craved and could not find in the dying habit of recitation and contrition.[29]

Is it relevant to note that voluntary confessionalism turns up in all sorts of cultural arenas where the United States can claim precedence and/or a disproportionate following for the practice? Two offbeat sites are the courts and income taxes. Uncoerced truth-telling has long been an American trademark in criminal law. The sources here are multiple, with the Fifth Amendment's ban on involuntary self-incrimination inspiring repeated Supreme Court attempts to define, and ensure, the rights of the accused. (The best-known such decision is *Miranda v. Arizona* [1966], which requires the police to inform suspects of their right to remain silent.) What stands out as remarkable is the extent of the United States' reliance on confession to solve crimes and convict wrongdoers. Guilty pleas account for 92 percent of felony convictions, a far higher rate than in almost any other nation. We approach totalitarian regimes in our determination to prove responsibility "from a defendant's own mouth." The premise, consonant with evangelical soul baring, is that only the subject can truly know what is in his or her heart. Countries with histories of state intimidation tend to be more sensitive to the duplicitous nature of inculpatory speech. In present-day Germany, a society seared by Nazism, confessional statements are not admissible unless substantiated by other evidence.[30]

Possibly still more curious is the reliance on willing confessionalism in the preparation of personal income tax returns. With this telling exception, American experience neatly inverts the British pattern. During the nineteenth century, Britain was the global champion of free trade and depended on income taxes for public revenues. The United States, seeking to develop domestic industries, erected high protective barriers. Individuals were not taxed on their earnings (save during the Civil War), and the government stocked its coffers from the tariff and from the sale of public lands.

In the twentieth century, and especially since World War II, the United States steadily displaced its erstwhile colonizer as the stronghold of open markets. The passage of the Sixteenth Amendment in 1913 permitted the imposition of an income tax, and Congress added the distinctive twist of self-assessment. This was a departure from the British, otherwise a statutory model; there taxes were collected through government assessment or through withholding (what came to be known as PAYE, or "Payment As You Earn"). The American taxpayer had to take upon himself or herself the burden of disclosure, reporting all sources of income and calculating the sum owed to the Internal Revenue Service. Truthfulness, not coercion, was, and to a large extent has continued to be, the taxing power's signature. Justice Robert H. Jackson of the Supreme Court put the matter succinctly in 1953: "The United States has a system of taxation by confession." The British, renowned for self-reticence, did not adopt the American method until 1996.[31]

I began this discussion of Winthrop's "Model" by noting its apparent social conservatism. What could be more supportive of birthright than his notion of an ordered community where "variety and difference" foster interdependence? Yet just as the Puritan governor privileges second birth over birth, so his sermon tacitly militates against the idea of inherited rank. Its first sentence, on "the condition of mankind" (quoted after the heading), contains a significant omission. Winthrop stipulates the necessity for rich and poor, high and low, but he does not mention aristocracy. Nowhere in his discourse does he use that word or refer to lords. "Estate" gets a nod but as "the estate of regeneracy" opposed to "the estate of innocency" (p. 84). The one time Winthrop speaks of earthly rank, he does so by way of an analogy indicating that the colonists' business is with heaven's ruler: "As it is the glory of princes to have many officers, so this great king [God] will have many stewards, counting himself more honored in dispensing his gifts from man to man, than if he did it by his own immediate hands" (p. 83). Steward, servant, serving: the terminology of social subordination gets transferred to religious duties, and liberality and sacrifice are prescribed as "service to the Lord" (p. 89).

Winthrop's contraction of social hierarchy might seem no more than an oversight or a fleeting concession to reality—no aristocrats sailed aboard the *Arbella*—were it not for the fact that the Puritans proceeded to legislate it. They dislodged birth from its European eminence by refusing to confer upon it the guarantee of governance. *That* privilege they reserved for the saints. Six years after landfall in New England, the Reverend John Cotton spelled out this implication of Winthrop's speech in responding to an inquiry from the Puritan nobleman, Lord Say and Seal, who was contemplating removal to America. The lord wrote to ask about the Bible Commonwealth's requirements for citizenship. Cotton minced no words in stating that all church members, regardless of station, could vote and were eligible to hold office. And only church members: godliness instead of ascriptive rank ruled in Massachusetts. Cotton's letter not surprisingly dissuaded his correspondent from emigrating; and no hereditary aristocracy arose in the New World, not even in the "Cavalier" South.

This devaluing of pedigree, though its full consequences would not be realized for a century and a half, amounts to still another blow against the hidden. It is the parallel in politics to the reformed abolition of monasticism. Aristocracy and monarchy are engines of exclusivity. A political regime ruled by either king or lords arrives at its decisions without popular dialogue. It takes for granted that the practice of governing belongs to a tiny, hereditary minority and is not to be shared. Secrecy, not openness, is its guiding principle. Publicity, on the other hand, always presumes choice. Voluntarism, as in the exiles' shipboard covenant, runs counter to in camera decision making because those who choose have to be consulted. They have to be brought into the deliberative process and given options in order to judge among them.

Not that the American Puritans were democrats. Far from it. They restricted leadership roles to the elite and demanded deference and obedience from the many. Here I want to touch briefly on only one aspect of their exclusionary side, an antidemocratic strain that seems at once to be the antithesis of New World legibility and to epitomize it. The Puritans were among the earliest Americans to codify chosenness. Perhaps, indeed, the New Englanders were the first to do so, for while seventeenth-century Virginians passed laws governing slavery, they evidently did not equate race with permanent bondage at the initial stage of settlement. Whiteness did not necessarily equal freeman's status, nor was blackness as yet a guarantee of subordination.

The Massachusetts colonists, on the other hand, slotted persons according to election, and they professed to be able to tell with inerrancy who among them were the saved and who were destined for damnation. They believed that their congregations could access a reality deep within the individual's soul. The transforming inflow of grace could not be discerned by human eyes, though behavior hinted at it. But it could be described in a narrative, and the saints could therefore identify who had it. They could also be confident about who did not have it, even though that person's outward conduct might differ little from their own.

In effect, the Puritan exiles reinscribed the caste system they had left behind in England. They ceased to uphold aristocracy as a social code, but they did not abjure the aristocratic principle, with its presumption of irrevocable inclusion and exclusion. Instead, they reconfigured that principle as a theological-political divide, a split between those inhabitants of the Commonwealth who could take communion and vote for officeholders, and those who were denied those privileges. A people apart, the exiles decreed apartness to be a fundamental law of their society. They shone the light of holiness on the saints and consigned sinners to the purgatory of never belonging. Subsequent generations of Americans did not hesitate to apply the clarifying law of difference to the vexed subject of race. Like the Puritans, they invoked categorical otherness even when the marks of difference could not be observed externally, on the flesh.

This is not to say that Southern Jim Crow codes somehow replicated Dissenter separateness. It *is* to suggest that English Protestant sectarianism translated into a stark binarism of light and darkness, racial as well as spiritual, whereas a less restrictive Spanish and French Catholicism fostered interracial societies with a spectrum of colors. Tocqueville was to make a point much like this in the nineteenth century when he noted how loath white Americans were to mix their blood with that of red and black strangers. The religious urge toward ever greater purity, combined with the refusal of admission to the unworthy, encouraged egalitarianism among believers and the systematic dehumanization of those outside the circle of the elect.

R eformed resentment of the hidden in religion did not die out with the Puritans. It has erupted numerous times in United States history. A much-publicized protest occurred in the antebellum era, fittingly enough in Massachusetts. The cinder was the influx of Irish immigrants to the Commonwealth, and nativist reaction unleashed its fury against Catholicism's labyrinthine, closed-off interiors. In 1834, rioters demolished an Ursuline convent in a Boston neighborhood. The English diarist Frederick Marryat, traveling in America, had this to say about the perpetrators' motives:

> The Americans are excessively curious, especially the mob: they cannot bear anything like a secret—that's *unconstitutional.* . . . [T]he majority of the mob were influenced more by *curiosity* than any other feeling. The Convent was *sealed* to them, and they were determined to know what was in it.[32]

Marryat's insight about the popular frenzy for accessibility points to American politics as a complement to Protestant demystifying. The Englishman's use of the word "unconstitutional" was a cliché at the time. Reporters of the riot and its aftershocks invariably remarked that the convent's Charlestown address was within sight of the Bunker Hill Monument, memorial to the Revolutionary hostilities that culminated in the writing of the federal compact.

William Penn's Plans for Philadelphia (and Pennsylvania)

> Since (by the good providence of God) a Country in America is fallen to my lot, I thought it not less my Duty than my honest Interest to give some public notice of it to the World, that those of our own, or other Nations, that are inclin'd to Transport themselves or Families beyond

the Seas, may find another Country added to their choice, that if they shall happen to like the Place, Conditions, and Constitutions, . . . they may, if they please, fix with me in the Province hereafter describ'd.[33]

So begins *Some Account of the Province of Pennsilvania* (1681), one of a barrage of promotional tracts, letters, maps, and agreements with would-be purchasers, by means of which Penn sought to realize his "Holy Experiment" of a New World sanctuary for Quakers. Pennsylvania, with Philadelphia as its capital, was to be the Friends' city on a hill. It was meant to rival—no, to outshine—its neighbor to the north as an exemplary Christian community.

Yet the passage's offer of unrestrictive welcome strikes a very different tone from Winthrop's Puritan chosenness. The "we" of "A Model" is gone. (It will return in Jefferson's Declaration and in the Constitution.) Penn's model commonwealth is to be inclusive and consensual. Birth does not bring special privileges, and neither does rebirth. (Unless we think of voluntary uprooting and redefining of allegiance as acts of rebirth, an inference strongly encouraged by naturalization ceremonies.) "No Law can be made," Penn writes, "nor Money raised, but by the Peoples Consent," and he lays it down as a colony-wide rule that neither office holding nor political rights are to depend on a religious test. The only condition he insists on is that the settlers be righteous men and women, well disposed toward the Indians, and prepared to work hard to improve their lot.[34]

Penn's visionary project thus represents a dramatic extension of American accessibility. He would banish the hidden or closed not by externalizing the soul's contents and not by narrowing eligible membership but by breaking down barriers and encouraging freedom of movement. He arranged for his pamphlets to be translated and distributed throughout Europe. Although most of the so-called First Purchasers of Pennsylvania were Friends, even this early group included pietists from Holland, Germany, Ireland, Sweden, and Wales. And though a nobleman himself, Penn took precautions to guard against the few monopolizing property (and with it, power). In his pamphlets he offers to sell tracts as small as 125 acres and scripts in a measure of social mobility by promising grants of 50 acres to indentured servants who complete their terms. The result of these provisions was to transform the province, circa 1750, into a preview of the twenty-first-century United States. "All religious sects are tolerated there," said a German visitor:

We find there Lutherans, Reformed, Catholics, Mennonites or Anabaptists, Herrnhuter or Moravian Brethren, Pietists, Seventh Day Baptists, Dunkers, Presbyterians, Newborn, Freemasons, Separatists, Freethinkers, Jews, Mohammedans, Pagans, Negroes and Indians. The Evangelicals and Reformed . . . are in the majority. But there are many hundred unbaptized souls there that do not even wish to be baptized.[35]

Penn's commitment to openness operates on other registers besides tolerance. Whereas secrecy invariably foments resentment, publicity figures in his writings as a surety of social peace. He wants disputes between natives and whites to be resolved by a publicly convened jury consisting of six members from each race. He orders business deals to be conducted in the open market, and he forbids buying and selling in private to prevent deception. No detail seems too trivial to escape his vigilance. How cattle and sheep are branded gets a paragraph. The markings must be plainly visible, Penn states, so as to dispel the uncertainty about ownership that can lead to strife.[36]

But what may be Penn's most influential contribution to American legibility lies elsewhere: in the recording and patterning of space. If Winthrop directs us inward, to the redeemed heart necessary for a covenanted society, Penn's focus is outward and environmental. His pamphlets for prospective immigrants contain detailed descriptions of his province's physical charms. And then he punctuates this vision of plenitude with a projected metropolis, Philadelphia, in which every piece of land is to be allocated, measured, and numbered. Penn's ideal city of brotherhood is the material world rendered transparent through human agency.

His accounts of Pennsylvania belong to the genre of promotional literature, the age's typology of surfaces. Like such forerunners as John Smith's *A True Relation* (1608) and William Bradford's *Of Plymouth Plantation* (begun in the 1620s, though not published until 1856), and such successors as Hector St. John de Crèvecoeur's *Letters from an American Farmer* (1782) and Jefferson's *Notes on the State of Virginia* (1787), Penn's advertisements abound in lists: lists of animals, trees, fruits, flowers, vegetables, waterways, bays, fish, natural boundaries, and native inhabitants. The pamphlets bristle with names: of towns, counties, falls, rivers, and creeks. Numbers come in abundance: rainfall, miles, acres, sizes, prices, populations, frequencies.

This parade of facts is an embryonic example of an "attestive" visual code.[37] At least in theory, the code can be tested and verified. Its aim may be celebratory, but it does not try to awe us with spectacle; it purports to persuade with objectivity. Penn's tracts can be thought of as simultaneously verbal and ocular. While they are in language, they want to set the world before us with the impartiality of a photograph—or, less anachronistically, with the clarity of a drawing or map. Indeed, by distilling description to notation—the sites of the principal rivers, the names of Kent, New Castle, and Chester Counties, the number of laws passed by the General Assembly—they strive to purge the rhetorical impurities from language itself. The tracts pretend to give us textual translucence without the distorting hand of authorial intervention. They are hybrids, and they mobilize the "scrutable" resources of both words and pictures to pass the reader/would-be settler's inspection. They must do this because the reader *is* a would-be settler and has the choice of staying put or emigrating.

The hybridity of the pamphlets culminates in the "portraiture" of Philadelphia, as Penn calls the combined "plat-form" (or plate) and explanatory narrative supplied by Thomas Holme in 1682 (and appended by the proprietor to his *Letter to the Society of Traders*). Holme's map is a bird's-eye-view of the city. Philadelphia appears as a grid of rectangular lots, extending for "two Miles" on a neck of land between the Delaware and "Skulkill" Rivers. At the center of the model is a square of ten acres reserved for public buildings. A High Street plus eight smaller streets run the length of Philadelphia from river to river; these are intersected at right angles by twenty streets crossing the city from top to bottom. According to Holme, each street will be exactly fifty feet wide.

The whole metropolis is organized on a clearly delineated system of lines and numbers. The numbers refer to the size and position of the lots, a distribution determined by Penn when he first imagined his capital city. Ten acres in Philadelphia were reserved for every five hundred acres purchased in the province as a whole. Holme indicates that purchasers of one thousand acres or more are to have the choice lots along the riverfronts and High Street, with lesser purchasers assigned locations "in the backward Streets." The two sets of lots are numbered from one upward, "whereby may be known each mans Lot and Place in the City."[38]

Penn may have had Roman antecedents for his city plan, but his orientation is futuristic, not retrospective. Philadelphia is to develop into its identity over the years ahead, filling in the blank lots and perpendicular streets on Holme's map. But its growth will always have a stable starting point. Penn's metropolis is the analogue in environmental configuration to Winthrop's spiritual summons: the moment of inception made evident to all. The origins of European and Asian cities are lost in the mists of the remote past. The origins of Philadelphia are recoverable in time as well as space.

The phenomenon of blankness in the landscape calling forth prodigies of diagrammed intelligibility reaches an early plateau in Penn. But the composition of nature would not attain its apogee until a century after his design. In 1785 the Continental Congress passed a Land Ordinance for settlement of the western territory that has left its imprint on roughly two-thirds of the contiguous United States. Penn's Philadelphia grid was a possible source for the legislators, who may have simply wished to transpose his urban framework to the wilderness.

If so, they both elaborated his model and made it the prototype for the ordering of a continent.[39] The 1785 Ordinance established a rectangular cadastral survey as the American method of geographic inscription. Six-square-mile townships were to be created, subdivided into thirty-six numbered sections of 640 acres apiece. The system had multiple advantages of accessibility, which would have pleased Penn: its accurate, government-run surveys expedited the making of maps, ensured unambiguous property titles, facilitated purchase and sale, and deterred speculators by eliminating insider information.[40] The Ordinance promoted knowledge in another respect, too: it required that the sixteenth lot of each township be set aside for school land. With minor refinements, the uniform grid with subdivisions has governed the American landscape ever since. The Homestead Act of 1862 mandated settlement by quarter sections (160 acres); and to this day, developers think of quarter quarters, or 40-acre parcels, as the modular unit.

The Ordinance and its successors in governmental land policy updated Penn's emphasis on the general availablity of property. This has been a crucial ingredient in the American rebuke of secrecy. Property is like knowledge or information in that it can be monopolized, made the exclusive possession of a few, and its engrossment leads inevitably to great disparities of power (a point emphasized by, among others, Georg Simmel, Jeremy Bentham, and Thomas Jefferson).[41] For more than two centuries, realty could never be so hoarded in America because there was simply too much of it to go around, a continent's worth. The Ordinance's wide distribution, its tacit endorsement of economic mobility, helped to underwrite an open society. "Yes" to rich and poor—as in Winthrop's "Model," as in the Declaration's "pursuit of happiness"—but a resounding "no" to hereditary nobility and a permanent servant class. (Penn, an aristocrat, visited his vast holding in the New World, but he had no intention of staying there.)

The arrangement of nature into a geometric pattern of straight lines has had lasting effects. The landscape's regularity became so reflexive that it infiltrated speech with its numeracy: nineteenth-century farmers in quest of adjoining lots spoke of "swapping forties." Frederick Jackson Turner, deeply impressed by the census of 1890 (another institutionalized fetish for numbers, this one dictated by the Constitution), put "lines" at the center of the most famous essay ever written on the country's geography, "The Significance of the Frontier in American History" (1893). Turner's argument for a "democracy born of free land," and now jeopardized by the frontier's passing, is obsessed with linearity: "the lines of settlement," "lines of western advance," "the frontier line," "boundary lines," "lines of trade," and so on. The renowned historian envisions the American landscape as a ruled piece of paper, in which time traverses space with its orderly march: "The United States lies like a huge page in the history of society. Line by line as we read this continental page from West to East we find the record of social evolution."[42]

Perhaps it is foreigners (especially Germans) who have been most sensitive to the country's relentless rectangularity. Wolfgang Langewiesche, a German-born pilot who emigrated to America in the 1920s, may have been the first to describe the continent's "mathematical gridwork" as observed from the air, a sight he characterizes as "one of the oddest . . . of the world." To Langewiesche, the landscape is like a sheet of graph paper on which are written out the basic principles of American identity. The townships, their boundary lines plainly visible ten thousand feet above the ground, are the antithesis of Old World towns. None has walls (barriers excluding outsiders), or a cathedral (no state religion as birthright), or a castle (no aristocracy to husband power and information). Yet every one of them can boast of "a giant high school," testimony to the nation's commitment to mass education and social mobility.[43]

True, "it all looks pretty much alike," Langewiesche concedes. But that is the point. The landscape, with the "strong plain writing" of the section lines, is exemplary of the nation, "a diagram of the idea of the Social Contract." Every parcel equals a man, and every man is a free and equal citizen of the Republic. From the air, the topographical coherence of the landscape "is a design for independent men."[44]

Or is it really a recipe for regimentation? Critics of such enforced patterns, usually scholars of Asia or Africa, deplore territorial uniformity as an effort by the centralized state to impose control.[45] Another often-cited example of sinister planning, this time involving urban (European) space, is Baron Haussmann's redesign of Paris. Haussmann, at the directive of Louis Napoleon, replaced narrow, clogged alleys with broad avenues and so expedited governmental surveillance. One can grant these points without assenting to their overkill. Democratic polities also have a stake in openness (as a two-way, not a one-way, process); and the very category of free citizenship, as Langewiesche recognizes, presupposes equal units, persons as interchangeable as forty-acre lots. Furthermore, the disorder associated with medieval cities hardly guarantees political liberty. *That* advance in governing had its modern birth in the artificial municipality whose setting between two navigable rivers "is scarce to be parallel'd": Philadelphia.[46]

The continental expanse has never looked so pellucid as from the sky. Langewiesche's piece is both admiring and prescient here. Admiring of the way the landscape shows itself like "a palimpsest," with the section lines visible beneath the present-day writing of forests and farms.[47] Prescient of the collusion between the aerial view and the total disrobing of the physical environment that, half a century after "The U.S.A. from the Air," has become the deadly reality of American military technology. ("The foreground doesn't hide the background. Looking down . . . from the air, you see everything, literally, that's there.")[48] Thanks to the "precision revolution" of the 1980s, a revolution powered by satellite reconnaissance, electronic sensors, lasers, robots, and microwaves, American weaponry has now achieved such perceptual mastery of the earth's surface that it can strike its target over 90 percent of the time. The battlefield of the future will be a place where everything can be seen and nothing hidden. American technological know-how has transformed the entire globe into a knowable landscape, at once a modernization and a lethal inflection of the originary longing to rationalize the wilderness.[49]

Penn's design inspired American city planners as well as legislators of the hinterland. The urban grid influenced new settlements like Indianapolis (1821) and long-existing ones like New York, which sought to control its chaotic expansion in 1811 by applying the system on a scale never before attempted. (The New York plan spared Broadway as the only irregular avenue.) Where the grid was bypassed, the goal of legibility was retained. In Washington, D.C., the United States built a synthetic capital city from scratch. As a concession to the southern states, the administrative hub of the newly independent Republic was relocated from Philadephia to the banks of the Potomac. A French architect, Pierre Charles L'Enfant, was commissioned to devise a plan. L'Enfant transformed the muddy, unattractive site into a neat lattice of streets crossed by diagonal avenues, the latter named for individual states.[50]

Cities like New York and Washington and neighborhoods like Boston's Back Bay remain among the world's easiest to "read," with numbered streets and avenues or named streets arranged in alphabetical order. In Salt Lake City, the state capital of Utah, streets are identified by their distance and direction from the Mormon Temple (Fourth East Street, Second West Street, etc.). The New World metropolis lays itself bare much as the landscape does. A visitor has little difficulty finding his or her route from a starting point to a destination. The same visitor, on a walking tour of London or Tokyo, will need a detailed map to get around. (Even a map will not do much good in Tokyo, an aggregation as "closed" as New York is open.) Another defining feature of these cities is the skyscraper, an American innovation that replaced the family farm as a national symbol. The towering buildings take the compositional repetition of the countryside and turn it into a vertical principle. The intermediate zone between the lower floors and the top one displays tier after tier of identically shaped windows in a recurrent rhythm of glass, masonry, and steel.[51]

The city of the skyscrapers was also the city of the tenements. And the tenements, a by-product of industrialization and immigration, triggered an exit of the middle class to the suburbs. White-collar families of mostly native stock sought to flee the overcrowding, crime, and disarray that by the 1890s were swamping the nation's urban centers. They found an attractive residential harbor in the intermediate space between the dense metropolitan clusters and the countryside—in the partly rural, partly townlike belt that has been labeled the "crabgrass frontier." The suburbs gradually overtook both the grid and the skyscraper as the distinctive American locale. "In 1970," as Kenneth T. Jackson says, "for the first time in the history of the world, a nation-state counted more suburbanites than city dwellers or farmers."[52]

Suburban flight—a bit like the migrating of self-disclosure into the analyst's office—promised a combination of privacy and revelation. The suburbs beckoned with their ideal of a detached single-family dwelling, set down in the imitation rural landscape of lawn and bushes. Freed from the city jungle, the homeowner could recruit his spirit in the blissful solitude of protected space. As this description suggests, however, the suburbs were also a return to the section's openness. They renewed the legibility that seemed destroyed by the foreignized metropolis, with its confusing jumble of sounds, sights, and strangers. The freestanding houses with their well-tended yards echoed nothing so much as the demarcated parcels of the grids. Unlike Europeans of comparable affluence, American suburbanites did not erect walls around their homes. They left their property exposed, and their inviolate sanctuaries could be scrutinized by every passerby.[53]

Moreover, the rush to suburbia was coterminous with a change in the nature of the middle-class house itself. An alteration in domestic architecture subjected the hitherto off-limits interior to the examination of non–family members. The parlor, long considered the "face" of the American residence, was supplanted by the living room as the place for receiving guests.[54] The parlor had been a formal chamber set apart from the private regions of the house. It was the public front the occupants showed to the world. The living room, in contrast, was a relaxed, informal area "lived" in by the family. It was the house's "heart." Its furniture, decorations, books, mirrors, and pictures encoded the family's secrets and were now thrown open to outsiders. While visitors socialized, the interior held forth (or "talked," to use the Freudian terminology) without restraint. In suburban living rooms across America, the private and the exhibitionistic freely commingled in a version of the same dynamic being played out on the analyst's couch.

The expulsion of secure privacy from the private home had no shortage of critics among both foreigners and natives, especially among expatriates familiar with European norms. One of the earliest to object was Henry James. When he came home for a visit in 1904, after twenty years abroad, James discovered a social order consumed with telling all. In "social notes" on Manhattan, he reports his horror at the promiscuity common to both glass-encased office buildings and individual residences. New York, in his view, is a city afflicted with the "original sin" of "perpetual" pendendicular avenues and not a sheltering deviation anywhere, its "glass towers" presenting "window upon window" to the eye. Elegant private homes are constructed on the same principles as the public thoroughfares. Rooms flow one into another with a "vagueness of separation" that effectively abolishes any interior. Or, rather, that effaces the interior's difference from the exterior and so does away with "the guilt or odium or responsibility, . . . of its *being* an interior." To one accustomed to European arrangements, James writes, the American home's endless vista of "doorless apertures," so that every part is "visible, visitable, penetrable," has the oppressive effect of "serving you up for convenient inspection, under a clear glass cover." (James's trope eerily prefigures George Orwell's metaphor for life in Oceania, in *1984*.) Private conversation is out of the question, as every word said "must be said for the house." How can there be anything less than total candor when the very domestic architecture prohibits secrets and forces one to take "the whole world" into confidence?[55]

Another critical comment comes from James's friend and fellow Europhile, Edith Wharton. In her first published book, *The Decoration of Houses* (1897), which she co-wrote with Ogden Codman Jr., Wharton takes up cudgels against the fad for structural indiscretion. Sheets of plate glass between rooms (rather than walls) and the elimination of doors highlight "the absence of privacy in modern houses." Americans are the worst offenders, Wharton asserts, because they regularly confound entertainment areas with family space. Doing away with the vestibule, they place the main artery for intimate domestic business, the staircase, directly in the entrance hall. As a result, "there is no security from intrusion."[56]

What is at fault here, Wharton shrewdly notes, is a categorical confusion. Americans, with their reverence for "sincerity" as a moral precept, assume that the same standard should apply to art (or architecture). Every detail of the house should be arranged to promote truthfulness. Concealment, dividers, *trompes d'oeux*, all are forbidden as dishonest. This is a grave error, according to Wharton. Artistic sincerity means nothing more (or less) than pleasure to the eye, and this end is best achieved through fitness and restraint.[57]

Carl Jung, of all people, provides my last quotation on the American confusion of domicile and confessionalism. Freud's quondam disciple accompanied the founder on the visit to Worcester in 1909 and left a record of his impressions. He points to the "boundless publicity" of American life as its "most amazing feature" and complains of the zest for annihilating boundaries and interiors. The visitor, Jung says, feels assaulted in residential landscaping, in gossip, and in social interactions:

> To a Central European like myself the lack of distance between people, the absence of hedges and fences around the gardens, the belief in popularity, the gossip columns in the newspapers, the open doors in the houses (from the street one can look right through the sitting room and the adjoining bedroom into the backyard)—all this is more than disgusting; it is directly terrifying. You are immediately swallowed up by a hot and all-engulfing wave of emotional incontinence that knows no restraint.[58]

America's love affair with the nonvarying grid has given rise to a multitude of comparisons: to a painting by Mondrian, to a checkerboard, to a patchwork quilt. (In the Far West, the symmetry is true of the states themselves. Wyoming, Colorado, and the Dakotas form near-perfect rectangular swatches on the cartographic canvas.) Other cultural phenomena have more of a conceptual affinity to the landscape's order. As I have emphasized, the duplicating of the same can be felt in democratic egalitarianism. It also lies behind the American system of manufactures, the use of interchangeable parts to machine-produce goods, rifles in the late eighteenth century (coeval with the 1785 Ordinance), automobiles in the late nineteenth and twentieth, computers and software today.[59]

Then there are photographs and movie screens. The motion picture camera records its images as a sequence of frames. Each celluloid rectangle on the reel of film is different from and yet the same as its predecessor. This isomorphism with the grid goes beyond the repetition of fungible units.

The photographic or cinematic and the terrain share a mutual emphasis on visual access, and the affinity has had a significant impact on American warfare. United States preeminence in military "eyeshot," noted earlier, reaches back to Mathew B. Brady's photographs during the Civil War and the propaganda footage compiled for the Allies by D. W. Griffith in World War I. The use of the moving camera to scan the battlefield has progressed from aerial reconnaissance, radar, and infrared imaging to today's stealth weaponry and totalized video surveillance.[60]

American bellicosity suggests another comparison, this one to the classic work of nineteenth-century literature with which I began this chapter. William Penn has an unexpected, and anything but pacifistic, heir in Melville's Ahab. The captain of the *Pequod* is a Quaker like the father of Philadelphia, and he is similarly bent on inscribing marks on a blank surface. Penn's inviting canvas was the landscape; Ahab's is the looming white hump of Moby Dick. Cinema, colonial proprietor, and whale hunter meet in the ambition to fill the empty screen with narrative. "That inscrutable thing is chiefly what I hate": Ahab's monomaniacal war on vacancy repeats itself in the settlement of the continent and in the flooding of the movie theater's white rectangle with light.

The *Pequod*'s voyage reminds us that the grid is a tool of conquest over nature, an attempt to gain some purchase on the monstrous size of the continent. Here, again, the landscape is prolific of analogies. Take the "control" revolution of the nineteenth century, harbinger of the computing and Internet revolution of today. The sheer magnitude of the United States called forth innovative strategies to regulate machinery and consumer goods at a distance. These included the Morse code, direct-order mail houses, telephones, the chain store, punch-card systems, and so forth—all seeking to bring knowledge up to speed with new technologies of production and distribution. Communications networks to prevent accidents and manage equipment marched across the continent in tandem with the railroad. By the end of the nineteenth century, the country led the world not solely in miles of track but also in miles of telegraph wires humming with information.[61]

Might the discipline of mental health supply yet another candidate for our list? I refer not to psychoanalysis per se but to the specifically American variant known as ego psychology, which flourished from the 1940s through the early 1960s. Ego psychology basically reified scrutability. It took Freud's illumination of the mind's interior to the extreme of bracketing, and practically denying, the indecipherable as an integral component of the self. This theoretical construct—like the "discovery" of the homogeneous and pacified landscape west of the Alleghenies—was the work of German emigrants to the United States, most notably Heinz Hartmann, Karl Kris, and Erik H. Erikson (a Dane partly raised in Germany). Ego psychology subordinated the ferocity of the id to the adaptive power of consciousness. Hartmann in particular reconceived the ego as a relatively autonomous entity capable of mastering instinctual urges when they threatened the subject's well-being.

Freud's ego had been the helpless rider of the horse of the id. Hartmann's rider was in charge, the reality principle bringing order to the lawless frontier of the drives. (Freud himself wrote of the unconscious as "a stretch of new country.")[62] Reason and insight vanquishing primitive nature: this much-reviled contribution to analytic thinking—reviled as vapid not just by Lacan and the French but also by many Americans—parallels the nation's geographic project, that of composing the virgin wilderness into regular, readable sections. Did Penn's 1682 vision of an urban epicenter find a climax of sorts in Hartmann's *Ego Psychology and the Problem of Adaptation* (1958)?[63]

We cannot leave this discussion of the environment without acknowledging the costs of its transformation. While the casualties have been many, three vectors of occlusion require comment here. The first is that the entire premise of a virgin land was unfounded. The North American continent perceived by whites as a void was in actuality anything but. Perhaps two million natives, with their distinctive patterns of settlement and cultivation, lived here before the European invasion. Penn's sympathy toward the Indians, his willingness to find their customs meaningful, was highly anomalous. To settlers and policy makers, the unimproved terrain and its dark-skinned inhabitants were opaque obstructions. What the six-mile townships with their geometric survey lines swept away was the custodial relation to the natural world observed by the natives. The Indians themselves were virtually eliminated from the earth. Not entirely, but close; and literature in the genre of the Western popularized the presumption of their disappearance.[64]

Second, the suburbs imitated the grid in the high toll they exacted on nonwhites. As the sections effaced the Native Americans, so the affluent communities around the cities ostracized American blacks. The corollary to the detached semirural dwelling, with its telltale interior, turned out to be the compulsory invisibility of some categories (or rather, as it proved, one particular category) of persons. The residential "new frontier" began its explosive growth during the period framed by *Plessy v. Ferguson* (1896) and Woodrow Wilson's election to the presidency (1912), events confirming segregation as the nation's official policy on race. Redlining, racial covenants, and "gentlemen's agreements" ensured that the low-density developments would be safe from black invasion. The country's tax code did its part to subsidize white suburbia by allowing deductions for mortgages and property taxes but not for the payment of rent.[65]

Third is the matter of those lines, another in the culture's inexhaustible armory of clarifying demarcations: the moving line of the frontier memorialized by Turner, and familiar to every reader of Westerns as the divide between civilization and primitivism; and the sharply etched boundary lines between holdings, sections, and townships bequeathed to generations of homesteaders by the writing on the soil. The lines have been no less durable than the evangelical Protestant sorting of the elect from the damned. They have been refashioned in the relentless fissuring of races: the aversion of white skin for red skin, and the wall erected between the Euro-American and the black. If the seams could be imposed on nature, could they not be stitched into the genes, used to prohibit interracial mating? Americans have not scrupled to think so, nor to stigmatize the mixing of peoples through the fetish of a single drop of tainted blood.

Thomas Jefferson, son of the Enlightenment, foe of aristocracy and all forms of hereditary privilege, has a unique standing in the history of American legibility. Authoring the Declaration was but one of his many relevant achievements. He had a role in bringing Penn's vision of topographical candor into the eighteenth century. First chair of the committee for the Northwest Territory, Jefferson in 1784 proposed a scheme of land allotment according to "hundreds" (ten-square-mile townships, subdivided into a hundred sections of 1,000 acres apiece). He drew up a map of possible future states, sketching them with gridlike boundary lines for maximum clarity and assigning numbers from "one" in the North to "fourteen" in the South.[66] Although these proposals were not adopted, Jefferson's enthusiasm for exact measurement and numerological simplification carried into the decimal system for American money, which he conceived and lobbied for; into the statistical data on climate, volume of foreign trade, manufactures, mines, rivers, slaves, and "aboriginals" with which he packed his *Notes on the State of Virginia*; and into his schemes for a democratic school sequence for Virginia's youth that would, he hoped, "rake" precisely ten geniuses "from the rubbish annually" and send them to university to be educated at the public expense.[67]

Comparable initiatives circulated in other nations besides the United States. Rationalizing paradigms were instituted during the French Revolution, and English proponents of statistics as unbiased representation have a long and illustrious history, beginning with William Petty's advocacy of "political arithmetic" in the seventeenth century. But in the case of the French, the decree of more accessible dates, codes, and weights and measures was allied to tyranny; and the Crown more often rejected than followed the advice of Petty and his successors.[68] Jefferson exemplifies the relatively smooth rapport in late-eighteenth-century America between political and other forms of transparency, including the environmental. The Constitution, written while he was out of the country, has given us a lasting icon of the two modalities, civic and cartographic, merged into a single entity. The Constitution was signed by the framers grouped according to state. The signatures were arranged in geographic order from New Hampshire in the North to Georgia in the South. "The United States," as Robert A. Ferguson puts it, "thus appear on the page in familiar map form,"[69] the nation knowable both as a written statement of governing principles and as a pictorialization of physical identity.

The Declaration of Independence

> The history of the present King of Great Britain is a history of repeated injuries and usurpations, all having in direct object the establishment of an absolute Tyranny over these States. To prove this, let Facts be submitted to a candid world.

What follows are eighteen sentences charging regal misrule, each starting with the pronoun "He," and an additional eight dependent clauses starting with "For," each accusing George III of giving his "Assent" to criminal acts passed by the British Parliament.[70]

There can be few more dramatic—one might almost say paranoid and novelistic—uses of an attestive code than in this call for revolution. (Paranoid, among other reasons, because there was no plot or conspiracy to enslave the colonists.) The "facts" crying out for public recitation constitute a "history" that, like other "histories" of the era, has a strong generic flavoring. Jefferson and his co-authors marshal King George's outrages in order to win the colonists to independence, not so much as a logical syllogism convinces—the customary comparison—but rather as one is persuaded by a narrative: by events related in temporal sequence, by vivid and formulaic language, by highly emotive portrayal of motivation. In its crystalline triumphalism, the Declaration allies itself with modes of expression, including popular fictional genres, with which it would seem to have little in common. Moreover, it stands in relation to *The Federalist Papers* and the Constitution much as popular literary materials stand in relation to a "canonical" writer like Nathaniel Hawthorne: as a model to be imitated and as an excess to be chastened.

But I want to defer the "literary" aspect until later and start by considering how this American genesis authorizes a culture of civic accessibility. The first thing to be said here is that the Declaration scourges "the monster aristocracy" and its "associate monarchy." (The phrases are Jefferson's, from a letter to the Marquis de Lafayette.)[71] Ascriptive rank is the text's principle of darkness. The truth that "all men are created equal," that birth confers no right of authority over others, indicts noblemen everywhere for obfuscating the light of "self-evidence" and using force to secure and maintain their position.

Hereditary privileges can have no place in a polity based on free choice. (The abhorrence of rank would be formalized in Article 1, Section 9, of the Constitution, which prohibits officials from holding or receiving titles of nobility.) Voluntarism is the rudiment of a republic, just as it is of Winthrop's city on a hill and Penn's holy experiment. As Jefferson famously puts it, paraphrasing Locke's *Second Treatise of Government*, governments derive "their just powers from the consent of the governed." His wording takes us to one of the Declaration's favorite contrasts: that between "consent" as a right of the people and "assent" as a monarchical or hierarchical prerogative.

Jefferson and the other Founders knew full well that the king's authority had been whittled away significantly by Parliament since the Glorious Revolution. George III's was a much weakened power of assent, not the arbitrary exercise of will suggested by the founding document. He could give his blessing to acts of Parliament; he could no longer dictate or invalidate laws on his own. But the Declaration overstates royal might in order to sharpen the contrast between a free and open polity and a closed one. It harps on "We consent" versus "He assents": the first denoting a deliberative process among equals, carried out in public; the second an act of concurrence by an individual, usually a superior. The text encourages a historically inaccurate notion of the monarch meeting with his counselors behind closed doors and exercising his "Will alone" (in the Declaration's language) by either agreeing to something or refusing agreement without any obligation to explain his reasons. Royal government by "assent" is *le secret du roi*, statecraft as whim or mystery, the analogue in politics to the arcana of monasticism. It is the nemesis of a democratic government by "consent."[72] The Constitution does away with the monarchical nomenclature altogether: whereas "consent" recurs throughout the federal compact—"without the Consent of the Congress" (Article 1, Section 9), "with the Advice and Consent of the Senate" (Article 2, Section 2), and so on—"assent" is absent from the text. The president does not assent to legislation; he signs bills passed by the Congress if he "approves" of them.

Jefferson's is also a voice of voluntarism in his endorsement of immigration. The Declaration contains an attack on the king for impeding settlement of the New World: "He has endeavoured to prevent the population of these States; for that purpose obstructing the Laws for Naturalization of Foreigners; refusing to pass others to encourage their migrations hither, and raising the conditions of new Appropriations of Lands." By listing "the pursuit of happiness" among humanity's "inalienable rights," Jefferson implicitly generalizes the principle of immigration into a defense of people's freedom to relocate wherever they wish.

"Consent of the governed" applies with signal force to the individual who leaves his or her natal country to reside elsewhere, and here we come back to the idea of voluntary migration as "second birth." Or not migration so much as citizenship: Jefferson's naturalized "Foreigner." Sometimes the American welcome has been expansive like Penn's, at other times exclusive like the Puritans', but the applicant for membership in the polity—much like the believer seeking admission to a sect—has always had to publicize an inner change. Manuals on naturalization typically state that citizenship is "a glorious possession" capable of being appreciated only by those who have had instilled in them "the spirit of this land." Either in "open court" or in some other setting, possibly a stadium filled with thousands, the new citizen delivers a narration of conversion. He renounces his loyalty to his native country, pledges "his faith and sole allegiance to the United States," and "begins life anew in the land of his adoption."[73]

Whereas malice toward consent taints all the king's acts—from dissolving freely elected assemblies to turning a deaf ear to the colonists' pleas—the advocates of independence aim for publicity in everything. Actuated by "a decent respect to the opinions of mankind," the Americans explain themselves before the world. They submit a long list of grievances. They "solemnly declare and publish" their intentions. And they do not send their utterance into the world as a foundling. Against English custom, and at grave risk to their lives, they acknowledge paternity by jointly signing their names.

For the members of the Continental Congress, then, the cause of freedom is bound up with the uncensored circulation of information. This commitment had diffuse sources and correlatives in the Revolutionary era, and it has had diffuse legacies. A contemporaneous impetus was the rise of a noncoercive, "print" public sphere in which authority was required to present itself before an audience of readers. A position could only prevail in this arena (at least theoretically) because it commanded the better argument.[74] The expanding public sphere made it all the more essential to nurture a literate populace able to reach informed decisions. The Puritan demand that the laity be readers, competent to parse God's word for themselves, evolved into a civic insistence on common or "public" schools. The difference from Great Britain would prove to be highly instructive. In the mother country, schools were called "public" if they were open to the public for admission; but they remained effectively private because they were financed by the tuition fees charged to students. In the United States, a "public" school was by definition free, open to all, and maintained at the community's expense.[75] (Free mass education at the high school and then the university level were additional American reforms of the nineteenth century.)[76]

The most immediate post-Declaration result of the attachment to publicity/information is of course the Constitution. Britain's unwritten constitution lodged an invisible core at the heart of politics. The American federal compact guarantees popular accountability by spelling out the government's powers and limitations in a form available for all to see. Moreover, the Constitution consolidates public access to information as a fundamental "law of the land." The First Amendment prohibits Congress from passing legislation abridging freedom of speech and of the press.

Beyond stated guarantees, the very structure of the new government promotes the gathering and exchange of information. Two features stand out here: the separation of powers, and the requirement of regular elections.

On the first, the United States institutionalizes distrust, even paranoia, set-ting itself apart from parliamentary systems where the legislature and the executive are more closely integrated, and the judiciary lacks independence. *The Federalist Papers* are a paean to suspiciousness as a democratic virtue. The division of authority into state and federal governments, and of func-tion into the executive, legislative, and judicial branches, builds into the sys-tem a habit of "watchful attention" (p. 357).[77] The states keep an eye on the central power, the central power on the states; and each separate branch of the government is a sentinel over the others, ever on the alert for encroach-ments upon its terrain. This ceaseless observation is not a closed circuit, moreover. To be effective, vigilance has to make known its findings, so the "compound republic" (p. 303) needs "a regular and effectual system of intel-ligence" (which the new government moved swiftly to establish through the mails). Those who detect abuses can thus "communicate the same knowl-edge to the people" (p. 516).

Thus far, information for protection; but facts are also necessary for predictive purposes. Hamilton's *Federalist* No. 35 expatiates on this idea. The government official, facing elections on a regular basis, has to familiar-ize himself with "the interests and feelings of the people." Because he de-pends on his constituents' support "for the continuance of his public hon-ors," he will want to do everything possible to act and vote in a manner consistent with their inclinations. And the only way he can be sure of this is through "extensive inquiry and information" (pp. 216–17). Judith N. Shklar has credited Hamilton with formulating an informal political science in this essay, one that grasps the essentially democratic character of electoral survey research. The voluntarism of democracy, the need to consult the popular will, injects the unpredictable into politics; and representative government will always try to limit this uncertainty by learning as much as it can about popular wishes.[78]

What better method for implementing these several objectives than a postal system? It would disseminate the news, and it would bring reports from the four corners of the land. Hence the Post Office Act of 1792, fore-runner of the Internet, another state-sponsored information technology. The act's success dazzled foreign visitors, Tocqueville among them. Forty years after its passage, he reported with amazement on the long-distance distribution of letters and newspapers in what was, by Old World standards, still a primitive society. On his travels to thinly populated regions of the Midwest, the Frenchman found backswoodmen keeping up with the latest affairs in Washington and Europe through the mail delivered by stagecoach. The American postal system employed more personnel than the federal army and had many more offices than either France or Great Britain (five times and twice as many, respectively).

More vital than the size of the operation was its single-minded focus on the flow of information. The American government effectively subsidized the communication network. Hinterlands unable to meet the cost of delivery and so forced to make do elsewhere without routes or facilities could boast of regular service. Rather than raising revenues from the press, moreover, the post office transmitted newspapers at highly favorable rates. Its stated policy was "hands off." In contrast to the British, whose "secrets office" monitored papers and routinely opened correspondence, postal employees were forbidden to use the mails for purposes of surveillance.[79]

The Constitution gives a hitherto unimaginable centrality to the role of numerical information in governing. Its cataract of figures is meant to banish the hidden and ambiguous and to erect an objective standard for regulating public officials and policies. The national compact is arranged according to numbered articles and sections, and has appended to it numbered amendments (twenty-seven as of the year 2002); its primary supporting brief is a collection of numbered essays (*The Federalist Papers*, consisting of eighty-five commentaries); it provides, in Article 1, Section 2, for a decennial census, the first modern nation to do so; it specifies the ages that must have been attained by congressmen, senators, and presidents; it gives the proportions of votes necessary to impeach, to confirm treaties, and to override presidential vetoes; and it even casts racial oppression as a problem in quantification, mandating that every slave shall be counted as exactly three-fifths of a free person for purposes of apportioning representatives.

Most telling of all, the Constitution enumerates the precise terms of elected officials. The purpose, to minimize the unknown, is again made evident by the difference from the British system. A prime minister can call elections up to five years after forming a government. He or she, acting entirely on discretion, can schedule a vote in the second year, or the fourth year, or the fifth year. No American president enjoys such leeway. He (or she) serves for a stated term, the length of which is known to everyone, and then can run for reelection for the same term, not a single hour more or less.

The mystique of numbers retains a determinative power in American governance. Polling to track popular sentiment, the translation of Hamilton's science of politics into arithmetic, has been employed in every presidential election since the early nineteenth century; candidates for office tailor their views accordingly. American bureaucracies have tended to diverge from their European counterparts because of their susceptibility to numerical oversight. British actuaries, to cite one example, were long able to resist the standardization to which accountants in this country assented early on. The British fended off parliamentary supervision by invoking patrician shibboleths such as "judgment," "character," and "discretion." The actuaries were gentlemen, and gentlemen could be trusted more than numbers. Their American equivalents, on the other hand, invented strict cost-accounting procedures because they knew they could not escape external inspection. (Supporters of Jefferson's decimal system regarded the pound sterling, with its confusing shillings, pence, halfpence, farthings, and guineas, as complicit in this sort of elitism. They excoriated the British mode of monetary reckoning as a "policy of tyrants," intended "to keep . . . accounts in as intricate, and perplexing a method as possible.")[80]

By the same token, French state engineers, the Corps des Ponts, have traditionally closed their deliberations to the public. They have argued that statistics cannot be shared with laymen in their raw form but have to be interpreted by experts. No "mere calculators," French technocrats pride themselves on being answerable only to their superiors. The United States Army Engineers, lacking comparable insulation, have been forced to regularize their methods and to devise cost-benefit analysis to pacify congressional monitors. Whereas the English operate on an Old-Boy network, and the French hunker down behind bureaucratic walls, American civil servants constitute a "government of strangers" accommodating outside scrutiny through calculations.[81]

Nowhere else have numbers been granted so much respect as a tool of measuring value. Their reach covers the entire cultural gamut. In what other society does the broadcast of major sporting events come complete with "statisticians"? Everyday speech displays a similar intoxication with figures. One of the more amusing asides on America as "an Eden of abstractions, . . . in which numbers have taken on an existence of their own," comes from László Moholy-Nagy, the Hungarian-born photographer and painter who settled in Chicago in 1937. In his "U S A number collage," Moholy-Nagy records illustrations from slang and advertising such as 7-Up, one-up, fifty-fifty, 5 and 10, behind the eight ball, 4F, 23 skidoo, and Heinz 57 Varieties.[82]

Tributes to numeracy have not been wanting in more sophisticated discourse either. The most celebrated statement in canonical literature about the honesty of numbers was penned by Ernest Hemingway in his 1929 novel about the First World War, *A Farewell to Arms*. Sickened by the phony rhetoric of wartime patriotism, the hero, Frederick Henry, reflects:

> I was always embarrassed by the words sacred, glorious, and sacrifice and
> the expression in vain. . . . There were many words you could not stand to
> hear and finally only the names of places had dignity. Certain numbers
> were the same way and certain dates and these with the names were all
> you could say and have them mean anything. Abstract words such as
> glory, honor, courage, or hallow were obscene beside the concrete names
> of villages, the numbers of roads, the names of rivers, the numbers of regi-
> ments, and the dates.

Hemingway's unadorned style is an attempt to pare down language to the clarity and unsentimental exactitude of figures.[83]

Americans have especially prized dates and numbers for their supposed competence to predict and control future events. In business, for instance, the United States took the lead in what was called, in the mid–nineteenth century, "forward contracts." These were agreements between farmers and merchants to deliver a stipulated amount of grain on a particular date some months away. Speculators began to buy and sell these contracts on the Chicago Board of Trade, and the first "futures market" in commodities was born.[84] (The natural sympathy between securities exchanges and the craving for data, in this case accurate information about the day's closing prices, led to the establishment in 1896 of the Dow Jones Industrial Average, the oldest stock index in the world.)

Speculation as "reading" or unveiling the future has assumed less pecuniary forms. Indeed, religion offers what may be the most tenacious strain of American prediction-mongering: the appetite for prophecy. Again, one confronts the paradox of a postmodern, college-educated people professing unconditional faith in the Second Coming of Christ. Millions of Americans, taking the Scriptures as a factual (though coded) scenario, enthusiastically mine past, present, and upcoming events for signs of Jesus' imminent return. These believers take an almost scientific relish in unearthing the hidden pattern of history. Anything but "ignorant," the prophecy popularizers and their followers are proof of the compatibility of technological and evangelical Protestant modes of knowing. Many writers have backgrounds in science and engineering, living (if bathetic) reminders that Isaac Newton was as fascinated by eschatology as he was by mathematics.[85]

And to say that "millions" of Americans devour the prophetic speculations is not hyperbole. The best-selling nonfiction book of the 1970s was Hal Lindsey's *The Late Great Planet Earth* (1970). One hundred and fifteen printings of this millenarian treatise had appeared by 1995, and total sales to date are well over twenty-five million. Lindsey's book is filled with integers that hold the key to history: the mark of the Beast (666), which will be tattooed on the foreheads of those who defect to the False Messiah; the seven-year countdown to Christ's Second Coming, which could not begin until sometime after the creation of a Jewish state ("14 May 1948"); the saving remnant of Jews who will convert to Christianty at the last minute (144,000). ("If you have no interest in the future," Lindsay thoughtfully warns potential readers, "this isn't for you.")[86] The prophetic reliance on numeracy has always rivaled that of politics. After much study, John Cotton thought Jesus would dispatch the Antichrist in 1655; the nineteenth-century Millerites picked the year 1843 (and then 1844); and in our own time, Pat Robertson calculated doomsday for 1982.[87]

Arguably, these prophetic speculations are marginal paroxysms, numerological pathologies with little relevance to mainstream urban and suburban culture. So let us shift to an arena in which the twentieth-century mainstream has had an incontestable stake: quantification as an index of individual potential. Numbers have succeeded phrenology as a key for unlocking the mysteries of mental aptitude, and their pretensions to authoritativeness sustain a venerable American tradition of intelligence ranking. The SATs, the most recent example of such schemes, claim the dual ability, in Nicholas Lemann's words, "to see the invisible (what was inside people's heads)" and "to predict the future (what someone's grades would be in courses he hadn't even chosen yet)."[88]

IQ tests were the original mind openers. Although the tests were the creation of a Frenchman, Alfred Binet, the United States and not France proceeded to apply them universally. The man who institutionalized intelligence measuring, Henry Herbert Goddard, was in the audience when Freud lectured at Clark in 1909; a student of Stanley Hall's, Goddard was instrumental in putting "psychology on the map of the United States."[89] Beginning with the diagnosis of mental impairment in children, he branched out into the examination of immigrants and soldiers, conducting testing at Ellis Island and, most influentially, on army recruits in World War I. His procedures, having been tried out on hundreds of thousands of ordinary citizens, won general acceptance as a device for classifying human beings.

As with all such sorting mechanisms, intelligence evaluation has advantaged some groups and persons while penalizing others and shunting them from sight. The Ellis Island results were pounced upon by nativists. They cited the low scores to press their campaign for immigrant restriction, and Goddard's numbers eased the passage, in 1924, of the Johnson-Reed Act, which virtually closed the United States to newcomers. The army tests, a prototype for college entrance exams, appeared to prove the inferiority of blacks and of poor native-born whites. Goddard himself concluded from the scores that only a tiny minority was fit to govern. Those arguing that intelligence is inherited and unaffected by the environment brandish the tests as corroboration to this day.[90]

Numbers have also had a starring role in American paranoia. In the Declaration, George III's plots to destroy the colonists are ticked off in a nightmare inventory, with twenty-six crimes alleged in all. A century later, Populist distrust targeted the ultimate quantifying medium, that of exchange, and decried the unavailability of money. And in the twentieth century, Senator Joe McCarthy, ever ready to haul iniquity into the sunlight, was fascinated by numbers, which he relied on to give his accusations a specious objectivity. The senator from Wisconsin broke into public notoriety in 1950 by waving a list of 205 reputed Communists employed by the State Department. (The figure later fell to 57, then climbed back up to 81.) McCarthy described five Democratic administrations as "twenty years of treason"; owing to this outrage, he complained, "a good 40 percent of all men living" groan under Moscow's writ.[91]

One might sum up this tale of statistics with a glance at two of the most long-standing American romances with quantification: the dollar and the vote. Money and majorities are constitutive reasons for the privileged place of numbers in a republican society without a hereditary ruling class. Democracy, however equipped with constitutional brakes on majority power, is a political order of tabulation in which the greater number almost always dominates (even the electoral college counts votes). The system elevates a (supposedly) nonsubjective and accessible criterion over less palpable touchstones such as bloodlines or connections. Americans worship the dollar in part because it is felt to possess some of the same impartiality. He or she who has accumulated great sums of money is, in the United States, likely to be judged more successful and to enjoy more prestige than other people. As a character observes in Philip Roth's *I Married a Communist* (1998), "Money's the democratic way to keep score."[92] To be sure, nothing could be less admirable as a test of worth than the possession of wealth—unless it is a society in which family pedigree determines how one is valued.

All men are created equal: in 1776, the category was anything but inclusive. Only males were meant, and not all of them (Jefferson's denunciation of slavery was excised from the original draft). But if the promise of the Declaration's words has been blunted in practice, the credo has given cheer to all who would open up the political nation. American women, led by Elizabeth Cady Stanton (later joined by Susan B. Anthony), took the document as their archetype when in 1848 they became the planet's first movement to organize for female suffrage.

The date, 1848, is no accident, and it serves as a useful reminder of what Jefferson's words *did* accomplish. In that year revolutionary movements spread throughout Europe, seeking, along with other goals, to bring the working classes into the polity. (White) laboring men already enjoyed the vote in the United States; the circumscribing of the franchise was along the lines of gender (and race), not class. This injustice heightened American women's collective consciousness and helped to propel early militancy.[93]

The injustice rankled for many reasons, not least because it marked a retreat from the Declaration's rewriting of Aristotle. While Jefferson's phrase aimed a blow upward, at aristocracy, the "equality of all men" also signaled a beaming of the civic spotlight downward, into regions that Western political thought, following Aristotle, had relegated to the darkness of private life. The key distinction, set forth in *The Politics*, was between *oikos* and *polis*, the economic and the public spheres. The former encompassed women, children, and servants (or the laboring classes), the latter, property-owning heads of households. The United States, as the first modern republic to abolish property requirements for the suffrage (in the early nineteenth century),[94] was the first to admit into the visibility of the polis persons who had previously had no public existence.

Foreign travelers, particularly during the antebellum period, marveled at the sheer *pervasiveness* of the American civic realm. The United States had a skeletal state compared with great European empires like France and Great Britain. Expenses were low, bureaucracies few, and regular military forces almost nonexistent. Yet Americans from all social classes participated in public life on a scale unknown abroad. They attended political rallies, joined parties, and voted for a variety of officeholders. Their voluntary associations shouldered responsibilities that monarchical or aristocratic regimes arrogated to themselves. Francis Grund observed: "Every town and village in

America has its peculiar republican government, based on the principle of election, and is, within its own sphere, as free and independent as a sovereign state." Tocqueville asked how it happened that newly arrived immigrants showed so much patriotism. His answer seconded Grund: "It is because everyone, in his sphere, takes an active part in the government of society."[95]

Stirred by the Revolution's ideals and by the reality of widespread popular involvement, some states moved in the aftermath of independence to abolish slavery and enfranchise women. While these efforts came to little, the Declaration's implied vision of an all-inclusive civic domain did contribute to keeping alive the dream of women's rights. Just how much the text mattered can be seen in the "Declaration of Sentiments and Resolutions" adopted by the Seneca Falls Convention seventy-two years after the original (and, to engage in a bit of numerology, seventy-two years in turn before women gained the vote). Stanton, the principal drafter, was a tireless campaigner against "an aristocracy of sex." The phrase indicates her insight into the national imaginary, the discomfort, as old as the Puritans, with birthright monopolies. In the "Declaration of Sentiments," the monarchical "He" of the Founders is retained and redefined as "man," and one gets a similar litany of "facts" indicating a design to establish "an absolute tyranny" over woman.

Stanton and her coauthors pay the 1776 Declaration's strategists the supreme flattery of imitation and paraphrase: the gesture of explaining themselves before "a candid world"; the reliance on numeration (eighteen charges, followed by twelve resolutions, the ninth of which refers to "women's sacred right to the elective franchise"); and the decision of the delegates to go public by affixing their signatures, a hundred in all, sixty-eight women and thirty-two men. The Seneca Falls declaration insists even more firmly than its predecessor on the "self-evident truth" of what it has to say. The phrase is repeated at least four times, with the first appearance being the most dramatic and revisionary: "that all men *and women* are created equal."

The movement to include women in the electorate obviously built on other factors besides Jefferson's manifesto. The scarcity of women on the frontier is often mentioned as a cause; increased female participation in the workforce contributed as well. What makes the Declaration so significant, giving it inestimable value in struggles for rights, is that it provides a bedrock rationale for inclusion in the polis. And entrance into public life, into the glare of politics, has always been the driving force in American protest. The U.S. women's movement was the world's largest in the nineteenth century, with significant influence on state and federal lawmaking (this in spite of not being able to vote); and although British suffragettes prevailed two years before their American counterparts, the ballot in the United Kingdom was restricted to those over thirty (hence more likely to be married and amenable to husbandly persuasion). The Nineteenth Amendment (1920) brought all American women into the electorate, a condition not duplicated by the British until 1928.[96]

Mass movements that try to elect officeholders and shape legislation have evolved into a defining feature of twentieth-century democracies. The United States has ceased to be unusual, but the diffusion of the phenomenon strengthens this country's claim to be the cutting edge of the modern. The continuity of popular participation, stretching back without interruption to the eighteenth century, is what constitutes the uniqueness of the American experience. Civil rights, feminism, and the fight for gay rights have all pursued the goal of pressuring the polis; all, arguably, have their roots in the ringing phrases of Jefferson's call for independence.

Which is not to deny that racial injustice has been the great failure of the Declaration's universalism. The promise of equality has had a twofold legacy: as an inspiriting benchmark, and as a history of betrayal. On the positive side, the Fourth of July has resonated as powerfully for African-Americans as it has for anyone. Nat Turner chose the birth date of national freedom to launch his uprising in 1831, and Booker T. Washington picked the same day fifty years later to open Tuskegee Institute, his vocational school for Southern blacks. Antislavery activists such as David Walker repeatedly invoked Jefferson's words to excoriate antebellum hypocrisy. Even so severe a critic of the republic as W. E. B. Du Bois believed there were "no truer exponents of the pure human spirit of the Declaration of Independence than the American Negroes." And not to be forgotten is the striving of the polis to be formally inclusive. Once slavery was abolished—thirty years after Britain, thirty-five after Mexico, but twenty-three before Brazil—the nation moved with speed to incorporate freedmen into the polity. Formerly enslaved males got the franchise in 1870, with the Fifteenth Amendment, at a time when most white workingmen in England still could not vote.[97]

But of course violence and intimidation belied paper grants.[98] The original denial of the right of consent was the "piratical warfare," as Jefferson called it, of seizing Africans and transporting them to the New World as involuntary immigrants, with no voice in their uprooting. Subsequent bars to the visibility of political life follow from that difference. The dropping of antislavery sentiments from the Declaration would be high on the list, as would the passage of the country's first naturalization law in 1790 narrowing the offer of citizenship to whites. Until the Civil War, the United States was an oxymoron, a slaveholding republic, and the nation's minority population paid the price for that contradiction until well into the twentieth century. When the Voting Rights Act of 1965 finally opened the voting booths to black people, Jefferson's beacon to humanity stood convicted of being the last advanced democracy to achieve the universal suffrage it had pioneered.[99]

It may seem strange to turn from this review of the Declaration's attestive credentials to its novel-like character. Not, of course, that the colonial brief for separation is a fiction (though the Crown certainly thought it was). Rather, the text deploys the kind of overwrought presentation and melodramatic cast of characters that contemporaneous readers would have had no trouble recognizing as novelistic. The accusatory voice, piling on charges of iniquity, evokes popular tales of seduction and betrayal, most of which advertised themselves—however improbable their actions—as based on "Facts," "Truth," or "Recent Events." But if the Declaration *were* a piece of fiction, one would have to differentiate it from the many narratives, such as Charlotte Temple's or Eliza Wharton's, that lovingly detail acts of rebellion only to recant their radicalism in the end. Jefferson's manifesto would have to be described, more boldly, as a sentimental novel with the courage of its beliefs.

Jefferson's manifesto: the generic strain is more accentuated in the initial draft, and I will quote freely from that version as well, italicizing passages that did not survive to July 4. For example, the famous sentence "To prove this let facts be submitted to a candid world" originally included an impassioned clause, *"for the truth of which we pledge a faith yet unsullied by falsehood."* This could have been uttered by the female protagonist of a seduction novel, vowing fidelity to her lover while warding off the designs of a would-be Lothario. The Second Continental Congress chose succinctness over sentimental echo and canceled it.

Even denuded of these flourishes, the document bristles with melodramatic rhetoric and plot devices. It tells a story of "repeated injuries and usurpations." It surveys the most extraordinary outrages, among them "invasions," "convulsions," plunder, ravage, destruction, war, captivity, insurrection, treason, "Cruelty & perfidy," "death, desolation and tyranny." A despot and indifferent brethren are the villains, while the cast of secondary characters includes rebellious bondsmen and "merciless Indian Savages." The slaves, so that *"this assemblage of horrors might want no fact of distinguished die,"* have been incited to murder the masters on whom the king imposed them in the first place. The Indians, loosed on the frontiers, direct their cold-blooded warfare against "all ages, sexes and conditions," lacking, like their sponsors, even the smallest sense of civilized honor.

The targets of this Gothic train of evils, and the text's heroes and heroines, are the inhabitants of the thirteen colonies. These people command our compassion through their remarkable sufferings and forbearance. Their goals, it must be said, are modest: they want only to live and be happy. They submit patiently to troubles. They hesitate to protest. When, pushed past endurance, they finally plead their cause, they suppress any anger they might feel and speak "in the most humble terms." And always they are models of "rectitude." No wonder Jefferson announces his narrative as "scarcely paralleled in the most barbarous ages" and fears that *"future ages will scarcely believe"* it.

The narrative itself has a conventional tripartite structure, a beginning, a middle, and an end. (Though, with armed hostilities under way, there will definitely be a second volume, in which the colonists will either secure independence or be hanged for their efforts. But we, if not the signers themselves, await the sequel without trepidation, aware that popular fictions usually find a way of punishing wrongdoers and rewarding the deserving.) It begins by locating the reader temporally, "When in the course of human events . . . ," a grandiose variant of the conventional "Once upon a time . . ." Next comes the meat of the action, the many abuses the Americans have suffered and their struggles to mollify and restrain their tormentors. Finally, we arrive at the climax, in which the colonists, provoked beyond measure, rise up against the British imperium—unmasked as a foe only through repeated crimes—and announce their resolve to go it alone. Their elected representatives stride off the page in the shining confidence of divine protection.

If the villains and the victims/heroes of this piece are crystal clear, they are also, typically enough, members of the same family. The British monarch as "Father" of the colonists was a commonplace (to be superseded, after nationhood, by the collective and benignant "Founding Fathers"). The king's immoral character shows itself most plainly in his tyrannical behavior toward his children. George III is high-handed and obtuse, unable to hear entreaties, and so infatuated with his own authority that he has ceased to care about the welfare of his offspring. To top off his misdeeds, he blames the colonists themselves for the current troubles and, showing them the door, has waved them *"out of his allegiance and protection."* His countless injuries against the young brand him as unfit for parenthood.

Just as bad, in their way, are the siblings of the Americans, their British sisters and brothers. The colonists have been unstinting in their attentions to these presumed "friends"—a term widely used in fiction to denote both family members and close acquaintances. Tearfully recounting their plight, they have looked for relief to the "native justice and magnanimity" of their British connections. Always they have clung to the hope that the "ties of our common kindred" would prevail over expediency. But these overseas friends have proven untrustworthy. "Deaf to the voice of justice and of consanguinity," they have condoned every crime of *"the disturbers of our harmony."* The Americans have been left no choice but to separate from their blood relations and declare their autonomy: " *These facts have given the last stab to agonizing affection, and manly spirit bids us to renounce forever these unfeeling brethren. We must endeavor to forget our former love for them. . . . The road to happiness and to glory is open to us too. We will tread it apart from them."*

A heartless parent, the violation and forsaking of familial responsibilities, selfish siblings, and a resolution to make a fresh start: Jefferson's Declaration calls upon memories of fictional formulas to color its message of separation's necessity. Where most eighteenth-century novels tend to depart from the call for independence is in their caution or ambivalence. This is definitely true of those yet unwritten stories that a handful of Americans were to publish between 1789 and the 1820s, when Cooper and Irving put this country's literature on the map. (*The Power of Sympathy*, the first native novel, appeared in the same year that Washington assumed the presidency.)

Early fictions commonly waffle on the question of whether their desiring heroes and heroines ought to revolt against paternal power. "Separation" in pursuit of liberty and happiness often turns out badly, as characters without filial loyalty die at sea, or by their own hands, or in solitary childbirth, abandoned by family and friends. Admittedly, most of the protagonists are young women, girls even, not "sons of liberty," and so presumably not in a position to demand their independence. Still, a number *are* men, and as a group they are far more sinned against than sinning. But their sufferings are seldom rewarded, and precious few manage to defy parental wishes and emerge triumphant.

Popular tales of sentiment trail behind civic culture's foundational utterance. The lag between the polis and the aesthetic, so familiar from the modern period as to have been naturalized, is reversed, and the political order runs ahead of a literary tradition just beginning to materialize. That tradition's scattered first shoots owe more to the English past than to the ascendant politics of legibility. They lack the Declaration's assurance of rectitude, its transparency of right and wrong. Popular literary genres would not catch up for a half century. Not until the antebellum era, and the development of distinctive American forms, would stories composed and printed in the United States duplicate the Declaration's boldness of accessibility. The narration of solving crimes, the tale of Western exploration and conquest, the celebrity fiction, in which the private life of a prominent figure is disrobed—these and other genres would finally translate Jefferson's revolutionary luminosity into the register of mass culture.

The civic sphere itself was poised to move, if not in a different direction, then along the same route at a decidedly different pace. *The Federalist Papers* and the charter those essays support share with Jefferson's text a commitment to the ideal of government by consent. But for all their advocacy of political openness, Madison, Hamilton, and Jay are quick to demonize the impetuous sensibility common to populist agitation, to the Declaration, and to popular literature. Distrust is for them a cornerstone of the Republic, and they distrust all forms of absolutism, including the absolutism of a vigilance that respects no limits.

The Federalist Papers are explicitly an antinovel. They castigate the opponents of the Constitution for being more conversant with "the regions of fiction" than with American political realities (p. 407). Madison warns of "unhallowed language" conjuring a "gloomy and perilous scene" (pp. 103–4). Hamilton is still more outspoken. He relentlessly accuses the anti-Federalists of trying to alarm people with overblown rhetoric and "frightful and distorted shapes." So extreme are the apprehensions of abusive power circulating in the press, according to Hamilton, that the unsuspecting reader might imagine "he is perusing some ill-written tale or romance" (p. 186).

The anti-Federalists, in other words, have seized upon the rhetorical and narrative strategies of the Declaration and repackaged them for the purpose of discrediting the national compact. *Their* fictitious libel elaborates "the gross pretense of a similitude between a king of Britain and a magistrate of the character marked out for that of the President of the United States." Has there ever been a more unwarranted case of recycling than the depiction of the innocuous leader of a free people as a replica of the repudiated monarch? And "not merely as the embryo, but as the full-grown progeny of that detested parent." Anti-Federalist fantasy represents the president as a rival in depravity to the potentates of trashy literature: "The images of Asiatic despotism and voluptuousness have scarcely been wanting to crown the exaggerated scene. We have been almost taught to tremble at the terrific visages of murdering janizaries, and to blush at the unveiled mysteries of a future seraglio" (pp. 407–8).

The defenders of the Constitution fare no better: they are pilloried as an updated version of the Declaration's coldhearted English brethren. Scurrilous voices accuse them of being domestic enemies who alternate between indifference to their countrymen and active plotting against the common good. Opponents of the charter even argue, as Jefferson did, for terminating the *"perpetual league and amity"* that binds together the whole people. In the most "unnatural" scenario, the anti-Federalists seek to reanimate the spirit of separation in order to destroy the Republic. Madison pleads with readers to eschew the falsehood that Americans, "knit together as they are by so many cords of affection, can no longer live together as members of the same family." The "kindred blood which flows in the veins of American citizens" should produce nothing but dismay "at the idea of their becoming aliens, rivals, enemies" (pp. 103–4).

These extravagant fictions are an index to the intemperance of anti-Federalism. They cater to prejudice and passion. Their traffic in Gothic villains, "discontented ghosts" (p. 438) haunting "the labyrinths of an enchanted castle" (p. 196), and "shameless" and "prostitute" eloquence (p. 411) is not intended to encourage serious thought but to stampede readers into immediate emotional response. The spinners of such "incoherent dreams" (p. 299) bear an unmistakable resemblance to that staple of antifiction polemics, the novelist as seducer. Hamilton rails against the "very specious and seducing form" of disunionist folly, which "is well calculated to lay hold of the prejudices of those to whom it is addressed. But when we come to dissect it with attention, it will appear to be made up of nothing but fair-sounding words" (p. 214). A person "of calm and dispassionate feelings," observing the appeal of anti-Federalist histrionics, can only "sigh for the frailty of human nature" (p. 160).

Yet according to *The Federalist Papers*, there is reason for optimism in the safeguards provided by the Constitution. The impressionable mind can in some measure be vaccinated against the enravishment of partisans (and novelists). It can be protected from its own susceptibility to rhetorical extravagance and superheated narratives. The solution is to temper the effects of popular rule with a steady diet of mediation.

Hamilton, Madison, and Jay lose no opportunity to rehearse this virtue of the national charter. Madison's famed No. 10, his rebuttal to Montesquieu's claim that a republic must be limited in size, reviews the peculiar vulnerabilities of free societies. A proneness to turbulence, to irrationality and hasty action, heads the battery of dangers. The cause is an excess of direct democracy. But the way to alleviate the problem, according to Madison, is not to eliminate popular input: it is to insert distance between the people and their government. Delegation and magnitude thus emerge as the chief guardians of liberty. First, the public voice, passed "through the medium of a chosen body of citizens," will find it easier to rise above "temporary or partial considerations." The views of the many, pronounced by their elected representatives, "will be more consonant to the public good than if pronounced by the people themselves." And second, the larger the society, the greater will be the "variety of parties and interests" in the federal legislature. This will make it more difficult for a majority to "have a common motive to invade the rights" of the minority (pp. 81–83).

Madison follows up these arguments by applying them to temporality. Just as great size shields against "vicious arts" and "local prejudices" (p. 82), so does extension in time defeat the winds of popular passion. (Time is declared to be an "auxiliary precaution" to geographic size [p. 385].) Lengthy terms—Supreme Court justices for life, senators for six years, presidents for four with the possibility of reelection, even biennial as opposed to annual races for the House of Representatives—will enable public officials to gain knowledge and experience. Just as important, the terms will provide "sufficient permanency" so that governors can take the long view and reach decisions without being unduly influenced by "temporary errors and delusions" (pp. 332–33, 383). Duration, too, insulates the rulers from the ruled.

Three of the examples just cited underline the Constitution's investment in mediation. Supreme Court justices are not voted into office but appointed by the president with the "Advice and Consent of the Senate." Senators are selected by the state legislatures and not directly by the people (a provision not overturned until 1913, with the passage of the Seventeenth Amendment). And the president has to be ratified by the electoral college, which on three occasions has reversed the popular will.

Extension in space and time, both complementing the premise of delegation—we could be describing the constitutive elements of print or writing as opposed to speech. Or rather not speech as such but any verbal communication that aims for immediacy and proximity, that wants to ape the affective impact of "in person" importunity (p. 81). The eloquence of demagoguery is high on *The Federalist Papers'* list of bugbears. It was the bane of the Greek democracies, says Madison: "In the ancient republics, where the whole body of the people assembled in person, a single orator, or an artful statesman, was generally seen to rule with as complete a sway as if a scepter had been placed in his single hand" (p. 360). The rhetorical equation with monarchy is deliberate. Madison is rejecting the whole world of intimate, personalized authority, a world reconstructed in his own time, so he and many Federalists believed, by extempore preachers, disaffected radicals like Daniel Shays, and all those who took too literally the Declaration's impassioned periods. (The Declaration, according to Jay Fliegelman, was meant to be read or spoken aloud to audiences of citizens.)[100] To this catalogue may be added the sentimental or Gothic novelist, sweeping away self-control and manipulating readers as if a magic "scepter had been placed in his [or, quite as often, her] single hand."

It follows that a written body of foundational principles has two, seemingly conflicting, objectives. Most obvious, the Constitution makes the polity's structure legible to ordinary men and women. It abstracts the government into a readily available form that anyone can examine. But at the same time, and insofar as the document is consistent thematically with its scripted identity, its "writtenness" mitigates its legibility. The text as a text blunts or attenuates its proffer of participation. It opposes the face-to-face democracy of oral culture with sobering doses of temporal and spatial delay. It thus reduces the risk to the political order from instability and tumult.

Madison, Hamilton, and Jay, deeply appreciative of this advantage, lay great stress on the interdependence of the federal system and writing. The large size of the country would otherwise be incompatible with the vigilance necessary for freedom. Citizens at a distance cannot make a practice of journeying to the government seat to monitor the legislature or the executive "on the spot." "Of personal observation they can have no benefit." Instead they must gather information "from the public prints, from correspondences with their representatives, and with other persons who reside at the place of their deliberations" (p. 516).

The Federalist Papers constantly advertise their own character as pieces of writing. For starters, there is the title: these are pages with script on them. As the papers accumulate, a growing self-reflexivity develops about the work's status as a book. (The first thirty-six essays were collected as a volume in 1788, followed by a second edition of forty-nine.) Beginning with No. 66, footnotes to other documents and to earlier numbers become common. "*Vide* no. 81"; "No. 32"; "*Vide Constitution of Massachusetts*"; "*Vide Protest of the Minority of the Convention of Pennsylvania*"; "*Vide* Blackstone's *Commentaries*, Vol. I, Page 136." These aids inhibit quick consumption, encouraging the reader to consult, to study, and to cross-reference. They privilege reflection over immediate response.

The point is that textuality requires interpretation. A written framework cannot spell out everything, nor should it aspire to do so. It should set boundaries to what can be known with certainty, especially when dealing with future possibilities and private affairs. The authors of *The Federalist Papers*, while in favor of listing the government's powers, take it for granted that any human document will leave important things unsaid. Reticence and omission are inevitable, though one should always bear in mind "the wide difference between *silence* and *abolition*." Add to this the complexity of government and the "inadequateness" of language, a finite resource, and no wonder ambiguities will abound even in a document as devoted to transparency as the Constitution. The "unavoidable inaccuracy" of a political charter is one quality it has in common with the Scriptures: "When the Almighty himself condescends to address mankind in their own language, his meaning, luminous as it must be, is rendered dim and doubtful by the cloudy medium through which it is communicated" (p. 229). This is not, Madison adds, a bad thing but an emphatic reminder that caution and objectivity are essential in parsing the federal compact.

Then there is the matter of authorial identity. The three contributors are concealed under the single pseudonym of "Publius." Their persons, effaced by print, are irrelevant; what matters is the persuasiveness of their position. (In actuality, of course, the authors are no mystery, and were not much of one at the time.) The more important act of masking involves motivation. The writer's heart is off limits. No matter how much he protests his good intentions, readers *cannot* know what he really thinks or feels, and this opacity, this check on confessionalism, is as it should be. "A city on a hill cannot be hid": in *The Federalist Papers*, the ancient ideal that quickened the Puritans coexists with the necessity for discretion. As Hamilton puts it in the very first number, in a classic defense of "public-sphere" impersonality, "My motives must remain in the depository of my own breast. My arguments will be open to all and may be judged of by all" (p. 36).

It would be tempting to read these words as a case of Enlightenment sobriety disavowing romantic self-revelation, Washington victorious over Rousseau.[101] But thanks to Oscar Wilde, we already know that the austere Washington's inability to tell a lie enjoined full disclosure upon his countrymen. Hamilton's arguments, in the American grain, are "open to all," and the federal compact is a revision, not a rupture, of earlier certitude. In this, civic culture was the model, the pathfinder, for literary development. The melodramatic truth-telling integral to the Declaration would filter into mass culture. Works of the emergent canon would feed off the same commitment to legibility even as they qualified it. So the case proved with Hawthorne. *The Scarlet Letter*, the American romantic spirit embodied in fiction, is not the antithesis of constitutional ambiguity and restraint but rather their consummation in the domain of "high art."

North's ministry tapped Samuel Johnson to reply to the Continental Congress in 1775, a year before the Declaration of Independence. Johnson responded with a stinging riposte to American publicity. He produced a pamphlet, *Taxation No Tyranny*, in which he took aim at colonial presumption. The work is best remembered for its rebuke of hypocrisy: "How is it that we hear the loudest yelps for liberty among the drivers of negroes?" No less revealing is the introductory assault on the entire worldview of the Americans. In contrast to their relations who stayed home, the rebellious colonists, according to Johnson, routinely cause truth to become "less evident" by seeking clarity in everything. They discover hidden designs in innocent policies and demand explicit representation when tacit understanding suffices for everyone else. The fallacy of their position, in a phrase, is "trying to make that seen which can be only felt."[102]

CHAPTER **2**

Majoritarian and Racial Tyranny: Tocqueville and Beaumont

Tocqueville conceived the most notorious stricture on American legibility as second nature. The United States, which he toured midway through the administration of Andrew Jackson, and in the same year as Nat Turner's rebellion, seemed to him a culture from which independent thought had been eradicated. The cause was that very "equality of condition" or absence of social rank that demarcated the young republic from the nations of Europe. Where all are fundamentally alike, according to Tocqueville, none can hold out against popular consensus.

Another interpretation of the "tyranny of the majority" was proposed by Tocqueville's fellow traveler, Gustave de Beaumont. A student of customs rather than democratic institutions, Beaumont does not write of the republic as an ominous preview of Europe's future. On the contrary, he sees a nation mired in backward-looking attitudes that stem from the prevalence of a condition the opposite of Tocqueville's: inequality. In *Marie; or, Slavery in the United States* (1835),[1] Beaumont focuses on race, and he claims that racial prejudice has effectively reinstated the European class system. He does not dispute his friend's insight about Americans all being alike; "there is only one class" (p. 21), he admits, but its membership is restricted. Beaumont's study is truly the companion piece to *Democracy in America*: the two works leave no doubt that the dictatorship of race is rooted in the soil of white equivalence.

Tocqueville, the infinitely more acclaimed of the two Gallic visitors, has a battery of names for democracy's inner trespass. He denominates it "the absolute sovereignty of the majority," "the omnipotence of the majority," and, most pejoratively, "the tyranny of the majority." His criticism boils down to the argument that public opinion far exceeds the power of any Old World despotism. A king's authority is physical, and while he may compel the obedience of his subjects through the threat of force, he cannot subjugate their wills. There will always be a clandestine realm that eludes him: "Thought is an invisible and subtle power that mocks all the efforts of tyranny. At the present time the most absolute monarchs in Europe cannot prevent certain opinions hostile to their authority from circulating in secret through their dominions and even in their courts."[2]

The American case is different, Tocqueville says, because there the majority enjoys moral as well as physical power. Debate thrives until the moment a decision is reached, whereupon all parties unite in bowing to the popular verdict. Opposition does not simply vanish from the public forums; it ceases to exist anywhere. Even the dissenter learns to be silent lest he alienate his neighbors; finding no one to agree with him, and attacked by self-doubt, he imperceptibly comes around to the prevailing viewpoint. The American mind has no shelter from consensus, no place where impermissible thoughts can safely hide, and neither "fetters" nor "headsmen," the crude methods of foreign monarchies, can duplicate this level of insidious conformism. Autocratic regimes only go after the body, but democratic republics enslave the soul.[3]

Tocqueville's argument is the political analogue to Henry James's reflections on American domestic architecture as proscribing a discrete interior. For both men, the reign of publicity colonizes everything. The Tocquevillean critique has, in one form or another, been reworked by a long line of French intellectuals for whom the United States has represented the quintessence of the modern (as it did for Tocqueville himself). Advertising, conformity, "friendliness," the cinema, the promiscuous exposure of the psyche—the New World menace has been summed up by Georges Duhamel as "a kind of masturbation of the eye." Indeed, anti-American feelings have fueled the twentieth-century French quarrel with ocularcentrism. One need only tick off some of the principal names: Guy Debord, indicting the "society of the spectacle" at the apogee of postwar American power; Michel Foucault, dissecting panoptic mechanisms of control just as the American Cold War state succeeded to France's role in Indochina; Christian Metz and Jean-Louis Baudry condemning the infantilizing allure of the popular, that is, the Hollywood, movies; and Jacques Lacan, simultaneously battling his expulsion from the American-dominated International Psychoanalytic Association and dismissing the coherent self championed by ego psychology as a fiction of the (visual) mirror stage.[4]

At the end of his first volume, Tocqueville turns his attention, almost as an afterthought, to race. He considers the topic only "collaterally connected" to his main subject of equality, and he stops well short of characterizing white treatment of Indians and Africans as another species of majoritarian absolutism. Although he does say that both racial minorities "suffer from [the] tyranny" of Europeans, he does not bother to develop the idea and clearly does not regard the subjection as somehow produced by popular rule. Americans, he insists, have never founded an aristocracy and will never do so. A social system institutionalizing a privileged class is simply too "repugnant to natural equity." The spectacle of a democratic people gradually establishing "inequality of condition, until it arrived at inviolable privileges and exclusive castes, would be a novelty in the world; and nothing indicates that America is likely to be the first to furnish such an example."[5]

Tocqueville's blind spot is corrected by his compatriot Beaumont; but the fact that even so penetrating an observer misses race's ideological effects suggests how thoroughly the contradiction rubs against the American grain. The careful reader of *Democracy in America* can find plentiful evidence, if not argument, for the proximity of racism and equality. For example, Tocqueville famously remarks that prejudice against Africans cannot be ascribed entirely to slavery because there is actually *less* segregation in the South. Racism diminishes where hierarchy is an accepted fact of life; where slavery has been abolished, on the other hand, antipathy reigns, and European-Americans show the most intolerance of all "in those states where servitude has never been known." Moreover, democratic and Protestant mores appear to breed a greater degree of pride in "whiteness" than exists in other cultures. The English, with their tradition of liberty, are much more resistant than either the French or the Spanish to intermixture with dark races.[6]

Beaumont's text, a hybrid of novel and sociological treatise, picks up these themes and gives them a centrality lacking in *Democracy in America*. For Beaumont, color—not individualism, nor democracy, nor slavery—is the great fact and dividing line of American life. Color solidifies the community of equals by setting limits on its membership. Color also allows a democratic society to smuggle back the gratifications of hierarchy. It resurrects aristocracy in the guise of race. But "inviolable privileges and exclusive castes" (Tocqueville's words) so outrage American principles that they cannot be admitted into consciousness. A kind of contradictory double movement results: a fanaticism to search out, and an equal determination not to perceive. Paranoia strives to unmask and extirpate any trace of "amalgamation" as an insult to pure bloodlines. At the same time, whites impose a rigid system of segregation meant to spare them the proximity, even the sight, of blackness.[7]

The hard truth of *Marie* is that color functions as a hereditary privilege and as a hereditary curse. In passage after passage, Beaumont ponders the "two contrary codes of morals" (p. 73) that make the freest nation on earth a simultaneous site of the feudalism of race. Americans forbid "distinctions among men," yet they are "proud to be white," as though fair pigment were proof of titled ancestry: "With strong and philosophical mind condemning the privilege of birth, and with stupidity maintaining the privilege of color!" (p. 120). Will not emancipation dispel this ignorance? asks the Frenchman

Ludovic, only to be assured that the prejudice is immutable. "To free the Negroes in the United States is to create an inferior class, and whoever is a pure-blooded white belongs to a privileged class. A white skin is a mark of nobility" (p. 62). Marvels the Frenchman: "If your custom is not to admit the transmission of honors by blood, why does it sanction inherited infamy?" (p. 63). And another character, the heroine Marie, who has inherited a tiny fraction of black blood, complains: "My birth condemned me to the contempt of men" (p. 66).

Tocqueville despaired of overcoming a division erected on the "visible and indelible signs" of race.[8] Beaumont recognizes that "color" is not even a color; or rather, it is a good deal more than visible skin shade. It is a pathogen that must be isolated and destroyed most of all when it is imperceptible and has the temerity to venture out of its cordon sanitaire.[9] Marie herself is physically indistinguishable from Anglo-Europeans. Her "complexion was even whiter than the swans" (p. 58). Sixty years before *Plessy v. Ferguson*, a solitary "drop of black blood" in a distant forebear is enough to taint an entire family (p. 55). Even though nothing can be spotted on the flesh, the stigma is so abhorred that even if its possessor flees to a distant city and assumes a fresh identity, he or she will be hunted down and humiliated. "Public opinion, so indulgent to adventurers who hide their names and antecedents, pitilessly searches for proofs of African ancestry." The entire society turns into a DNA-scouring private eye on the issue of race: "The color may be blotted out; the stain remains. It seems that people find it out even when it is invisible; there is no refuge secret enough, no retreat obscure enough, to hide it" (pp. 78–79).

The other side of this frenzy for detection is a fiat of disappearance. Americans go to extravagant lengths to seal off Negroes and prevent them from interacting with whites. Ludovic reports that black children are denied access to public schools; injured or ill blacks are treated at separate hospitals; black criminals are incarcerated in separate sections of the jails. The two races do not reside in the same areas, nor do they worship together. "Who would have believed it! Rank and privilege in Christian churches! The blacks are either relegated to some dark corner of the building or completely excluded." Every town has its pair of cemeteries, "one for the whites, the other for colored people" (pp. 75–76). And the requirement of segregation that accompanies Africans into the grave also reaches back to the beginnings of time. Although Beaumont does not mention it, contemporaneous American scientists were elaborating the theory of polygenesis, the doctrine of separate origins for the different races. They would outlaw integration in the Garden of Eden, as well as in the afterlife. (Polygenism came to be known as the American school of anthropology.)[10]

This is boundary patrolling gone mad, changed from an instrument of democratic knowing into a weapon of ostracism and tyranny. And the word "tyranny," in this context, is deliberate: Tocqueville's smothering of intellectual dissent becomes, in *Marie*, a community-wide attack on those who are

different. The passage on American conformism surpassing European au-
tocracies from *Democracy in America* darkens in Beaumont into a
Hamilton-like comparison to "Asiatic despotism," only this time the
tyrants encompass the whole population of American whites:

> In a barbaric country, one has but one hate in the presence of the greatest
> misery—hate against the despot. To him alone belongs all the power;
> through him alone comes all the evil; against him alone are aimed all im-
> precations. But in a land of equality all citizens are responsible for social
> injustices; each is a party to them. Not a white man exists in America who
> is not a barbarous, iniquitous persecutor of the black race.
>
> In Turkey, there is but one tyrant responsible for the most frightful dis-
> tress; in the United States, there are, for each act of tyranny, ten million
> tyrants. (pp. 73–74).

Such total dictatorship, Beaumont adds, can happen *only* with popular
rule, and he proceeds to underscore the link between government by the
majority and the tradition of English Protestantism. In an appendix to
Marie, he acknowledges the prominence of religious sects in the struggle for
abolition. Some translate their faith in "the moral equality of man" into an
"ardent zeal for the cause of human liberty" (p. 201). Yet that same egalitarianism makes other Protestant congregations all the more unwilling to
combat bigotry. The sect is a mini-democracy, and every flock elects its
minister. Since he depends on his constituents for his livelihood, the Protestant pastor dare not offend them by opposing their racial attitudes. A
Catholic priest, in contrast, is appointed by the church hierarchy; he answers only to his bishop and enjoys "absolute master[y]" over his congregants. The upshot is a tolerance rare among decentralized denominations:
"The Catholic churches are the only ones that will allow neither privilege
nor exclusion; the black population may enter there like the white"
(pp. 76–77).

With the advantage of hindsight, one might indulge a certain skepticism here: New York's Irish Catholics rioted against blacks during the Civil
War, and their religious leaders did little to curb their racism. But thirty
years after Beaumont's travels, Catholicism had become markedly more
American, and priests more responsive to the sentiments of their parishioners. Which simply underscores the iterated theme of *Marie*: democracy
in America is the "tyranny of the people's will"; far from being an improvement in human affairs, it is, for the black race, a political system "of hatred
and scorn." Beaumont sums up his impeachment of popular sovereignty in
terms reminiscent of Tocqueville on the tyranny of uniformity: "Public
opinion, so charitable when it protects, is the cruelest of tyrants when it per-
secutes. Public opinion, all-powerful in the United States, desires the oppression of a detested race, and nothing can thwart its hatred" (p. 77).

Beaumont, in his foreword, warns readers that there is a palpable "dis-
sidence" between his own work and that of his companion (p. 7). Yes and

no. There is obvious disagreement in that Tocqueville emphasizes democracy (and maintains a guarded optimism) while *Marie* foregrounds racial prejudice (and presents a tragic picture of the new nation). Yet the two accounts of the antebellum United States belong together in theory just as they do in historical fact. Egalitarian liberty is the foundation for the aristocracy of color. It at once allows the return of feudal hierarchy and hustles it out of sight. Perhaps partly for this reason, because caste is an inadmissible affront to democratic ideals, *Marie* itself was lost from view for more than a hundred years. It suffered a very different fate in the New World from *Democracy in America*. Tocqueville's two-volume study was instantly hailed as a classic and translated into English almost immediately by Henry Reeve. It has never been out of print. Published simultaneously in 1835, and reissued several times in France, *Marie* was not made available as a book in English until 1958, four years after the Supreme Court called for an end to school segregation in *Brown v. Board of Education*.

CHAPTER 3

Popular Forms

Three popular and enduring genres take recognizable shape in the works of Cooper, Poe, and Fanny Fern: the Western, the detective story, and the celebrity fiction. Each genre is built on a grammar of visibility. The Western irradiates the wilderness; the detective tale, the city and the human heart; the celebrity novel, the newly consolidated zone of the private. Two of the authors, Poe and Cooper, have strong claims to having pioneered their generic categories; the third, Fern, writes within a tradition. However, Fern's text presses a strain in the domestic novel to an extremity of exhibitionism that amounts to originality.

My illustrations, the Leatherstocking Tales, "The Murders in the Rue Morgue" and "The Purloined Letter," and *Ruth Hall*, are not uniformly straightforward narratives. All possess complications and ambiguous elements, although all share a thrust toward the legible. The textual peculiarities count less than the intentions of a prototype. It is the forms themselves, not their discrete avatars, and certainly not their canonical debuts, that constitute a cultural legacy. The Indian and cowboy saga, the mystery story, and the exposé have flourished in American popular arts—as literature, radio programs, movies, and television shows—for two centuries. They have gone through dizzying permutations (as narratives of space travel, war with aliens, etc.). Their health and longevity as mass entertainment are beyond dispute, not just in the United States but throughout the globe, often enough in American productions.[1]

Cooper and the Western

The Western is a novelization of the grid, a translation into literary genre of the drive to visualize the physical environment. Its very setting is evocative of the linearity through which the framers of the Land Ordinance of 1785 sought to pacify and standardize a continent. The action of the typical Western unfolds at or near a frontier, the boundary line between the Indian- and outlaw-infested backcountry and the town, fort, or other settlement where the emissaries of civilization have planted their farthest outpost.[2]

Cooper, in *The Pathfinder* (1840), has crafted a scene that is exemplary of the Western genre's scopic power. As the novel begins, a group of characters has gathered on an acclivity. The gentle height has been piled with uprooted trees by some miraculous force of nature, thus creating an extended opening from which the travelers can gain an elevated view of the forest. These privileged spots go by the name of "wind-rows." (The pun on "window" is a subject to which I will return.) Cooper devotes several pages to describing the extraordinary vista, with the trees "forming one broad and seemingly interminable carpet of foliage, that stretched away towards the setting sun, until it bounded the horizon, by blending with the clouds, as the waves and sky meet at the base of the vault of Heaven" (p. 9).[3]

Moments like these, in which Cooper's art abounds, have always impressed readers of the Leatherstocking Tales with their painterly, visual qualities. The novelist's earliest critics allied him with members of the Hudson River school as a master at representing natural settings. D. H. Lawrence, who did more than anyone to revive Cooper's modern reputation, praised his prose for its "Pictures! Some of the loveliest, most glamorous pictures in all literature."[4] And even Mark Twain was struck by the vividness of Natty's adventures, although Twain of course lambasted those pictures as hilariously inaccurate, filled with details of almost supernatural prowess that had no business in a realistic narration.

Twain in some ways is closer to the truth than Lawrence. It tells only a part of the story to label Cooper's descriptions as painterly or lithographic. They are a good deal more than that in their penetration into invisible recesses that no brushstroke could capture without shattering verisimilitude. Cooper writes as his hero sees and hears, with cavalier disregard for the laws of nature. In the passage on the wind-row, the "surface of verdure" is likened several times to bodies of water, an entirely apt comparison in that much of *The Pathfinder*'s action occurs on and around Lake Ontario. Indeed, this opening scene is replayed about a hundred pages later when Mabel Dunham scales another boundary line, a bastion from which she can behold, on the one side, the "apparently endless forest," and on the other "the still broader field of fluid" that is the lake (p. 109). Her Uncle Cap, a saltwater seaman, voices disdain for the wilderness as a "tame surface" beside the Atlantic (p. 10); but Mabel, as well as Natty's readers, knows that the woodsman's domain is as rich in hidden dangers as any ocean: beasts, Indians, Frenchmen, desperadoes, subterfuges, and ambushes all lie in wait beneath the treetops.

Pathfinder's senses ferret out every one of them. His hearing and above all his sight routinely dig under, through, and around the surface to detect—with Cooper in tow—things impossible for unaided human organs to perceive. His "vigilant ear," we are told in *The Pathfinder*, can catch the sound "made by the parting of a dried branch of a tree" on a distant shore (p. 99). His "vigilant eye," according to *The Last of the Mohicans* (1826), suffers "no sign, whether friendly or hostile, to escape him" (p. 316).[5] In *The Deerslayer* (1840), Cooper's frontiersman acquires his nickname "Hawkeye" when he thwarts an attempted ambush, and his dumbstruck Iroquois victim bestows the title. Natty glimpses a rifle muzzle and a pair of eyes—black eyes, at that—through a minuscule opening in the bushes, aims "almost without sighting," and gets off his shot a fraction of a second before his enemy. He then stands impassively while the Indian bursts from the woods and rushes toward him, tomahawk in hand, only to crumble helplessly to the ground from his fatal wound (p. 110).[6] Recurrent versions of this scene, often as a harmless but sense-defying shooting match, appear in all five of the Leatherstocking novels. Hawkeye displays his preternatural marksmanship by seeing and hitting a target, such as another bullet embedded in a tree, or the narrow mouth of a gourd, at a distance of hundreds of feet. Disbelieving onlookers have to approach the target and examine it closely, sometimes with their fingers, to convince themselves of his accuracy.

Cooper wants the reader to extrapolate from these exhibitions to the Western as a form of literature; I want to add a related point about the genre as the cinematic apparatus in embryo. Natty's exploits, as well as those of his Indian companions, Chingachgook and Uncas, are possible because the wilderness never lies. The twig breaking a mile away, a barely perceptible motion through the leaves, a moccasin footprint so faint that ordinary eyes pass over it: "These infallible signs," Cooper insists, provide the "undeniable testimony" from which "the practiced woodsman arrive[s] at the truth" (*Last*, pp. 221, 258). Deciphering such signs is no different from conning a text, the novelist goes on to suggest. Though Hawkeye is himself innocent of book learning, he often speaks of his survival skills as an act of literacy. In *The Last of the Mohicans*, he exclaims to David Gamut that he has "never read but in one [book], and the words that are written there are too simple and plain to need much schooling; though I may boast that of forty long and hard-working years." When Gamut, perplexed, asks the volume's title, Natty gestures toward the forest and says, "Tis open before your eyes" (p. 138).

Natty's virgin continent as transparent sign system is both subject matter and model for the Leatherstocking Tales. Mark Twain notwithstanding, the tales are fictional equivalents to a nature rendered "simple and plain" to "a practysed eye" (*Pathfinder*, p. 375). They provide an education in the utter truthfulness and ultimate legibility of the Western form, and they turn the genre's readers into metaphoric woodsmen. We acquire expertise by following Hawkeye through his sixty-year odyssey from the youth of *The Deerslayer* to the dying old man of *The Prairie* (1827), and by participating in his victories over perils and deceptions. Every textual obscurity, every apparent obstacle to understanding, can be overcome if we take Cooper's heroic Pathfinder as our guide.

True, even Natty can be baffled for a moment. But the Tales never allow us to remain in darkness. Some character, usually an Indian, always steps forward to solve the puzzle, and he does so in terms that underscore the parallel between comprehending the text and tracking the wild. In *The Last of the Mohicans*, Chingachgook and Uncas are able to ascertain the tribe of a dead Indian by studying his scalp as if it were "the leaf of a book, and each hair a letter" (p. 232). They can tell who an individual brave is from the faded footprint he has left on a trail, for, as Natty reminds an astonished Duncan Heyward, "one moccasin is no more like another than one book is like another" (p. 220). What is mute to untrained eyes and ears speaks volumes to the natives, and through them, to Natty, and through Natty, to the reader. As in the detective story and the celebrity fiction, the challenges of the wilderness adventure are there to whet our curiosity, but they are not meant to stump us. They exist in order to be dispelled.

The feats of percipience that master those challenges prophesy the cinema. The movies, in other words, have not just a geographic or thematic bond with the Western—as suggested by the choice of a train robbery for the first feature film, and by the genre's lasting popularity with Hollywood—but a perceptual or epistemological connection as well. The frontier narrative, as exemplified by Cooper, heralds the motion pictures in its sensory hyperreality; it is the site where visual and aural potentialities were auditioned before the mass public in advance of their mechanical incarnation.

Here Twain is remarkably astute on the "literary *delirium tremens*" of his romantic predecessor. (The phrase is Twain's term for *The Deerslayer*.) In "Fenimore Cooper's Literary Offenses," the humorous attack he first delivered as a lecture in 1893, and then published in 1895, Twain charges Cooper with violating eighteen of the nineteen rules governing literary art. What the infractions add up to is a wholesale disrespect for "the eternal laws of Nature." All the absurdities I have noted are ridiculed as affronts to credibility. Characters trying to move silently through the woods are sure to "step on a dry twig and alarm all the reds and whites for two hundred yards around." About a shooting match where the target is a nail head, Twain marvels:

> How far can the best eyes see a common house-fly? A hundred yards? It is quite impossible. Very well: eyes that cannot see a house-fly that is a hundred yards away cannot see an ordinary nail-head at that distance, for the

size of the two objects is the same. It takes a keen eye to see a fly or a nail-head at fifty yards—one hundred and fifty feet. Can the reader do it?

Hawkeye hits the invisible nail head with ease, and Twain mocks him as someone who could command a princely salary in Wild West shows hunting flies with a rifle.[7]

Twain has Cooper dead to rights: the all-seeing Hawkeye is a human movie camera, capable of acts of telescopic and microscopic vision that would not materialize as a popular possibility for half a century. But the very supernaturalism that disqualifies Cooper as a realist constitutes his modernity. In this respect, Twain's piece is an *ave atque vale!* Cooper, he says, "saw nearly all things as through a glass eye, darkly."[8] The glass eye of the camera lens revived the Western as a cinematic spectacle at the very moment that the older writer's brand of romantic fiction was becoming obsolete. While Twain worked on his critical obituary for the Leatherstocking Tales, the first of Edison's kinetoscopes were being shipped to arcades across the country, and the filmed Western prepared to displace the written one as a centerpiece of mass entertainment.[9]

Toward the end of *The Pathfinder*, Cooper claims a superiority for literature over the "lame sciences" of physiognomy and phrenology. The two interpretive systems too often jump from outer signs to erroneous conclusions, he says. His own novel, on the other hand, has consistently exposed the traitor Davey Muir as one whose "air of supererogatory courtesy" invariably "denotes artifice." We "hold," Cooper continues, "that there is no more infallible evidence of insincerity of purpose, short of overt acts, than a face that smiles when there is no occasion, and the tongue that is out of measure smooth" (p. 414). Literature is an unerring judge of motivation. No amateur psychology can match its ability to see through smiles and flattery to the inner truth of character. (A similar preference for literary analysis over phrenology will appear in *Ruth Hall*.)

The discriminations of the Leatherstocking Tales are not, then, limited to nature and warfare. They radiate into arenas that seem far removed from the gridwork clarity of the physical environment. Along with character reading, one such arena is race, and no book in the series is more lucent on this score than *The Last of the Mohicans*. Lucent and fanatical, not to mention North American: "Cooper's obsessive social neatness," as Doris Sommer has put it, demarcates him from his Latin American heirs, who dissent from Yankee intolerance toward class and racial crossings.[10]

The pathology grips both the author and his protagonist: Natty rambles on endlessly about his purity as "a man without a cross" (p. 138), and Cooper endorses this boundary policing by killing off Cora Munro and Uncas lest they consummate their attraction to each other (this despite Cora's already tainted bloodlines as a product of white-black mixture). The insistence on legibility and the anathematizing of racial uncertainty go well beyond surface appearance. Cora is not recognizably black, and Natty's hint of defensiveness about his "genuine" whiteness (p. 35) probably stems from the fact that his complexion has been burned by the sun. He tells anyone who will listen that his skin "has no tinge of red to it that the winds of the heavens and the sun have not bestowed" (p. 318).

The problem, of course, is that Hawkeye, as the hero of the Western, is that familiar "man in the middle," a mediating figure between the wilderness and civilization. (The renegade Indian Magua speaks of him as "one whose skin is neither red nor pale" [p. 344].) This makes Natty peculiarly susceptible to the danger of miscegenation, a lurking possibility that the whole thrust of the narrative works to prevent. In the end racial hybridity can be ensured against only by abstracting Natty from sexual relations altogether and turning him into the "hard, isolate, stoic" killer recognized by Lawrence.[11] The one time the hero comes close to marriage, with Mabel Dunham of *The Pathfinder*, the consequences prove disastrous for his ocular hegemony. Romantic desire converts his very nickname of Deerslayer, a title more deserved, he boasts, than that of "many a great lord" (p. 18), into a misnomer. Whenever he dreams of Mabel, "The young does sport before me, and when I raise Killdeer, in order to take a little venison, the animals look back, and it seems as if they all had Mabel's sweet countenance, laughing in my face, and looking as if they said, 'shoot me, if you dare!'" (p. 445). Even the remote prospect of mating (and thus, more chillingly, of interracialism) disorders the "practysed eye" that gives the Leatherstocking saga its haunting grandeur. The legibility of the Western can no more survive the smudging of racial divisions than could the legibility of the West endure without the section lines.

The descriptions, strikingly similar, are yet significantly different. The first, to which I will return momentarily, appears in "The Murders in the Rue Morgue." Poe's unnamed narrator finds himself shaking his head in awe at C. Auguste Dupin's "peculiar analytic ability." Dupin, Western culture's first "private eye," has an uncanny gift for intuiting people's thoughts and histories. "He boasted to me," says our informant, "with a low chuckling laugh, that most men, in respect to himself, wore windows in their bosoms" (p. 144).

The second description, from *The Deerslayer*, occurs toward the end of a long passage on Judith Hutter's unexpected romantic interest in Natty Bumppo. The novelty of the attraction, for her, consists in the fact that she is a renowned frontier beauty, while Natty is neither handsome nor polished. But Judith has tired of designing admirers from the British army, and she feels instantly drawn to the hero despite his plainness. The reason, according to Cooper, is that Deerslayer "had a window in his breast, through which the light of his honesty was ever shining" (p. 153).

In the Poe, Dupin's singular acuity enables him to peer through the windowlike fronts of other men into their hidden depths. In the Cooper, it is Natty himself whose bosom is made of glass, but his windowlike aperture does not so much bare his interior to scrutiny as beam light outward from his heart. In part this is the familiar romantic idea of the self as a lamp that subjectively colors what it sees rather than passively reflecting the real like a mirror. Given Natty's miraculous sensory range, however, it is tempting to read the image of light shining from his breast with reference to the future as much as to the past: as a foreshadowing of the radiance streaming onto the screen from a motion picture projector.

I have called Natty a human movie camera, but this emphasis inverts the process of consumption. It slights the cinema's democratizing power. The projector, after all, is the technological invention that enables the popular audience to see and hear as Natty does. The flickering light on the silver screen multiplies *our* ocular and auditory reach until it equals Hawkeye's. Like a window (or a "wind-row," to return to the pun with which I began), the filmic image opens unimaginable vistas to perception. In nickelodeons, movie palaces, and finally cineplexes, the tracery on a fly's wing is visible in close-up to every ticket holder, and, after the talkies, the sound of a breaking twig reverberates in the dullest ear.

Poe and the Detective Story

One approach to Poe's Dupin narratives would be to read them as urban variations on the Western. The material correlative in this case would be not the uniform sections of the territories but the planning of the New World metropolis on a grid. When Poe was writing, in the antebellum period, American cityscapes tended to be worlds apart from their European equivalents. They were smaller, more coherent, less densely populated. Consider Poe's comparison of London and New York in "The Man of the Crowd" (1840). The narrator has been tracking his quarry through a rainy English night:

> The street was a narrow and long one, and his course lay within it for nearly an hour, during which the passengers had gradually diminished to about that number which is ordinarily seen at noon on Broadway near the park—so vast a difference is there between a London populace and that of the most frequented American city. (p. 479)[12]

Historical evidence bears out this contrast. Mid-nineteenth-century Manhattan, having outgrown the face-to-face relations of the past, maintained legibility through its physical layout and relatively small size and also through a network of textual aids: street signs, sandwich boards, advertisements, newspapers, handbills, shop signs, banners. A public culture of "brazen visibility" defined the city as an apparent conundrum ripe for decoding.[13]

In "The Man of the Crowd," the opaque European epicenter and the textual rendering of it in Poe's story are identified with "a certain German book that *'es lasst sich nicht lesen'*—it does not permit itself to be read" (p. 475). The detective tale is the antidote to this obscurity. It unravels the city mystery through a plot that moves ineluctably toward an outcome of solution or transparency. It might be said, then, that in the Dupin stories, which are set in Paris, Poe imposes an American urban lucidity upon the unreadable European cityscape: that he looks upon the Old World's textual-spatial enigmas with eyes sharpened by experience of antebellum Richmond, Baltimore, and New York.

Other inferences are possible from the French setting of the narratives. Dupin's Paris might be interpreted as a precursor of the American future, an omen of the massive urbanization of the late nineteenth century. The detective's resourcefulness could thus be taken as forecasting an entire culture's "search for order," in Robert Wiebe's serviceable phrase, as the American people sought to make sense of the change from predominantly rural society to metropolitan behemoth. A third possible reading, and the one to which I will return later, might see Poe's French capital as an image of the American city already being transformed by immigrants, but threatened less by the arrival of European newcomers than by racial otherness. This perspective invites a pair of juxtapositions that will bring our urban and cultural themes into dialogue with the psychological. I will weigh Poe's stories against two classic European exercises in detection: Freud's *The Psychopathology of Everyday Life* (1901) and Lacan's analysis of Dupin's method as an "allegory of psychoanalysis." Revisiting the critical chestnut about Poe's Parisian detective as a proleptic Freudian will reveal the extent to which he is also an American in disguise.[14]

How does Dupin know? His belief, that "most men, in respect to himself, wore windows in their bosoms," seems to place him at the opposite pole from Natty. A "private eye" to Cooper's Hawkeye, he comprehends men's secret thoughts, their interiors, not the vast outdoors as seen by a bird in flight. Dupin's domain is insight, deduction, verbal analysis. But if his boastful metaphor cannot literally refer to the eyes—he does not, after all, observe organs and skeletons like an X-ray machine—it does suggest an ocular facility that enables him to spot what others overlook. Poe describes his hero as a composite knower, one who "makes, in silence, a host of observations and inferences" (p. 142). The detective's reach is imperial, encompassing both visual mastery over surfaces and analytic penetration into the invisible depths. It is the professional police, not the freelance investigator, who consistently misapply the two techniques and deduce instead of looking, or scrutinize instead of thinking.

Despite its title, sight holds center stage in "The Purloined Letter." "Policial eyes" (p. 216) are thoroughly blind in this story even though the prefect and his assistants excel at minute visual inspection of persons and premises. They ransack "every nook and corner" of Minister D's hotel, using microscopes to probe for secret compartments, and they twice waylay and search him physically (pp. 210–13). Dupin's observation proves superior to the police's, and a match for the minister's cleverness, because it perfects, as it were, the direct spatial apperception of vision. Pretending to suffer from weak eyes, the sleuth pays a visit to the minister wearing "a pair of green spectacles," and under cover of his glasses, he discerns the stolen letter on a pasteboard rack, crumpled as though to disavow its importance. The letter escaped the notice of the police, Dupin explains to the narrator, because it was "too palpably self-evident," rather like the letters on a map that no one sees because they "stretch, in large characters, from one end of the chart to the other" (p. 219).

The reference to cartography is a nice touch for our purposes, a reminder of the instantly accessible American terrain as observed from the air. The detective, as a connoisseur of visibility, can perceive things that the authorities dismiss as unworthy of notice because *anyone* can see them without the least exertion. As Dupin puts it: "Thus there is such a thing as being too profound. Truth is not always in a well. In fact, as regards the more important knowledge, I do believe that she is invariably superficial. The depth lies in the valleys where we seek her, and not upon the mountain-tops where she is found" (p. 153).

This quotation comes from the second of Poe's mysteries (the first in order of composition), "The Murders in the Rue Morgue," and is something of a paradox in that the method of analysis in *this* tale is more logical and systematic than visual. To solve the identity of the killer, Dupin borrows some of the police's strategy from "The Purloined Letter." He carries out a meticulous physical examination of the crime scene and infers from accumulated evidence—the stupendous strength and agility required to enter through the window, the texture of a hair, the mutilation of the corpses—that the assailant could not have been a mere man. Sightless musing replaces sudden revelation. As Dupin explains his step-by-step deductions to the narrator, "his eyes, vacant in expression, regarded only the wall" (p. 155). "Murders" foregrounds language, as crucial to the process of reasoning. Dupin learns the details of the tragedy from reading newspaper accounts. The ape targets his deadly violence at the throats, mouths, and vocal chords of the victims. And the voice overheard by the witnesses is imagined to be conversing in all the vernacular tongues of Europe.

The master of appearances possesses equal adroitness at analytic thinking, once again in contrast to the prefect. And once again, Dupin supplies the moral, apparently contradicting, or at least amending, his earlier stricture on the police. The official crime solvers have more ingenuity than substance, he says, and "our friend the Prefect" could never have gotten to the bottom of the Rue Morgue murders because he "is somewhat too cunning to be profound" (p. 168).

The deployment of different techniques in these tales is more a matter of degree than kind. A second look all but dissolves the opposition in tactics. "The Purloined Letter," as its title will not let us forget, is obsessed with writing and depends for its denouement on Dupin's ability to enter the mind of his adversary. Insight rather than sight *really* outwits the minister, and the story begins, accordingly, with the prefect happening upon Dupin and the narrator sitting together in darkness in the hero's library. Dupin rises to light the lamp, but he decides not to do so once he realizes the reason for the visit. If it is a matter demanding reflection, he tells the bewildered police chief, "we shall examine it to better purpose in the dark" (p. 208). The visual can provide little help where reconstructing the minister's thought holds the key to success, and indeed Dupin reasons his way to the likely solution *before* he puts observation to the test. Policial failure, from this angle, flows less from blindness than from stupidity, sheer incomprehension when it comes to understanding a subtle intellect like the minister's. The prefect simply lacks the psychological acuity to see through men's bosoms as though they were windows.

In "Murders," to continue with our methodological about-face, depth-seeking—attempting to be "profound"—positively hinders the police's efforts to apprehend the criminal. Optical alertness, on the other hand, turns out to be an essential. Dupin figured out the hiding place of the purloined letter while meditating in his windowless library. Now the order is reversed, and he pieces together a solution *"a posteriori"* (p. 157). Newspaper reports are insufficient: "We will go and see the premises with our own eyes" (p. 153). Moreover, psychology has no role to play in this story. The sympathetic insight necessary to best a prodigy like the minister is utterly irrelevant. What good is "an identification of the reasoner's intellect with that of his opponent" (p. 215) if animal instinct, not human greed or desire, can explain everything? The police go wrong because they assume that theft was the motive for the murders. But there was *no* motive, and no interiority either, precisely because the killer was an Ourang-Outang.

Poe's two stories, then, are thoroughgoing hybrids, and Dupin's genius consists in knowing when and how to exercise a particular faculty. Let us try to profit from the detective's cognitive and ocular versatility by applying some analysis of our own to that seemingly blank subject, the ferocious ape. The investigation will eventually return us to the psychological—the dimension presumably missing from the animal interior. But as a first step, it leads back to the social secreted within the psychological: the Freud of *The Psychopathology of Everyday Life* and the different fates of race and ethnicity in Europe and America.

We begin with our earlier suggestion that Poe's national provenance and, more particularly, his Southern outlook flavor his portrayal of Paris. Consider the profusion of foreign residents in "Murders." The fictional French capital has a level of ethnic diversity evocative of the antebellum United States. Early waves of European immigrants to these shores, combined with economic hard times (the long depression of 1837–43), had aroused nativist sentiment. In the narrative, various people come forward to testify about the violent crime, and each describes the killer's "gruff voice" as that *"of a foreigner"* (p. 155). The witnesses speculate that the language being spoken was English, or perhaps German, or possibly Russian or Italian. Not surprising, this confusion: those interviewed by the police are themselves evidence of an alarming heterogeneity. They include, besides several Parisians, an Englishman, a Spaniard, an Italian, and a Dutchman.

The guilty party speaks none of these tongues and is not himself, or itself, a European. The procession of suspects and witnesses belongs to the same species as the natives; they are therefore "innocent" and assimilable (though not as desirable as the indigenous Frenchman, the wrongly arrested but rightly named Adolphe Le Bon). The true culprit is the ape that escapes his master's control and commits atrocious, and vaguely sexual, violence against women, slitting one victim's throat and strangling the other before shoving her body up a chimney.

Poe, a rabid antiabolitionist, probably had in mind the black slave when he imagined his deadly animal.[15] Blacks were widely viewed as subhuman and routinely compared to apes. They haunted Southern sleep with nightmares of slave rebellion, homicide, and the violation of white women. (Even the enlightened Thomas Jefferson, a Virginian like Poe, believed that black men showed an erotic preference for white women, "as uniformly as is the preference of the Oranootan for the black women over those of his own species.")[16] The threat to civilization, in other words, emanates not from the ethnic strangers but from the African/beast, not from those who speak a different language but from those inhabit, and dare to rise up from, a different order of creation. Poe's tale teems with references to heads and bodies, and the Ourang-Outang's rampage is clearly meant to suggest the overthrow of rationality or mind by the brutely physical. A grim irony underlines the horror: the monster gets inside the women's apartment by scaling a lightning rod, emblem of man's conquest over nature.

Shift now to *Psychopathology*, a text with as great a faith in the pregnancy of trifles as Poe's private eye. Freud's book, published just four years after the election of the Jew-baiting populist Karl Lueger as mayor of Vienna, shows a comparable sensitivity, or, in this case, hypersensitivity, to ethnic difference. The basic thesis is that nothing human is unmotivated. The forgetting of words, slips of the tongue or pen, "bungled actions" like the breaking of things: none of these apparently accidental occurrences is in reality unintentional. All can be traced to their source in the *"incompletely suppressed psychical material"* that has found this indirect way of obtaining expression (p. 355).[17] The psychopathologist of the quotidian, therefore, scours speech, clothing, manners, and other details for the trivial but clamorous clues that establish hidden meaning.

The first example Freud gives of these "parapraxes" hints at other stakes besides the deciphering of daily phenomena. Recollecting his own repression of the name of the Italian painter Signorelli, he is led by a series of associations to reflect on the primitiveness of Bosnia's Turks, a people said to "place a higher value on sexual enjoyment than on anything else" (p. 12).

Freud next describes a young academic, a fellow Jew, giving vent to frustration that those of their "race" are condemned "to atrophy" in Austria (p. 19). His third illustration, also from a conversation with a Jewish colleague, involves a poem about intermarriage, heathens, and baptism. In this incident, Freud misreads his interlocutor's remarks as indicating a wish for union with a Christian woman.

Given these introductory cases, it seems undeniable that what was weighing on Freud's mind as he composed his ostensibly innocuous study was the plight of the backward Jewish "heathen" in a climate of escalating anti-Semitism. To rabble rousers like Lueger, Jews were cousins to the animal-like Turk. The Hebrew was no more a true civilized European than the Muslim on the margin of the continent who feared a disruption of his sexual activity even more than he feared death. Freud's cultivation serves to distance him, but all too incompletely, from the Turkish, that is, the racial other. For all his knowledge of Renaissance art, his "social status" is still that of a Jew (p. 19). His prospects remain circumscribed, and the only secure chance of preferment is through intermarriage and conversion.[18]

Freud's deepest concern was not for himself but for his intellectual creation, psychoanalysis. His often-expressed anxiety was that the heavily Jewish "complexion" of the field, as well as his own role as its founder, would permanently besmirch it in the eyes of the gentiles. Another parapraxis, this time borrowed from Freud's acolyte Sandor Ferenzci, goes to the heart of the problem: the sexual root of the neuroses. This was at once the great insight of psychoanalysis and the indisputable confirmation to anti-Semites of the carnality of the Jew, whose degraded nature could never serve as the template for a doctrine of universal application. Ferenzci describes an exchange with a friend who states, "Nothing human is foreign to me." In light of Freud's discoveries, Ferenzci reports himself as adding, "You ought to have gone further and have admitted that nothing animal is foreign to you" (p. 33).

The animal shadowing the detested minority: in one instance, the refined physician of the mind is degraded to the plane of the "Asiatic" Turk; in the other, the white foreigners are acquitted because the real culprit is a Negroid ape. Our two texts reveal the bestial and reviled other metamorphosing from an American black into an Austrian Jew. For Freud's disciples, of course, the geographic itinerary was otherwise: not to Vienna, but away from it, to the United States, where racism proved far more virulent than anti-Semitism. A century after Poe's death, generations of Jewish analysts fled to America to realize the ambitions denied them in Europe. Like other ethnic immigrants, they could "pass" as members of the white race, a condition proscribed to African-Americans, their talents doomed to atrophy in a land that judged them less than fully human.

Another area where Jews have enjoyed spectacular success in the New World is the movies; and here, too, a case can be made for the relevance of Poe's detective fictions. Not so much because crime and gangster films have been a staple of Hollywood, second only to Westerns and their offshoots. A more fruitful detail is the near simultaneity of Poe's tales with the invention of photography.[19] The writer, a polymath to rival Dupin, published articles on the new technology of daguerreotypy in 1840, less than a year before writing "Murders." He was right to sense a symbiotic connection. The police moved quickly to enlist the photographic image as an ally in solving crimes, eager to take advantage of its documentary (as in mug shots) and surveillance possibilities. The camera's ability to record reality "whole" made it unsurpassed as a tool of revelation, a mechanical double for the all-seeing private eye himself, especially as he functions in "The Purloined Letter." Such powers of detection were only enhanced by the improved realism of the moving pictures. As André Bazin once put it, in a formulation that captures the visual and linguistic doubleness of the medium, in film "reality lays itself bare like a suspect confessing under the relentless examination of the commissioner of police."[20]

Oddly enough, the French analyst Jacques Lacan was the first to theorize the filmic aspect of Poe's stories. Lacan noted that the privileged position in "The Purloined Letter" is that of the unseen seer, the character who watches others without being observed himself. (One is reminded of Stanley Cavell's contention that the moviegoer views the diegesis while enjoying the luxury of invisibility.) Lacan's emphasis on the cinematic ties in with his understanding of the psychotherapist's limits. I will conclude this discussion of the detective story with a brief glance at the Frenchman's colonization of the genre as a poststructuralist and (despite his protests of fidelity) anti-Freudian text.

Lacan's principal claim is that the interpreter, whether of crimes or psyches, cannot, in the end, burrow beneath the visible. In the "Seminar on 'The Purloined Letter'" and elsewhere, he emphasizes the linguistic structure of the unconscious and argues that just as language, or the "letter," circulates endlessly without giving us access to the referent or thing-in-itself, so analytic interpretation must forever play upon the surface. It is destined never to penetrate the depths. Poe's story is held to exemplify this truth. Dupin succeeds in retrieving the queen's missive and replacing it with a facsimile. But the incriminating contents of the letter, Lacan exclaims triumphantly, remain undisclosed.[21]

This is an ingenious reading (to paraphrase Dupin on the police), and it is supported by the passage in "Murders," already cited, in which the detective argues for the superficiality of truth. Thus far Freud would agree; the truth is in the symptoms. But he would add that the symptoms gesture beyond themselves to something deeper, not just to words but to the drives and unacceptable wishes seething within the unconscious.[22]

Lacan's analysis conflates the disease with its manifestations. Unconscious drives churn below the surface, inadmissible to consciousness, because they invariably concern a forbidden sexual desire—because, as Freud would say, they originate in the needs of the body. Poe might add that the superficiality of truth is a proposition about images, not language. Lacan gets stalled in a visual hermeneutic because he mistakes a verbal tool for decoding interiors with the object of its explorations, the subterranean mind. Let us return for the last time to the American storywriter's fascination with heads and bodies.[23] Recall that at the end of "Murders," Dupin mocks the Parisian police for being "too cunning to be profound." The rest of his critical judgment reads as follows: "In his [the Prefect's] wisdom is no *stamen*. It is all head and no body, like the pictures of the Goddess Laverna—or, at best, all head and shoulders, like a codfish" (p. 168).

Dupin thus acknowledges the body or "animal" side of his own analytic procedure, his attentiveness to the id-driven unconscious that only *appears* to speak a language. The gutteral sounds overheard in the Paris streets, and misunderstood as Russian, Italian, German, or English, are actually the grunts and cries of a beast. If in one sense the Ourang-Outang is the antithesis of interiority, in another it represents the baseline of depth, the savage id that is the very wellspring of illicit desire. Dupin's successful apprehension of the creature demonstrates his conviction that he, unlike the prefect, *can* get to the bottom of things. He restores the lethal body to the ownership of its master-head, the sailor who proceeds to sell the ape to a zoo, the mass-cultural exhibition of human dominance over the wild. Such optimism is neither Lacanian nor particularly French. The upbeat resolution of Poe's tale is, rather, the symptom or clue that unmasks the eagle-eyed crime solver as a countryman of Cooper and Fanny Fern.

Fanny Fern and the Celebrity Novel

R *uth Hall; A Domestic Tale of the Present Time* desires to be read, as its subtitle reminds us, as a sentimental fiction with home life at its center, a racier version, so to speak, of *Uncle Tom's Cabin* or *The Wide, Wide World*. The designation is appropriate but no more so than a rubric that I am proposing to call the celebrity novel. These are tales of the sort the French refer to as romans à clef, thinly disguised fictionalizations of well-known persons or events. They are in no sense unique to the United States, although they can claim a certain kinship with the nation of Hollywood as the breeding ground of modern celebrity culture.

What *Ruth Hall* illuminates is the way the two categories, fame and the home, feed upon and necessitate each other. The collusion of domesticity with the best-seller is no secret, of course. In the 1840s and 1850s, the family residence solidified its identity as a "private sphere" in which fictions about the "wide, wide world" could be consumed in leisure.[24] But the connection between the domestic and the fixation with celebrity has been largely overlooked. *Ruth Hall* is a good place to correct this oversight because in Fern's text the emergence of sheltered privacy invites or, rather, compels its violations. Fern, as the first celebrity columnist in America, knows perfectly well that mass culture's hunger for rooting in the hidden lives of famous people is energized by a taboo, the recognition that the details of those lives are pro-scribed to popular scrutiny.

I will begin by taking *Ruth Hall* at its word and treat it as "a domestic tale of the present time."[25] The first thing to be said in this vein is that the whole narrative labors to reconstruct the domicile as a place of secure refuge. The death of Ruth's husband, Harry, in the first quarter of the novel plunges the heroine and her two daughters into poverty and instability. Harry leaves no assets, only debts, and with the loss of middle-class stand-ing, the Hall women experience a series of shattering blows to their integrity as a domestic unit. These shocks drive a plot line that culminates in Ruth's determination to become a writer, enabling her not only to re-build her home but also to go public with her grievances and pay back her tormentors.

The initial shock, after Harry's passing, is that Ruth cannot support her children. She is forced to board her elder daughter, Katy, with her in-laws, Dr. and Mrs. Hall, who mercilessly pump the child for information about her mother. One trespass after another follows. Ruth and Nettie, her other daughter, take up residence in a crowded boardinghouse in New York and experience at first hand the intrusiveness of life among the downtrodden. (The antebellum decades, owing to commercial expansion and a stream of Irish and German newcomers, saw the first substantial growth of the Amer-ican metropolis.) They sleep and eat at close quarters with "red-faced" maids-of-all-work, apprentices, sewing girls, clerks, and drummers, none of whom shows the least respect for privacy. Across the way is a tenement filled with "poor emigrants" whose every activity is displayed for inspection through the curtainless windows (p. 90).

Behavior complements physical setting. A servant girl bursts in on Ruth to deliver a message, "omitting the ceremony of a premonitory knock, as she opened the door" (p. 84). The male boarders undress her with their eyes as she comes and goes, stationing themselves so as to get a "peep" at her ankles and loudly exchanging comments on her "deuced nice form" (p. 73). If Ruth's body is fair game in this environment, so is her biography. She tries to supplement her wages as a seamstress by tutoring students, but when she applies for a position, a prospective employer, "after putting Ruth through the Catechism as to her private history, and torturing her with the most minute inquiries as to her past, present, and future, coolly informed her that 'she had no children to send'" (p. 99).

Ruth is stung by such treatment, readers are led to believe, because she so thoroughly cherishes the private realm. She refuses to throw herself on the mercy of her hard-hearted relatives, since she would then have to reveal the extent of her need, and she counsels her daughters not to gossip about the family outside the home. A prying shopkeeper gets her comeuppance from Katy: "Mama does not allow me to talk to strangers" (p. 118). Despite her eventual notoriety as author, moreover, Ruth finds the idea of mounting the pulpit or lecturing to mixed audiences utterly unacceptable. She does her writing under the protective cover of a pseudonym, Floy, and has "as great a horror" of the self-exposure of speaking in public as she does of "the profession of an actress" (p. 173). We are encouraged to share her mixture of astonishment and dismay at the letters "Floy" receives from an adoring readership, who have never laid eyes on her yet pour out their innermost secrets, send proposals of marriage, and ask her to raise their children. These correspondents cannot seem to grasp the distinction integral both to the ideology of the separate spheres and to the rise of the celebrity: that between a public persona and a private individual. Ruth's struggles as a writer are crowned with the financial success that she values less for itself than because it permits her to reclaim her daughter.

So goes the sentimental narrative in which even Ruth's long days and nights of writing, which keep her from playing with Nettie, are justified by their outcome of salvaging the family. But a second strain in Fern's novel works against the conventionalism of the domestic plot. This other tale, by unsettling gender and biological categories, calls into question the private-public divide (which is calibrated along a female-male axis). Publicity regains the upper hand but not by an act of violence against the home. Rather, Fern abolishes altogether the distinction between commercial identity and private life. She draws the same conclusion as Henry James: there is no interior that exists apart from the surface. But she gives the conclusion a far more positive valence than the later writer: in *Ruth Hall*, the absence of a sequestered self is at once a triumph of legibility and a proof of women's superiority to men in the democratic marketplace.

Consider that pen name, Floy. It throws Hall's readers into confusion because they cannot tell whether their beloved advice giver is a woman or a man. The androgyny—part Flo, part Floyd—is deliberate and is meant to scramble domesticity's binaries. (Ruth does not pretend to be a man, which would simply reinforce the binaries. "George Sand" or "George Eliot" leaves undisturbed the assumption that only males enter the public arena of authorship.) Ruth's story teems with such disruptions, the most unexpected of which, perhaps, is the relentless unmasking of family. Not only her in-laws but also her own father, brother, and other blood relations systematically withhold assistance. Her father, Mr. Ellet, argues with Dr. Hall over who is better off and should therefore be responsible for supporting Ruth and the girls. Neither would contribute a dime were it not for that very public meddling in the private that sentimentalism abhors: they briefly relent from their stinginess because of the pressure brought by rumor and gossip, which threaten to damage their reputations within their churches.

Ruth's brother, Hyacinth, is even worse. A writer and nominal editor with good connections—he is based on Fern's actual brother, N. P. Willis, who was Hawthorne's favorite critic—he is both competitive with Ruth and dismissive of her. When she asks him for advice about getting started as a writer, he piously falls back on the separate spheres doctrine and urges her "to seek some *unobtrusive* employment" (p. 116). She persists anyway, and her popularity so angers her brother that he will not run her pieces in his magazine, "perhaps," as that publication's real editor speculates, because "he wants to be the only genius in the family" (p. 159).

These rebuffs announce the failure of biological connection, with all its messy ambiguities, and point toward the contractualism of laissez-faire as a cleaner and more trustworthy ally, especially for women. Ruth is approached out of the blue by another editor, John Walter, who sends her a letter offering his services as an agent. Walter has a high estimate of Ruth's "market-value . . . as a writer" and promises to get her paid what she is worth (p. 142). The two immediately begin addressing each other as "Sister Ruth" and "Brother Walter," but this is not, as it might seem at first, a familializing of business relations. On the contrary, their partnership represents the *supersession* of blood by choice, indicating that kinship should be based on mutual usefulness instead of family ties. With Walter's introductory note in hand, Ruth reflects: "If Mr. Walter *were* honest, if he *really* felt such a brotherly interest in her, how sweet it would be to have him for a brother; a—*real, warm-hearted, brotherly brother,* such as she had never known" (p. 144). An accident of birth, to this way of thinking, cannot fill the place of genuine fraternity. In replying "frankly and unreservedly" to Walter's inquiry, Ruth unbosoms herself to an unknown correspondent with no more sense of delicacy than is later shown by her fans. But no one can quarrel with the results: Walter becomes a stalwart champion whose guidance brings her the monetary independence she craves.

One does better, in short, to choose one's siblings—and one's parents, and one's cousins—from among strangers, valuing them for the help they can provide, than to submit to nature as a given. Ruth, or rather Fanny Fern, offers herself in a comparable capacity to her largely female readership. She sets out in easily accessible form the useful advice about launching oneself as a writer that her blood brother denied her and Walter supplied.

Ruth Hall, it should be noted, contains an abundance of male physicians, from Dr. Hall to Ruth's cousin, John Millet. These self-important doctors husband their knowledge of healing, yet they are basically quacks without the good sense of uneducated women like Ruth's black servant, Dinah. The novel is the antithesis of medicine's hoarding and exclusivity. It provides a model for other women who, penniless or not, may wish to try their hands at literature. Fern's how-to book opens up the arcana of professional authorship, the equivalent to *Moby-Dick* for would-be whalers and *The Deerslayer* for those contemplating survival in the wilderness. She shows us how to balance the demands of children and writing, how to go about negotiating contracts, how to arrange for publication and promotion. She explains what factors should be weighed when trying to decide whether to sell or retain copyright in one's writings. She holds back nothing from embarrassment or pride.

The contrast to a male novelist like Hawthorne is noteworthy. In the preface to *The Scarlet Letter*, Hawthorne offers his own version of what it takes to be a writer, but it would be hard to imagine a more dissimilar narrative. Hawthorne reduces everything to talent and temperament, and his account of overcoming a writer's block mystifies more than it reveals trade secrets. Occupying center stage are the unpredictability of the creative process and the chasm that gapes between the sensitive artist and the workaday world. No one who reads the preface will feel emboldened to follow Hawthorne's example. There is not a word in it about the actual mechanics of composing, securing the interest of publishers, or marketing oneself to the public.

These differences hint at a more theoretical claim very much encouraged by Fern's fiction (and by her personal history). Contrary to the standard identification of women with the organic, *Ruth Hall* implies that maleness is an aristocratic principle far more invested in bloodlines than are women. In its quarrel with ascription, femaleness is actually a democratic ideal congruent with the Declaration's statement of equality (or the more inclusive statement promulgated in the "Declaration of Sentiments," seven years before Fern's best-seller). Fern's celebration of volition comes out starkly in her cavalier approach to patronyms. A last name perpetuates pedigree. Ruth has two in the course of the story, Ellet and Hall, but as her husband dies early on, and her father fails her, the names seem more disposable than expressive of her identity. Indeed, she sheds them both unhesitatingly in her professional career, reinventing herself as Floy and embracing Walter as her "*real*" brother. Hyacinth, who affects an aristocratic, dandyish manner, proves to have a much greater stake in descent. The presumably more self-reliant male underscores his sister's independence by contrast: he clings to his own given names with as much tenacity as if they were titles.[26] (Hyacinth's floral and feminized Christian name suggests the limits of his masculinity.)

Historical realities from antebellum literary culture dramatize the contrast. The woman who was Fanny Fern wrote under a pseudonym, and she also had a list of surnames—Sara Willis Payson Parton—reflecting her metamorphoses through several marriages and one divorce (a rarity at the time, and a reflection of Fern's commitment to choice). Her male counterparts displayed little of her aptitude for nominative self-making. They were stuck in some kind of Anglophile or gentrified time warp, parading their ancestry through a string of tripartites: James Fenimore Cooper, Ralph Waldo Emerson, Henry David Thoreau, Richard Henry Dana, Henry Wadsworth Longfellow, James Russell Lowell, and Edgar Allan Poe.

There is another crucial divergence between a writer such as Hawthorne and Fanny Fern, one underscored by the Salem recluse's determination to preserve his "inmost Me behind its veil." For Hawthorne, as we shall see, the act of writing allowed for closeness to readers without undue proximity—truth-telling without violations of the private self. Fern understands that textuality can have a totally opposite effect. As in the case of Ruth Hall's intimacy-famished readers, the pen's apparent impersonality or security can act as a spur to self-revelation. It can function as a kind of doubling of the home to elicit the orgies of trespass and nakedness it was supposed to guard against.

In *Ruth Hall*, hiddenness in any guise—behind a pseudonym, or behind the closed doors of a family residence—creates the irrepressible appetite to know what is being concealed. Ruth's fans are consumed with curiosity about her, and John Walter is no exception. His excitement at the mystery of her identity is manifestly erotic. He sits in his office, finger pressed against "the right lobe of his organ of causality," and "searchingly" studies the "wail from her inmost soul" that is Floy's latest article. "Who *can* she be?" he asks himself over and over again, "who can she be?" (p. 140). Walter's journal, for which Ruth soon does most of her writing, has the suitable title *The Household Messenger*—suitable because her columns are bulletins from the private sphere, teasing glimpses into the off-limits corners of her life. The glimpses are what seduce and transfix her readers. Unlike her daughter Katy, who has been brought up to be closemouthed around people she does not know, Ruth cannot help herself. She makes a fabulously successful career out of talking to strangers.

It is no accident that Walter, intoxicated with the puzzle of Ruth's real name, should be caught fingering one of his phrenological bumps. Phrenology is the era's (pseudo)scientific equivalent to the editor's eagerness to deduce the private person from the public personality. The text later devotes an entire chapter to a visit the two of them pay to the offices of "Professor Finman," an expert at interpreting cranial conformations. The phrenological exam to which Ruth submits titillates readerly interest by providing a detailed analysis of the heroine's aptitudes and weaknesses: her sharply observant mind, too quick temper, and so on. But the novel clearly agrees with Ruth's disparaging comment that they have gotten their "$2 worth of flattery" (p. 171). Phrenology can never compete with literature as a description of character. *Ruth Hall* and Fanny Fern, because they can rove wherever they want, will always get the better of Professor Finman as analysts of the interior.

Fern's narrative is a phrenologist on the loose. It routinely forces itself into areas, usually domestic, where a genre more respectful of boundaries would be reluctant to intrude. The prefatory note, "To the Reader," takes this license as a structural raison d'être: Fern says she has dispensed with lengthy introductions and "entered unceremoniously and unannounced, into people's houses, without stopping to ring the bell" (p. 3). The four walls of the home, which Ruth spends prodigious effort to reconstruct, seem to exist in the text for no other purpose than to be breached. The novel consists of ninety fast-paced chapters, some as short as a paragraph or two, and chapter after chapter begins by bursting into a scene in media res.

Or, rather, in midconversation. Chapter 15 opens thus: "'Hallo! What are you doing there?' exclaimed the doctor . . ." (p. 35). Chapter 32: "'And is it because Biddy M'Pherson don't suit yer, that ye'd be afther sending her away?'" (p. 64). Chapter 75: "'Hark! Nettie, Go to the door, dear,' said Ruth, 'someone knocked'" (p. 161). Chapter 76: "'Have you ever submitted your head to a phrenological examination?' asked Mr. Walter, as he made a call on Ruth, the next morning" (p. 167). Chapter 83: "'I don't know about holding you *both* in my lap at once,' said Ruth smiling . . ." (p. 176). As a snoop, moreover, Fern is more than a match for nosy old Mrs. Hall. "Examine closely," she says to the reader on an inspection tour of Ruth's house. "Walk in; . . . Now, step into the nursery . . ." (pp. 34–35). And the boardinghouse's lecherous males have nothing on Fern as a voyeur: "Let us peep into the doctor's sitting room," she says, escorting us into Dr. Hall's airless office and waxing indignant at his confinement of Katy (p. 128).

Not to be forgotten is that the novel we are reading relates the ordeal of Fanny Fern under the diaphanous cover of a nom de plume. The antebellum public scooped up the book because it told curious readers everything they could ever want to know about its celebrity author. Fern figuratively undresses in its pages. She is voluble about her love life, the gruesome death and financial improvidence of her husband, her loss of a child, her uncaring in-laws, her brother's sexual confusions and cruelty to her, the grotesque selfishness of her father, her cousins' piggish eating habits, and much more. We even learn the circumstances under which the book itself was written. Fern relates how Ruth works at home, stealing moments from tending to Nettie to scribble her thoughts and interrupting her labors to wash "a little soiled face" or repair a doll. "There was *the* book," Fern exclaims on publication day, "Ruth's book! Oh, how few of its readers, if it were fortunate enough to find readers, would know how much of her own heart's history was there laid bare" (pp. 174–75).

In actuality, of course, the reader—*this* reader—witnesses the book's composition and gleans directly from the author how much of her personal saga has been condensed into its pages. Household, private life, and the making of a famous columnist converge in Fern's descriptions of each "little history" behind her articles:

> Little shoeless feet were covered with the proceeds of this; a little medicine, or a warmer shawl was bought with that. This was written, faint and fasting, late into the long night; that composed while walking wearily to or from the offices where she was employed. One was written with little Nettie sleeping in her lap; another still, a mirthful, merry piece, as an escape-valve for a wretched heartache. (p. 175)

Nothing escapes the reader's prying gaze in *Ruth Hall*, least of all the intimate details of writing, a process ruled out-of-bounds by every proponent of textual privacy. Yet the person who drags this offstage activity into the limelight, and thrusts it under the public's nose, is the pseudonymous Fanny Fern herself.

In the last few paragraphs, I have made little effort to differentiate between the surrogate struggling writer Ruth Hall, who is a fiction, and her creator, Fanny Fern, who was a historical inhabitant of Jacksonian America. The slippage has been intentional. After all, "Fanny Fern" is itself a kind of fiction, the alias under which the actual woman Sara Payson Willis achieved her celebrity. (As names go, Ruth Hall sounds less made up than Fanny Fern.) But it is a fiction, or public fabrication, that usurped the private life of its owner. Shortly after publishing *Ruth Hall*, Fern married the editor James Parton. He did not address his wife as Sara, and she did not sign her letters Sara Parton, or Sara Willis Payson Parton. Even in the seclusion of their bedroom, he called her Fanny, and she corresponded with her closest friends as Fanny Fern. She had ceased to exist as a private person. She had become her public persona, and the only thing that existed behind her assumed identity was . . . her assumed identity as Fanny Fern.

Fern's roman à clef has had a myriad of descendants. Joe Klein's bestselling novel about the Clintons, *Primary Colors* (1996), is a recent example. But *Ruth Hall* remains unusually audacious in that its public washing of dirty linen is performed by the subject herself. Or perhaps "discarding of linen" would be a better metaphor. Recall that Ruth Hall confessed to an insuperable prejudice against actresses, those brazen creatures who flaunt their bodies on the stage. She told Mr. Walter that she was too shy to expose her own "form" by speaking in public. But Nathaniel Hawthorne knew better. After reading *Ruth Hall*, he felt that the novel outdid any actress in shamelessness. Hawthorne was awed by Fern's feats of unselfconscious exhibitionism. He marveled to his publisher at her willingness to "throw off the restraints of decency, and come before the public stark naked, as it were" (p. xxxv).

CHAPTER 4

The Nineteenth-Century Canon: Hidden in Plain Sight

Four canonized texts offer themselves collectively as a rejoinder to the unbridled legibility of American popular literature. Not as a rejoinder that silences but as one that opens a colloquy, for the four works—*The Scarlet Letter*, *Moby-Dick*, *Walden*, and *The American*—all engage with the knowledge drive as a compelling societal edict. All share the exhilaration of the quest while in the end relinquishing the possibility of consummation. In *The Scarlet Letter*, Hawthorne probes the mania for unveiling and revenge as destructive of the private; he turns toward the written word as a space of secure because polysemous revelation. In *Moby-Dick*, Melville sees the same compulsions as imperiling democracy, and he implies a link between his own project and that of the Founding Fathers in the Constitution. Both authors construct puzzles that are hidden in plain sight; but, unlike Poe's purloined letter, and unlike the printed names that stretch from one end of the chart to the other, the scarlet letter and the white whale refuse to emerge from their hiding places.

In *Walden*, too, the magnetism of knowing exerts a strong if ultimately limiting attraction. Thoreau, the most "Jeffersonian" of the romantics, exchanges interventionism for a Hawthornian privacy. He asserts textuality as obscurantism and explicitly opposes his own literary enterprise to the readily absorbed entertainments of popular novelists. Henry James, my sole example from outside the antebellum era, announces in his very title of *The American* the national provenance of the fixation to understand and to expose. James counters with a Francophile appreciation of "painterly" impenetrable surfaces. But French stasis gets none of his sympathy. James's novel delivers a stinging rebuke to societies of birth. For all its high aestheticism, *The American* has a claim to being a successor to Beaumont's polemical *Marie*: it is that rare work of fiction by a non-European to suggest an analogical symbiosis between aristocratic segmentation and the unearned entitlement of race.

The Scarlet Letter

It is a curiosity of American literature that the novel that by near unanimous consent launches the canon or national tradition begins with a secret. Or, rather, with an unwillingness to divulge a secret in public. The novel of course is *The Scarlet Letter*, and the opening scene, in which Hester stands on the scaffold and defiantly refuses to name her lover, signals a complex swerve of high or elite literature from the popular pressure toward legibility. The pressure manifested itself across a continuum of social, political, and cultural practices emergent in the antebellum period. Hawthorne showed a troubled awareness of several of these phenomena: daguerreotypy, which he wrote about in *The House of the Seven Gables*, and the fads for mesmerism, phrenology, and physiognomy, which he addressed in both *The Seven Gables* and *The Blithedale Romance*.

Hawthorne's swerve or demarcation is complex because he at once shares and recoils from the demand for openness. In *The Scarlet Letter*, he labors to find some way to check the intrusions of legibility, while at the same time he strives to fashion a mediated or indirect mode of revelation that respects the need to "be true," as the text has it, without surrendering the right to privacy. Another way of framing this, which suggests something of Hawthorne's proleptic insight, would be to say that against the tyranny of knowing, he champions distanced and guarded forms of disclosure that, in the twentieth century, have been incarnated in the motion pictures and the analyst's couch.

Three historical periods, in other words, figure as the framework for this discussion. The first is Puritan Boston; the second, the antebellum years; and the third, the 1890s. To bring the three into conversation about the act of hiding in public is, on the surface, wildly anachronistic. In one era, the dream of a purified city on a hill installed a regime of "holy watchfulness." Every aspect of life was held up to public scrutiny, for sins committed by an individual could subject the entire colonial experiment to divine wrath. Hawthorne's time, two centuries later, brought the emergence of a private sphere. The growth of market society drove a wedge between work and the home. The isolated household, no longer a site of artisanal production, came to signify all those facets of the self needing shelter from the glare of politics and moneymaking. Another half century, and urbanization and industrialization, fueled by unprecedented numbers of foreign immigrants, combined to transform a still largely rural nation into a megalith of strangers. Millions hungered for the closeness and order of the past without, however, wishing to surrender the newfound freedom of anonymity.[1]

Hawthorne's novel, I am proposing, straddles the boundary between these three eras. He turns his searchlight on the Puritans from a present already conscious of privacy's value. And he gestures toward a future where new technologies of protected transparence were incubating in response to modernity's apparent chaos. I claim license for venturing this assertion from Hawthorne himself, who indulges in a few anachronisms of his own. Most relevant for my purposes, he overstates seventeenth-century Boston as an intimate community or gemeinschaft in order better to discriminate it from the more impersonal society or gesellschaft that was materializing as he wrote, and of which Hester, Dimmesdale, and Chillingworth are representatives in Puritan mufti.

The reader of *The Scarlet Letter* is immediately conscious of discrepant fictional worlds. There is the world of the Puritans, who recognize no distinction between the public and the private, and who assume that all should be bared before the multitude; and there is the consciousness of the three central characters, who wrap themselves in secrecy. In that remote, simpler past, in a tiny settlement no bigger than a village, nothing can be hidden from surveillance. Women thrust themselves into the public ways and speak boldly there; sinners are expected to confess openly and to endure punishment before their neighbors; and the separate sphere of family life, cherished in the mid–nineteenth century, simply does not exist as such. Hester's upbringing of Pearl is closely monitored by the entire community and is a subject "for the deliberations of legislators and acts of state" (p. 89).[2]

Into this setting of full visibility, of face-to-face dealings and oral discourse, is deposited the prescient threesome—to whose number should no doubt be added Hawthorne's persona, the narrator. This individual flags the crucial historical contrast when he can hardly contain his indignation at the "outrage" of the stocks, a penal technology that immobilizes the culprit before "the public gaze" and forbids him "to hide his face for shame" (p. 59). Hester, though spared this particular punishment, is forced to stand exposed in the marketplace "under the heavy weight of a thousand unrelenting eyes" (p. 60). She reacts to her sentence by figuratively absenting herself from the scene and returning, in thought, to her English home. She then literally duplicates this split of inner and outer by safeguarding her secret, the identity of Pearl's father, both from the Puritans and from her disgraced husband, whose importunities in prison she spurns.

Hester is a thoroughgoing anomaly in the Puritan past. Her subjectivity is structured along a public-private division that the seventeenth-century Bostonians have difficulty understanding, or even imagining. But her example is contagious. It has infected her partner in sin, the Reverend Dimmesdale, who vainly tries to persuade his fellow clergyman, John Wilson, "that it were wronging the very nature of woman to force her to lay open her heart's secrets in such broad daylight." Wilson, who has the disadvantage of not being familiar with the antebellum cult of true womanhood, simply does not get it. "The shame," he lectures his young colleague, "lay in the commission of the sin, and not in the showing of it forth" (p. 66). Dimmesdale's selfhood is so fractured that he has to appeal to someone else to make known who he is. He exhorts Hester to name her fellow sinner, aware as we are, but as his auditors are not, that the guilty party is himself.

And then there is Roger Chillingworth, né Prynne, Hester's long-absent spouse. The very surname he goes by is a disguise. Chillingworth's first gesture in the narrative is, by laying his finger on his lips, to admonish Hester not to breathe a word about his real identity.

These three principals, all guardians of a secret, spend most of the story in a state of tension with their society. For the Puritans, the penalty of the scarlet letter is an extreme but by no means atypical condition. Its normativeness consists in its advertising, its shrieking aloud, of the wearer's identity. Everybody in the theocracy is expected to be immediately recognizable to everybody else. Even Mistress Hibbins, the frequenter of black masses in the forest, is acknowledged to be, and more or less accepted as, a witch.

The anachronistic characters challenge this communal consensus with intimations of a far less transparent future. They have strayed, as it were, from "Wakefield" (1835), Hawthorne's story of the anonymous nineteenth-century city, that environment of strangers where all one knows of others is their appearance, into a Bible commonwealth of almost totalitarian luminosity. Hester, Dimmesdale, and Chillingworth go about in a condition of chronic masquerade. While they conform "with the most perfect quietude to the external regulations of society," as Hawthorne says of his heroine (p. 133), they shelter altogether different beings under their public roles: the freethinking subversive under the silent penitent, the self-lacerating adulterer under the pious minister, the demonic seeker of revenge under the impartial healer. The novel bristles with the words "secret," "riddle," and "mystery." And this duplicity, this modern burden of nurturing a second or hidden self, seems to spread like a blight into nature. During the forest scene, Hawthorne anthropomorphizes the murmuring brook as a source of thwarted revelation that keeps trying to tell "its unintelligible secret of some very mournful mystery that had happened . . . within the verge of the dismal forest" (p. 149).

An argument could be developed from this evidence that would place Hawthorne on the side of Hester against the colonial elders. He so abhors their treatment of her, their reduction of human variety to a single meaning and their refusal to allow any private act to remain private, that he writes his novel to reprimand the American lust for knowing. But one should not be too quick to portray Hawthorne as an admirer of opacity or hypocrisy. If he does not favor a reversion to the tribalism of the past, neither does he stint on his criticisms of Dimmesdale as an "untrue man" who knowingly deceives his congregation. "The only truth," he writes, "that continued to give

Mr. Dimmesdale a real existence on this earth, was the anguish in his inmost soul, and the undissembled expression of it in his aspect" (p. 121). What Hawthorne seems to want is to reconstruct legibility in a culture of segmentation. He craves truthfulness without the pitiless exposure, the violation of human personality, that he attributes to the Puritan gemeinschaft.

Not to be overlooked here is Hawthorne's flirtation with Roman Catholicism, in particular the confessional. This attraction crops up again in *The Marble Faun*, in the scene where Hilda enters an English-language booth at St. Peter's and bares her soul to a sympathetic priest; and, perhaps as tellingly, in Hawthorne's daughter Rose's conversion to Catholicism and taking of orders as a nun. In *The Scarlet Letter*, Hester is said several times to be performing penance, and Hawthorne speculates that if "a Papist" had observed her on the scaffold, he might have mistaken her and her infant for "the image of Divine Maternity" (p. 59). But the Reverend Mr. Dimmesdale is the character most tempted by Catholic rituals. He keeps nighttime vigils and flogs himself with "a bloody scourge," behavior, says Hawthorne, "more in accordance with the old, corrupted faith of Rome" than with the enlightened creed of the Puritans (p. 120).

Above all, Dimmesdale is shown in intimate colloquy with Chillingworth, in what might be described as an obsessive parody of the confessional or, with equal justice, as a prefiguration of psychoanalysis. Indeed, these scenes help to explain why twentieth-century Americans, deprived by their Protestantism of Catholic practice, hastened to embrace Freudian therapy as a substitute. As opposed to the public *confession* or relation demanded by the historical colonists, and still employed by evangelical Protestants today, the confessional/analyst's office offers the balm of self-disclosure in a context secure from "the public gaze." The two settings enable deep utterance through their promise of tongue-loosening confidentiality, permitting, in the terms I have been borrowing from Ferdinand Tönnies, the transparency of community to migrate into the guardedness of gesellschaft.

In Hawthorne's novel, these possibilities are suggested but not realized because Dr. (or Father) Chillingworth has neither absolution nor cure in mind, and the guilt-ridden minister, preternaturally sensitive as he is, intuits as much and refuses to unbosom. Noting, as a therapist might, that bodily infirmities are but "symptom[s] of some ailment" in the mind (p. 114), Chillingworth encourages his patient to tell all only in order to torture him. He burrows deep into the minister's interior, "delving among his principles, prying into his recollections, and probing everything with a cautious touch, like a treasure-seeker in a dark cavern" (p. 105). Through medical skill and pretended sympathy, he succeeds in bringing "the very inmost soul" of the sufferer "out before his eyes," the better to scrutinize and aggravate his victim's every pang (p. 115).

The Dimmesdale-Chillingworth relationship, however perverted in practice, dramatizes a hypothetical conjoining of revelation and privacy that fixates Hawthorne's imagination. The self-alienation with which Hester tries to shield herself on the scaffold, and which Dimmesdale manifests in asking her to confess for him—as he later implores her to "Think for me . . . ! Thou art strong. Resolve for me!" (p. 155)—is, paradoxically, both the predicament to be overcome and the pathway to a solution. Hester exhorts her former lover to desert New England and "Exchange this false life of thine for a true one!" (p. 156). But for Hawthorne, truth can be attained neither in flight and disappearance nor in the unwanted glare of exposure and public speech. It can be found only in a mediated or protected honesty, in the legibility of the written word.

Which is to say that Hawthorne's first important novel, the inaugural text of the indigenous canon, vaults its major characters out of the in-the-flesh, oral past and into the cosmos of writing or the "letter." (It is perhaps relevant to note here that in actuality letters were among the earliest acknowledged sites of privacy in the American republic. Unlike Great Britain, which permitted postal clerks to examine the contents of letters, the Post Office Act of 1792 prohibited government officers from opening the mails to spy on citizens.)[3] The essential action of the narrative occurs in the aftermath of the forest scene. As Dimmesdale heads back to the settlement, intending to flee to Europe with Hester and so, despite his self-loathing, to perpetuate for a few days longer "the contrast between what I seem and what I am" (p. 152), he is beset by an intensification of inner conflict so severe that he fears he is going mad. He has to struggle against the impulse to blurt out profanities to a series of people—a deacon, children, worshipful church members—who believe absolutely in his holiness. But this radical experience of self-division, or, if you like, of modernity, culminates in the writing of the Election Sermon, during which Dimmesdale feels that he is simultaneously inscribing his thoughts and standing apart and watching himself from a distance. And this experience in turn holds the key to his, and Hawthorne's, eventual reconciliation of the wishes both to tell the truth and "to hide [one's] face for shame."

The critical moment comes under the heading "The Revelation of the Scarlet Letter." What imagination, asks Hawthorne portentously in the lines leading up this chapter, can possibly connect the sainted minister in the pulpit with the adulterous woman on the margins of the assembly, the public figure with the private sin? What miracle can bridge the gulf between them? His answer is that writing or literature can, and his problem is that Dimmesdale cannot mail in his admission of guilt to the Puritans and thus spare himself the agony of confessing in person. But he can speak as though he were writing, and so convert a technology of presence into one of removal from the scene.

Dimmesdale's guilty plea has generated a great deal of critical comment, most of it noting, and criticizing, the minister's change of voice from first to third person. Standing where Hester stood seven years earlier, he begins by summoning the people of New England to "behold me here, the one sinner of the world!" Then, abruptly, as though referring to someone else, Dimmesdale announces, "It was on him!" and slips into using the impersonal pronoun "he" (p. 195). He concludes by tearing away his ministerial band to expose . . . what? Presumably the stigma on his breast, but we never know for certain because Hawthorne pointedly declines to tell us.

The majority opinion faults the clergyman for calculated obfuscation.[4] But if we give him a provisional benefit of the doubt, it becomes evident that Dimmesdale has hit on an inspired exit from his quandary. He has told the truth but told it slant—spoken as though he were somehow distanced in space and time from his own utterance. He is separated in space because the third-person "he" cannot physically occupy the same subject position as the first-person "I"; and separated in time because Dimmesdale almost immediately dies after confessing, ensuring that he is not available in person to be interrogated about his words. Even though he acknowledges his sinfulness and does so directly in his own voice, and in the presence of a thousand witnesses, he manages to achieve the absent position of every writer who ever addressed an audience on the page. Contrast this self-erasure, or mediated truth-telling, to the self-centeredness of his earlier confessions to his parishioners, where the litany of "I's"—"I, whom you behold in these black garments . . . I, who ascend the sacred desk . . . I, in whose daily life . . . ," (p. 119)—convert abasement into narcissistic falsehood.

Not only does the minister figuratively "write" his climactic admission; his Puritan spectators figuratively "read" it. Dimmesdale's disclosure has the inherent ambiguity of written composition, and the colonists receive it more like textual interpreters than in-person witnesses. They are unsure of the precise meaning of what they have heard (and seen) and spend days trying to decipher the minister's parting words, thereby transmuting themselves into forerunners of Hawthorne's present-day explicators, the perplexed readers whom he invites to "choose among these theories" (p. 197). Roger Chillingworth is surely correct when he hisses to his dying patient: "Hadst thou sought the whole earth over, there was no one place so secret, . . . save on this very scaffold!" (p. 194). Chillingworth's frustration is understandable. Dimmesdale has "escaped" him by hiding in plain sight. A single amendment would be in order, however: the choice of the word "secret," applied so frequently to the minister's concealed sin, no longer seems quite apt. A better, and more historically resonant, word would be "private," because it conveys the elements of choice and self-protection that enable Dimmesdale willingly to mount the scaffold and confess.

A respect for privacy, moreover, is what governs Hawthorne's narrating of these final scenes.[5] His increased authorial discretion becomes apparent as far back as the moment in the forest when the two lovers exchange vows. At the end of chapter 17, Hawthorne writes, "Then, all was spoken!" (p. 157), but he never reproduces the dialogue between the pair and puts off until chapter 20 a detailed summary of their intentions. Nor does he reprint the minister's Election Sermon; we experience it at a distance much as

Hester does and, like her, must work out its meaning "entirely apart from its indistinguishable words" (p. 187). As noted, Hawthorne even refuses to delineate "The Revelation of the Scarlet Letter." "It was revealed!" he breathlessly exclaims, immediately adding, "But it were irreverent to describe that revelation" (p. 196). The moral he extracts from his story is similarly reserved. "Be true!" he beseeches thrice, only to qualify his own admonition, and drastically so, by urging that one "show freely to the world, if not your worst, yet some trait whereby the worst may be inferred!" (p. 198).

Admittedly, Hawthorne's reticence is accompanied by the psychological acumen that so dazzled his contemporaries. But this, I have been arguing, is precisely the point. The man who hangs back from excessive frankness, who will not speak all, and who "blushes" to recount his minister's wicked thoughts (p. 171) is also the writer who gives us "Another View of Hester," as he calls the chapter where he traces her innermost thoughts, and who titles his in-depth study of Dimmesdale "The Interior of a Heart." Hawthorne's plumbings of the psyche are the corollary to his authorial restraint. He carries out his dissection of the human heart in the privileged sanctuary of literature, and he can afford to be candid because he has averted his face. Recall his autobiographical outpouring in "The Custom-House." This painfully shy individual goes on at length there about his family, his controversial dismissal from public office, and his difficulties in getting started on *The Scarlet Letter*. In the same breath he warns us that he will refrain from "confidential depths of revelation," and he says that he has only been able to "thaw" into talking at all because he preserves "the Inmost Me behind its veil" (pp. 22–23). The quoted phrase, from the second page of the novel, is a reminder of Hawthorne's attraction to Catholicism and might also be read as a prophecy of his daughter's novitiate: when a woman enters a religious order, she is said to be taking the veil.

I have suggested that *The Scarlet Letter*'s seemingly contradictory motives, in trying both to block revelation and to facilitate it, give the book its peculiar double identity as a reproof and as a refinement of American legibility. The combination evokes not only psychotherapy but also, and rather more improbably, the cinema. Or perhaps not so improbably, for the gesellschaft of Hawthorne's primary characters did not fully materialize in the antebellum era during which he imagined them. It came into being at the end of the century, when the American city finally reached the impersonal proportions of a European metropolis like London, that teeming environment where Wakefield, acting on a whim, disappears from his family by moving to a flat just a block away. The motion pictures and Freudianism arose in that not-too-distant future. They were eagerly adopted by Americans because they simultaneously advanced unveiling and allowed it to occur in a "private," sequestered setting: the doctor's consulting room and the dark and anticommunal movie theater, perfected in today's warrenlike multiplexes. One might recall here the well-known circumstance that the 1890s, decade of the two innovations, opened with a landmark defense of reserve:

the publication in 1890 of the *Harvard Law Review* article in which Louis D. Brandeis and Samuel Warren formulated a statutory right to privacy.

Would it be too far-fetched to suggest that Dimmesdale's mediated public confession is more like a film than a piece of writing? After all, he is seen as much as he is heard, and his interplay of proximity and nonpresence evokes the immaterial image on celluloid. (Arguably, he is *more* seen than heard. Visual imagery predominates at the moment of disclosure: "God's eye beheld it! . . . Behold! Behold a dreadful witness of it!" [p. 195].) But this *would* be carrying anachronism too far, so let us conclude with a more modest suggestion: that Hawthorne, writing on the cusp of celebrity culture, was haunted by its tribulations. The maintenance of a public-private division is essential to that culture, but it incites the very demand for knowing, for peeking behind the mask, that it is supposed to guard against. For that reason, it forces the celebrity, whether he be a successful novelist or a movie star, to thicken the wall between his putative real self and the self he shows his public. And the consequences of that balancing act, according to Hawthorne, may be fatal to a person's character. For as he says of Dimmesdale, "No man, for any considerable period, can wear one face to himself, and another to the multitude, without finally getting bewildered as to which may be the true" (p. 168).

Melville's *Moby-Dick*

Moby-Dick is the unavoidable centerpiece of the American tradition. The novel takes the quest for knowledge as the fundamental fact about the culture, and it records with single-minded focus both the fascination of that search and its capacity for unimaginable devastation. Ahab's hatred of inscrutability has been a catalyst for this study, and Melville's storyteller Ishmael is swept up in the hunt for the white whale. But the narrative as a whole never unequivocally endorses the mania for legibility. Melville lodges two potent objections to Ahab's takeover of the American ship of state: first, he queries the proximity, or rather the inextricability, of knowing and destroying, a dynamic that recoils back on the knower as well as targeting the object to be known. And, second, he warns of the facility with which the drive for "Truth" and revenge mutates into demagogic tyranny.

These are positions Melville shared with the Founding Fathers. More precisely, he shared them with the Founders who authored the Constitution and *The Federalist Papers*. Like other antebellum moderates, such as Lincoln, Melville feared moral absolutism as a license for lawlessness. Unlike Lincoln, specifically the Lincoln of the "Address to the Young Men's Lyceum of Springfield" (1838), he did not single out the revolutionary spirit as such as a threat to stability. But he did have a strong sense of the doubleness of the Founders' legacy, its incitement to zeal and transparency (in the Declaration), as well as its acceptance of limits (in the Constitution). To put it differently, Melville is both Ahab and Ishmael. He thrills to the *Pequod*'s commander's unyielding dedication to truth, but in the end he sides with his storyteller's recognition that knowing has to be relinquished. Melville joins Hawthorne and Thoreau in finding "redemption" in the sanctuary of writing, in the blockage and removal from immediacy of the text.[6]

An itch for explication is operative on every one of the book's levels. Start, as Ishmael does, with the "Etymology" and the "Extracts." The first, with its picture of the "pale Usher" dusting his grammars, introduces us to the bookish territory ahead, in which dictionaries, histories, biographies, epics, almanacs, primers, dissertations, novels, chapters of Scripture, sermons, short stories—in short, virtually every form of written discourse—will be mobilized to help us understand the whale. The "Etymology" itself scours space by reprinting the word for "whale" in a dozen languages, from Icelandic in the north to "Fegee" (Fiji) in the south. The "Extracts," supposedly supplied by a librarian, follow and do the same for chronology, ranging from Genesis and the classics (Plutarch and Pliny) at the dawn of recorded time to contemporaneous fictions, whale songs, and accounts of voyages.

Our narrator, whom we meet immediately after these prefatory materials, is a sometime schoolteacher, and his profession's trademark curiosity permeates the tale. Ishmael's concern with knowing has a touch of obsession, even of paranoia, about it. At the Whaleman's Chapel, he cannot restrain himself from imputing hidden meaning to everything he observes. Of Father Mapple's pulpit, which is shaped like the prow of a ship, he asks, "What could be more full of meaning?" He broods over Mapple's drawing up his stepladder behind him, declaring that "there must be some sober reason for this thing; furthermore it must symbolize something unseen" (pp. 68–69).[7] Ishmael's faith in the ubiquity of meaning may be a response to the chapel and its renowned preacher. Mapple exhorts his parishioners to give "no quarter to the truth" and to root out sin no matter where it hides (p. 80). Later, under the influence of another fanatic for truth, Captain Ahab, Ishmael will exclaim that "some certain significance lurks in all things, else all things are little worth" (p. 549). But for most of the narrative, he needs no external prodding to consecrate himself to cognition. He differs from the two "old men," as Ahab and Mapple are endlessly referred to (and about which more later), chiefly in the irenic quality of his fixation.

Ishmael wants to understand; Ahab wants to exterminate that which eludes his understanding. To the ship's captain, the fact that Moby Dick sheared off his leg is secondary to the white whale's status as an enigma. When Starbuck objects that a dumb brute acts blindly from instinct, Ahab delivers his famous paean to scrutability:

> . . . the little lower layer. All visible objects, man, are but as pasteboard masks. But in each event—in the living act, the undoubted deed—there,

some unknown but still reasoning thing puts forth the mouldings of its features from behind the unreasoning mask. If man will strike, strike through the mask! (p. 220)

This passage expresses in extremity the suspicion of concealed meaning that overtook Ishmael in the Whaleman's Chapel. The animus is new, but the curiosity is consistent. Indeed, curiosity is what keeps Ahab's rage at the boiling point. His ardor for vengeance would inevitably dissipate were it not for the assurance of intent and conscious malice in his adversary.

Ishmael and Ahab are partners in an epistemological odyssey, and *Moby-Dick*, as a compendium of Americana, inventories the culture's favorite ways of knowing. Facts and numbers ("Cetology," "The Decanter") complement pictures ("Monstrous Pictures of Whales," "Less Erroneous Pictures of Whales") and eyewitness reports ("The Affidavit," "The Town Ho's Story"). Prophecy and millennialism are as essential as the most advanced scientific discoveries. Ahab sets sail on Christmas day, and he vows to fulfill the biblical scenario of a savior who will revoke the curse on Adam and his seed. Christlike, he would crush the serpent/leviathan's head on the fateful third day of the chase. Signs and wonders, as foretold by Elijah and Fedallah, accompany him on his journey. Technology, dispeller of mystery, is a stout ally. Ahab studies sea charts and quadrants to track the likely movements of his prey, and he constantly employs technological imagery in speaking of his resolve: "The path to my fixed purpose is laid with iron rails, whereon my soul is grooved to run. . . . Naught's an obstacle, naught's an angle to the iron way!" (p. 227). "The Try-Works" documents the industrial aspect of whaling; "A Bower in the Arsacides," where Ishmael measures a whale skeleton, figuratively transforms the earth into a factory, another emblem, like the railroad, of mankind's mastery over nature.

Yet all such moments of cognitive presumption prove hollow. (Even "A Bower" invites skepticism, as Ishmael has to tattoo the whale's statistics on his arm, which, he confesses, is not large enough to record all the numbers; moreover, the skeleton gives little idea of the actual shape.) Leviathan turns out to be far more perplexing than imagined. The monster not only thwarts Ishmael's repeated attempts at decryption but also emerges victorious from the battle with the *Pequod.* The book's chapters fall into a pattern. Ishmael undertakes a thorough investigation of some part of the whale's anatomy or behavior only to reach the conclusion that reliable knowledge is impossible. The whale's brow is "pleated with riddles" (p. 448), and neither phrenologist nor physiognomist can make sense of it. The linear markings on its skin are indecipherable. Its secret ways beneath the ocean's surface defy "the most erudite research" (p. 243). Countless essays to capture its form in pigment end in failure, the botched canvases proof that the whale is the "one creature in the world which must remain unpainted to the last" (p. 352). Ishmael's inability to describe the tail sums up his frustration: "Dissect him how I may, then, I but go skin deep; I know him not, and never will" (p. 486).

To denominate Ishmael's state of mind as "frustration" is not quite accurate, however. In repenting his oath to destroy Moby Dick, Melville's narrator abjures as well the compulsive pursuit of meaning that has gripped him from the novel's earliest pages. Ahab, not his quarry, perishes in the third day's battle, and the *Pequod*'s commander drags down the other characters with him. All but one: Ishmael escapes the fate of the crew because when the ship sinks, he seizes the coffin–life buoy on which Queequeg carved a copy of the tattooing from his own body. Symbolically, Ishmael is rescued by a puzzle. The scribbling on his friend's skin spells out "a complete theory of the heavens and the earth, and a mystical treatise on the art of attaining truth." But this vital communication confounds understanding; its very author has no inkling of what it means:

> So that Queequeg in his own proper person was a riddle to unfold; a
> wondrous work in one volume; but whose mysteries not even himself
> could read, though his own live heart beat against them; and these mys-
> teries were therefore destined to moulder away with the living parchment
> whereon they were inscribed, and so be unsolved to the last. (p. 612)

Ishmael's good fortune—or perhaps it is our good fortune as readers— is *textual*, Melville emphasizes. *Moby-Dick*'s storyteller owes his life to a floating coffin that is a proxy for his Spouter-Inn bedmate and tropes that beloved companion as a book. Literature's mediation somehow contributes to Ishmael's survival. The distancing of writing, the opportunity the printed page affords for reflection, has been an important subtheme in the novel all along. Ishmael greets us not as an actor in the present but as an author of past events. We learn in the first paragraph that the adventure he will narrate took place "some years ago" (p. 23). Although he is vague about precisely when the action occurred, he is exact about the time of writing: "fifteen and a quarter minutes past one o'clock P.M. of this sixteenth day of December, A.D. 1851" (p. 475). In the chapter "Cetology," he pointedly classifies the different species of whales according to terms derived from printing. The sperm whale is compared to a folio, the killer whale to an octavo, the porpoise (which Ishmael considers a small whale) to a duodecimo, and so on. Even the light by which his book is read derives from the whale, oil from blubber supplying almost all the world's tapers, candles, and lamps.

This iterated self-reflexiveness underlines the bookishness and indirection of the reader's encounter with Moby Dick. Ishmael endured the ordeal of the *Pequod*'s voyage and foundering, and he tangled with the deadly sperm whale on our behalf. We survive that peril because we have the "wondrous work in one volume" that is *Moby-Dick*. Ishmael's words are our cetological universe. And those words, Melville constantly reminds us, are already a secondhand rendering of Ahab's charismatic leadership, a necessary asylum from his establishment of a shipboard dictatorship in the name of truth.

If Lincoln had not written the speech, Melville might have. Perhaps he did. The anticipation of *Moby-Dick*'s language, imagery, even atmosphere, is uncanny. Alarmed by the spread of "wild and furious passions" (especially acts of mob violence against abolitionists and Negroes),[8] Lincoln lays out a blueprint for the emergence of an American tyranny. As Michael Rogin has pointed out, he would deny his generation the Declaration.[9] That passionate document and the Revolution it inspired belong to the past. "The game is caught," Lincoln tells his listeners, "and I believe it is true, that with the catching, end the pleasures of the chase" (p. 12). But the future president cannot shake the moment of origin; its magnetism compels his imagination. If the "mobocratic spirit" persists (p. 9), he warns, dangerous men of "towering genius" will arise among us. Such beings, who belong "*to the family of the lion, or the tribe of the eagle,*" will never be content to serve in the system erected by their predecessors. "What! Think you these places would satisfy an Alexander, a Caesar, or a Napoleon? Never!" The ambitious individual, thirsting for a distinction comparable to that of the Founders, "will have it, whether at the expense of emancipating slaves, or enslaving freemen" (p. 12). Only a renewal of "*reverence for the Constitution and laws*" (p. 14) can prevent the anarchy of the present from degenerating into the despotism of tomorrow.

According to Edmund Wilson, the Springfield Address allowed Lincoln to project his future role as wartime leader.[10] The more immediate, if fictitious, realization is Captain Ahab. Melville's truth-seeker—to describe him for the moment in Lincoln's terms—renews the chase after monstrous game. He "disdains a beaten path" (p. 12). He engrosses power by transferring all sense of grievance from America's historic foe, the British nation, to a new enemy and by capitalizing "on the deep rooted principles of *hate*, and the powerful motive of *revenge*" (p. 13). He even resembles one of the Revolutionary forebears whose dying out Lincoln mourns (right down to the "mutilated limb"):

> They *were* a forest of mighty oaks; but the all-resistless hurricane has
> swept over them, and left only, here and there, a lonely trunk, despoiled
> of its verdure, shorn of its foliage; unshading and unshaded, to murmur
> in a few more gentle breezes, and to combat with its mutilated limbs, a
> few more ruder storms, then to sink, and be no more. (p. 14)

Ahab and "Father" Mapple are aged men, Melville's giants from the past. The *Pequod*'s captain has wandered for "forty years on the pitiless sea." To the crew, he is "old man Ahab," and Starbuck labels him "Old man of oceans." He himself wonders, "Do I look very old, so very, very old?" (pp. 635, 683–84). His scar gives him the appearance of a stricken oak:

> Threading its way out from among his grey hairs, and continuing right
> down one side of his tawny scorched face and neck, till it disappeared in

his clothing, you saw a tender rod-like mark, lividly whitish. It resembled that perpendicular seam sometimes made in the straight, lofty trunk of a great tree, when the upper lightning tearingly darts down it. (pp. 168–69)

Ahab has returned, as it were, from the Revolutionary era to reawaken "furious passions" in his lawless crew and to channel their feelings of hatred and revenge against the mystery of Moby Dick. In the process, as Lincoln predicted, he becomes an American Alexander, Caesar, and Napoleon rolled into one.

Ahab accomplishes this by deploying a battery of demagogic stratagems. Melville's hymn to "the great democratic God!" (p. 161) reminds us that for all its formal hierarchy, the ship remains an assemblage of "freemen" (Lincoln's word) who could not be swayed to their commander's purpose without their voluntary if manipulated consent. The Pequod's perverse populist taps into the demos's paranoid suspicion of hidden malice in a world of pain. Nothing, he exclaims, has the right to exempt itself from accountability: "I'd strike the sun if it insulted me. . . . Who's over me? Truth hath no confines" (p. 221).

His is a war, Ahab insists, and Melville suffuses the novel with martial imagery. (Lincoln's three examples of "towering genius" were all celebrated military leaders.) As early as chapter 1, "Loomings," Ishmael imagines a "grand programme of Providence" in which his whaling voyage is juxtaposed with a "BLOODY BATTLE IN AFFGHANISTAN" (p. 29). Ahab, who converts the Pequod's crew into his private army, declares to Starbuck, "I am the Fates' lieutenant. I act under orders. Look thou, underling! That thou obeyest mine" (p. 707). But the old autocrat shrewdly supplements his commands with mesmerizing performances. His entrance in "The Quarter-Deck" is prefaced by stage directions: "Enter Ahab: Then, All" (p. 215). He is a masterful orator whose eloquence—like that the authors of The Federalist Papers warned against—overbears opposition and places a "scepter" in his single hand. In "The Candles" he uses dramaturgy and fiery stage effects to terrorize the sailors. By the time Moby Dick is finally sighted, the crewmen are little more than machines moving "dumbly" to his will (p. 674). They have coalesced into the "one man, not thirty" (p. 700) that consummates the ambition of every would-be despot.

The people's champion who hated inscrutability ends up a conundrum to everybody else, a near double of his prey. Ahab enshrouds himself in "magic" and elicits "servile wonder" (p. 655). He domineers through "bodings, doubts, misgivings, fears" (p. 674). Absolutism for legibility in the ruler results in abjection and mystification for the ruled.

Ahab's last chance to renounce his obsession with meaning and vengeance comes just before the three-day chase, in the chapter titled "The Symphony." For an instant he stands back from his monomania:

What is it, what nameless, inscrutable, unearthly thing is it; what cozzening hidden lord and master, and cruel, remorseless emperor commands me; that against all natural lovings and longings, I so keep pushing, and crowding, and jamming myself on all the time; recklessly making me ready to do what in my own proper, natural heart, I durst not so much as dare? (p. 685)

Unable to answer his own question, the captain rededicates himself to slaying the "nameless," "hidden," "inscrutable" thing that torments him, and the moment of hesitation passes. The scene contrasts to Ishmael's embrace of the unknowable as embodied in Queequeg's coffin-text. And that in turn brings to mind an earlier contrast, this one between Father Mapple's absolutist sermon—"preach the Truth to the face of Falsehood!" (p. 79)—and Ishmael's original bonding with Queequeg in the Spouter-Inn.

Melville's storyteller returns from the Whaleman's Chapel to find his bedmate sitting before the hearth fire with a large book on his lap. Though raised in "the infallible Presbyterian Church," Ishmael opts for connection on equal terms with a pagan idolator. He would rather "do to my fellow man what I would have my fellow man to do to me" than impose his version of the truth like Mapple. He sits down beside his friend, and the pair continues leafing through the "marvelous" volume while Ishmael explains "the purpose of the printing, and the meaning of the few pictures that were in it." They cement their goodwill with a smoke from Queequeg's pipe, and the experience relieves Ishmael's "splintered heart and maddened hand." As with his saving by the coffin-life buoy, a text—here identified with tolerance and open-mindedness—is integral to the redemptive incident (pp. 82–85).

Lincoln's Springfield speech climaxed with a reference to the shade of "WASHINGTON." Rededicate American liberty to the great hero's memory, Lincoln pleads, and "*the gates of hell shall not prevail against it*" (p. 14). Melville also concludes his novel with a mention of hell. Battered by the white whale, Ahab's ship, "like Satan," prepares to "sink to hell" under the shroud of the sea (p. 723). But Melville appeals to Washington, too. Queequeg, Ishmael's figurative life-saver, was said to be "George Washington cannibalistically developed" (p. 82). If Washington, titular head of the Founding Fathers, is the culture's foremost voice for the zealotry of truth, he is simultaneously a symbol of its Constitution and respect for law. The textuality of the Founders is the antidote to their own preachment of popular transparency.

And yet, as the turbulence of the 1850s increased, even Lincoln felt moved to reanimate the spirit of 1776. He invoked the Declaration's principles against the South's belligerent expansion of slavery. And Melville's novel, though it validates the haven of writing, dissents from the Constitution on slavery and race. Queequeg, text, riddle, and raft, is also a nonwhite. What the ending of *Moby-Dick* accepts as axiomatic is the integrity of blackness. Ishmael floats to safety because he allows the racial other his indecipherable, irreducible alterity. The South Sea islander can no more be distilled into meaning than Melville's other unforgettable figures of unavailability: Bartleby, the scrivener, the white-collar proletarian from the story of the same name; Babo, the leader of the slave revolt in "Benito Cereno"; and Moby Dick.

Thoreau's *Walden*

No writer appears to be more committed to translucence than Thoreau. In his advocacy of simplicity, his resolve to burrow to the truth buried beneath "the mud and slush of opinion" (p. 97),[11] and his wish to shed the encumbrances of daily life, Thoreau strikes an insistent note of American anti-obscurantism. One strain of *Walden* is a clarion call for renewal, for a return to the values his countrymen have allowed to decay in their haste to acquire. The conspicuous selection of July 4 as the day to start the experiment at the Pond leaves no doubt of the text's reformist intentions.

Yet the choice of July 4, date of the Declaration, proves problematic for Thoreau. Not that he ever abjures the culture's founding message of freedom. While living at the Pond, Thoreau also wrote "Civil Disobedience," and in that essay he attacks "the men of '87" (the writers of the federal charter) for their retreat from the Declaration's principles.[12] He lumps together the Constitutionalists with Daniel Webster as trimmers on slavery, voices of expediency and not "Truth" (which he capitalizes as ritualistically as Melville). So it might seem perverse to argue, as I plan to do, for a Thoreau, or a *Walden*, that basically follows the strategy of 1787. This Thoreau systematically blunts the themes of reform and revelation. He conjoins them with a progressive affirmation of opacity that threatens to engulf their meaning. Though *Walden* never quite reaches this point, it hints at a stage beyond even the ambiguities and anti-immediacy of *The Federalist Papers*. Thoreau's disaffection from modernity's clarifications culminates in an estrangement from writing itself, the text as a means of communication.

Thoreau the awakener and truth-teller is a figure familiar from the earliest pages of *Walden*. He comes before us in the nakedness of "the I, or first person," and promises to speak candidly about his time in the woods (p. 3). From start to finish, he would jar us out of our sleep of materialism into contact with the real. His neighbors, Thoreau says, wander clueless in "the dark unfathomed mammoth cave of this world," mistaking "shams and delusions" for "soundest truths," and he brings redemption from their lifelong habit of never penetrating beneath the surface (pp. 93–95).

The revivalist Thoreau does not waver in his belief that the Truth, or the bottom, or reality can be reached. A devotee of Poe's detective stories might be excused for thinking of *Walden*'s author as a kind of private eye of the woods, confident that every apparent mystery can be solved. In chapter 2, "Where I Lived, and What I Lived For," Thoreau vows to wedge his way down "to a hard bottom and rocks in place, which we can call *reality*"

(p. 98). In chapter 16, "The Pond in Winter," he refutes the rumors about the "no bottom" of the Pond by measuring its depth at "exactly one hundred and two feet" (pp. 285–87). And the last and eighteenth chapter, "Conclusion," reaffirms his conviction that "there is a solid bottom everywhere" (p. 330).[13]

Thoreau takes as much interest in nature's surfaces as in burrowing to the depths. He praises the hardiness of "a primitive and frontier life" (p. 11) and portrays himself as a man in the middle, a product of civilization who is conversant with native lore and customs. The woodsman of Concord can sound like Cooper's Hawkeye in his Indian-like ability to perceive what other white men overlook in their surroundings. For years he earned his living as a surveyor, and in the book he surveys in imagination. He inspects every spot "within a dozen miles of where I lived" as a possible house site (p. 81). When the Pond freezes over, Thoreau lies down on it not just to study the bottom but to make a thorough investigation of the ice itself, with its greenish blue tint and its minute bubbles "like a string of beads" (pp. 256–57). In "Spring," he devotes page after page to a painstaking description of the designs formed by the clay as it thaws.

Walden's surveyor and sounder takes a classic American delight in facts and numbers. We too often forget how much of the text is devoted to knowing. Thoreau describes in detail the building of his house and provides a whole chapter of instruction on the planting and harvesting of beans. He showers us with statistics. The reader-student learns how much he spent on food, seeds, clothing, windows, and boards (down to the quarter cent), and how much he earned from day labor and from selling his crop. He records the breaking up of Walden's ice in the spring, giving the temperature and the precise day of the month for every year from 1845 to 1854 (p. 303). He inscribes the date of his arrival (July 4, 1845) and of his departure (September 6, 1847). One thing no reader forgets is that Thoreau lived for exactly two years, two months, and two days in the woods.

The doubling or repetition of *Walden's* numerology—the two years, two months, and two days—is a tip-off, as it happens, to the text's reversal of its documentary legibility. It is a tip-off in two senses (if that is not belaboring the pun): first, because the call to awaken elicits its dark twin, a defense of textual aporia; and second, because nature with its cycles and repetitions becomes the template for *resistance* to knowing, for a strangeness that mocks the human passion to "strike through the mask." Near the end of "Spring," Thoreau is explicit about his doubleness of outlook: "At the same time that we are earnest to explore and learn all things, we require that all things be mysterious and unexplorable, that land and sea be infinitely wild, unsurveyed and unfathomed by us because unfathomable" (pp. 317–18).

This acceptance of inscrutability undoes the parallels to Poe's detective and Cooper's Western hero. *Walden* is rife in moments when nature balks Thoreau's incursions. For example, the plumbing of the Pond's bottom is balanced by the story of the loon in chapter 12, "Brute Neighbors." Thoreau relates his attempt to anticipate where a loon will appear on the Pond's surface after diving and vanishing from sight. He attributes mental nimbleness to the creature: "While he was thinking one thing in his brain, I was endeavoring to divine his thought in mine. It was a pretty game, played on the smooth surface of the pond, a man against a loon" (p. 235). This is not a case, as in "Murders in the Rue Morgue," of imputing motivation where none exists. Walden's loon is no Ourang-Outang but a match for human cunning, and Thoreau can neither outwit it nor reduce it to easily predicted instinct. His maneuvers to intercept the bird invariably fail because nature is a superior Minister D., an order of intelligence beyond even Dupin's. Its otherness forever confounds human comprehension.

Thoreau draws the same lesson as a direct reproof to societal modes of knowledge in "The Village." He compares the assemblage of citizens in Concord to "a great news room," with gossip "incessantly . . . circulating either from mouth to mouth, or from newspaper to newspaper." The villagers line the streets conversing and looking about themselves "with a voluptuous expression." Nothing seems to escape the floodlight of publicity: the very houses are arranged to front each other so that the residents "could most see and be seen." To visit the village is to run a gauntlet of scrutiny, and the hero makes haste to return to the woods again.

Against this ordeal of visibility and verbal intrusion, Thoreau contrasts groping his way at night, in pitch blackness, for his "snug harbor" beside the Pond. Again, he inverts the cultural ideal of the Pathfinder. What he values about the journey is not the ease with which he negotiates the course but the "perplexity" of traveling at nighttime, far preferable "to steering like pilots by certain well-known beacons and headlands." The rare and memorable bonus is the experience of getting "lost in the woods" and *not* knowing where one is. For "not until we are completely lost, or turned around," Thoreau says, ". . . do we appreciate the vastness and strangeness of Nature" (pp. 167–71).

The stark polarity here between the social requirement of transparency and the bracing consent to ignorance in nature becomes an emblem for the entire project of *Walden*. For Thoreau, as he revised his manuscript, the contrast of "The Village" was reinforced by popular indifference to what he had to say, and he began to champion the figurative blankness of night as an antidote to a sophomoric accessibility.[14] The correct parallel in this vein is not with popular literature but rather with the authors of *The Federalist Papers*, Madison, Hamilton, and Jay as proponents of textuality's obstructions.

Walden almost seems to paraphrase the Federalist and public sphere elevation of impersonality over presence. In his meditation "Reading," Thoreau trots out the standard arguments for the "reserved and select" medium that is writing as opposed to the "transitory" and "brutish" one that is speech. Inscribed language has the inestimable advantages of distance and duration. It outlasts the ephemeral, the perishable speaker as well as his momentary passion, and we can appreciate its subtleties because we can study it at leisure. Like a remote star, it never ceases to hold our attention. The same, according to Thoreau, cannot be said about even the most forceful verbal performance. No matter how intoxicating when heard, spoken language does not pass the test of a second visit:

> What is called eloquence in the forum is commonly found to be rhetoric in the study. The orator yields to the inspiration of a transient occasion, and speaks to the mob before him, to those who can *hear* him; but the writer . . . speaks to the intellect and heart of mankind, to all in any age who can *understand* him. (pp. 101–2)

Again like the advocates of the Constitution, Thoreau directs his most withering scorn at texts that emulate speech's facility of ingestion. He assails popular fiction for retailing "easy reading" about the trials of "Zebulon and Sephronia, and how they loved as none had ever loved before, and neither did the course of their true love run smooth." This kind of banality recalls our third example of popular forms, the novel as gossip, and indeed Thoreau compares its avid consumers to the villagers in the streets of Concord wagging their tongues over the latest news. "All this," he writes of the too-accessible novels, "they read with saucer eyes, and erect and primitive curiosity, and with unwearied gizzard." Literature as orality prefigures the mindless absorption of the image and, in the name of transparency, produces a comparable drugging of the higher faculties (pp. 104–5).

Not written language alone, then, but writing that taxes the reader and frustrates easy consumption: this ideal evolves as the book's counter to its own epistemological evangelicalism. The process of estrangement, or *"extra-vagance,"* to use a Thoreauvian pun for interpretive difficulty, culminates in the final chapter. *Walden*'s "Conclusion" transmutes speech into writing and writing into bafflement. No other chapter in the book is so lapidary and "worked on," so "reservedly" articulated. None can equal it in the generation of pithy and quotable statements. One has the impression that Thoreau is deliberately coining "written" proverbs. He is freezing the transitory into permanence, refining and elevating what ring like oral sayings into lasting aphorisms: "Only the defeated and deserters go to war, cowards that run away and enlist" (p. 322); "If you have built castles in the air, your work need not be lost; that is where they should be. Now put the foundations under them" (p. 324); "For the most part, we are not where we are, but in a false position" (p. 327); "Only that day dawns to which we are awake. There is more day to dawn. The sun is but a morning star" (p. 329).

Everyone will have their favorites among these epigrams, and most readers will agree that some of the best elude translation, or even understanding. Thoreau wanted it that way. He is explicit about his ambition to attain "to obscurity," to craft an account of his experience that emulates the Walden ice. To the "demand which England and America make, that you shall speak so that they can understand you," his reply is uncompromising: "As if there were safety in stupidity alone." Thoreau presses public sphere obliquity well beyond its political limits, drastically narrowing his audience from the collectivity in the "news room" to the rare and solitary scholar in his study. Or, rather, he comes close to lengthening the distance between author and audience until it verges on the impassable. "The volatile truth of our words," he says, "should continually betray the inadequacy of the residual statement" (pp. 324–25). Spoken language is no longer the problem to be transcended, the obstacle to a rarefied communication. Written words can prod and inspire, but *no* language can contain Thoreau's meaning.

One way to read *Walden*'s escalating crypticness would be to see it as an exercise in privacy. Thoreau states in "Economy," his first chapter, that although he would, if it were possible, "never paint 'No Admittance' on [his] gate," secrets are "inseparable" from his trade and total candor out of the question (p. 17). His cabin at Walden Pond gives him the spatial protection necessary to "transact some private business" (p. 19). His dwelling is situated "a mile from any neighbor" (p. 3), and even when entertaining visitors, he requires "sufficient distance" from his guest so that his thoughts can carom around the house. He and his interlocutor sit "so far apart bodily that we cannot possibly hear each other's voice in any case" (pp. 140–41). *Walden* the piece of writing reconfigures physical reserve as textual barrier. The book's conundrums weed out the slumbering and merely curious, all who are unwelcome gate crashers at Thoreau's experiment. Obscurity allows him to post "No Admittance" on his title page.

Here we can see Thoreau's exemplarity for the nineteenth-century canon. His retreat into darkness paradoxically illuminates American literature's premature modernism. Thoreau's attraction to textual blockage, a literary strategy he shares with Hawthorne, Melville, and Henry James, arises in direct response to his culture's hegemonic legibility. It replicates as "private" art the instinct for withdrawal from the "tyranny of the majority," which, according to Tocqueville, writing twenty years earlier, "disposes each member of the community to sever himself from the mass of his fellows and to draw apart with his family and his friends, so that after he has formed a little circle of his own, he willingly leaves society at large to itself."[15] The often-noted precociousness of American authors in devising near-unreadable books parries the oppressive lucidities of the first modern nation: the verbal and visual trespasses of "The Village"; the best-selling novels; the diffusion of communicative technologies, from newspapers and the post office to the telegraph; and the railroad that shatters Thoreau's silence at the Pond while carrying books from the city to the country but extinguishing "the wit that writes them" (p. 116).

And yet Thoreau's notion of the private cannot be reduced to a social category. The paradigm he cherishes is not finally cultural or political or even human; it is natural. Let us return to the passage in which he admits that his wish to explore coexists with a yearning for the wild to be "unfathomable." The thought continues with a celebration of nature's "vast and Titanic features," a pleasure in witnessing our human "limits transgressed, and some life pasturing freely where we never wander" (p. 318). Nature as the alien, the ultimately unknowable, is the text's lodestar. In a similar mood, Thoreau describes waking up one winter morning with an urgent sense "that some question had been put to me." A glance outside the window convinces him that nature is the "answered question." But beyond the serenity this brings, there is nothing further to be said, no attempt to paraphrase either the query or the retort. "Nature puts no question and answers none which we mortals ask" (p. 282). The only truly responsive gesture would seem to be silence, imitating nature's discretion by abandoning verbal interchange altogether.

By the end of his experiment, Thoreau has clearly absorbed the foreignness of nature into his writing. Or, perhaps more accurately, he has subordinated the written to the natural and ceased to put and answer questions. In "Spring," as he watches the land coming back to life, he feels by contrast the insignificance of "histories, chronologies, traditions, and all written revelations" (p. 310). It is well known that Thoreau sought to pattern the two books he published in his lifetime, *A Week on the Concord and Merrimack Rivers* (1849) and *Walden*, after the cycles of nature, in the first adopting the model of the week, and in the second condensing his time at the Pond to the progression of the seasons for a single year. Less often remarked is the fact that both volumes have the same ending date, September 6. *A Week* begins on August 31 and covers seven days; *Walden*'s two years, two months, and two days take us from July 4 to September 6. Thoreau cast his only "written revelations" as an act of repetition, a doubling or recyling of each other. Together the two books suggest textuality as nature scripted. But more than this, they exemplify writing as impasse. They go nowhere. They do not "advance." They bring no "news." They just return upon each other in an endless cycle of the same.

Thoreau published little after *Walden*. He did speak out against slavery, but more, one feels, because he could not otherwise live with himself than because he expected to be heard. The years left to him he spent writing in his journal. He filled up volume after volume, patiently documenting the monotony of seasonal change. Nature's "infinite self-referentiality," in Sharon Cameron's phrase, engrossed his attention until his death in 1862. Cameron believes Thoreau hoped for posthumous publication of this mammoth legacy, but her evidence is unpersuasive.[16] Thoreau appears to have been content to contemplate nature's strangeness in privacy, in the silence of a manuscript that would never see the light of day. In this he was simply being true to the attitudes forged in *Walden*. "Perhaps," he writes in "Higher Laws," "the facts most astounding and most real are never communicated by man to man" (p. 216). In the journal Thoreau has crossed out "perhaps" and washed his hands of communication.

James's *The American*

You are not a child," Christopher Newman exclaims to Claire de Cintré when the woman he loves bows to her mother's demands and agrees to break off their engagement. "You are not a minor, nor an idiot" (p. 348).[17] Claire has little to say in her defense. I must submit to my family, she pleads. "It's like a religion" (p. 353). And then she enters a convent, and Newman never sets eyes on her again.

In the terms of the novel—not to mention this study—the colloquy could hardly be more pregnant with meaning. Claire *is* an idiot, though not in the word's modern sense of a mentally deficient person. "Idiot" derives from the Greek for private. It signifies someone—a child, a slave, historically a woman—who is excluded from participation in public affairs: more narrowly, someone who has no determining say in the role and duties assigned to him or her. Newman's use of the word underlines James's vision of late-nineteenth-century France as an anti-America. In the Paris of *The American*, the reigning religion is an alloy of social rank and Roman Catholicism, and individual choice resides in the hands of the few. Even when the decision directly affects one's welfare—as calling off their marriage affects no one more deeply than Claire and Newman—those outside the privileged circle of authority have no claim to consultation. They remain in the dark. Whereas the United States as a Protestant, democratic, and egalitarian nation cherishes openness, France stands for occlusion. It is a culture of closure, limited access, and arbitrary power.[18]

But that is too simple a contrast. Though James articulates it, he also qualifies it. French blankness as the inversion of the postbellum United States commands his tempered respect precisely in its refusal of legibility. *The American* tells the story of a man who becomes "new" by learning to appreciate that which is "old": he is transformed, at least in part, into a European. (A more descriptive title than the one James gave it would be *The Europeanized American*.) Newman achieves this cosmopolitan condition by renouncing his own mania for exposure, as though Captain Ahab had good-naturedly acceded to Starbuck's request to desist in "The Symphony." The hero, that is, escapes the allegorical or "romance" confinement of his name/identity.

James's qualification of the Old World/New World contrast does not stop there, however. His fictional Europe is not just the opposite of America; it is, perversely, an allegorical, or rather an analogical, double for the country James left behind in 1875. The author of *The American* has been criticized for replicating a mystique of "discrimination" that lends support to racial hierarchy.[19] But the novel—serialized in the *Atlantic Monthly* in 1876–77, at the very moment when Reconstruction was being dismantled—is a sustained indictment of a social system based on pedigree or blood. And in 1877, the "inherited infamy" of blackness (Gustave de Beaumont's phrase, from *Marie*) was well on the way to becoming as much a principle of social regulation as the aristocratic reverence for family that causes the Bellegardes to reject Newman as a suitor for Claire, after having given their pledge that they would accept him.

Conspicuous in the narrative is the physical layout of dwellings, a phenomenon James always made much of on his periodic returns to the United States (more and more to America's disadvantage, as he grew accustomed to European arrangements). Newman's first attempt to call on Claire brings him to the Faubourg St. Germain. The houses are said to "present to the outer world a face as impassive and as suggestive of the concentration of privacy within as the blank walls of Eastern seraglios" (p. 79). The Bellegarde residence puts the hero in mind, ominously, of a convent, and his request for admittance is rebuffed by the marquis. But even the likable Valentin Bellegarde, who thinks of himself as the liberal "Opposition" to his monarchist brother, lives in a "contracted" apartment filled with "obstructive" furniture and featuring "a curtained recess with a sheet of looking-glass in which, among the shadows, you could see nothing" (p. 144). Newman, on the other hand, has rented an apartment with a parlor as large as a ballroom or a church, as Valentin observes with a smile, and he astonishes his guest by giving him "unlimited leave to laugh" at its palatial size (pp. 133–34).

These spatial differences are expressive of cultural ones. Bellegarde France translates impediment into a social principle. It esteems birth over talent or merit and proscribes mobility as a trespass of rightful order. All that counts in such a world, as Claire's mother sniffs to the hero, is one's "antecedents" (p. 308), and getting ahead materially carries a taint of immorality. One encounters no Parisian equivalents of Christopher Newman, who has acquired a fortune through energy and character. One finds only the titled beneficiaries of ascription and heartless bounders like Noémie Nioche. Valentin's sense of stasis—he could not go into business, or politics, or follow a profession, all because of his noble birth—complements Noémie's sense of herself as a pure commodity ("'Everything I have is for sale,' said Mademoiselle Noémie" [p. 199]), willing to do anything for a price.

Valentin's immobility pales beside his sister's. In her case the familial shades into the political. Claire is the will-less subject of an absolute monarchy. Her capitulation to Madame de Bellegarde over Newman marks the second time she has yielded to arbitrary dictates. She wed M. de Cintré "without her having any voice" in the matter (p. 153). The scene in which we learn why she cannot marry Newman reads like a formula for autocracy. "We have used authority," the mother states, and Claire confirms, "My mother commanded" (p. 315). When Newman objects and asks by what right they have done so, the old woman tautologically appeals to her power and her daughter's obedience.

It is no accident that Valentin fought in the armies supporting the pope's claims to earthly power, or that he muses to Newman, "I think I shall tie a rope around my waist and go into a monastery" (p. 141). Catholicism in *The American* is the religious corollary to the ideology of birthright. It functions overwhelmingly—and climactically—as an engine of exclusion. At the end of the novel, Claire transfers her reflex of submission from her family to the church and immures herself in a convent. The Carmelite building into which she disappears on the portentously named Rue d'Enfer presents an appearance distinguishable from the Bellegarde mansion only by virtue of its being an extreme of that prisonlike dwelling. It lies among "streets bordered by long dead walls." Its distant upper windows and blank masonry reveal "no symptoms of human life; the place looked dumb, deaf, inanimate" (pp. 444–45).

We have gone from the open vistas of the American continent (Newman is typed as a "great Western Barbarian" [p. 68]) to "pale, dead, discoloured" walls (p. 445); from the "visible sainthood" of Protestant evangelicalism to the "invisible sisterhood" of the Carmelite nuns (p. 404); and from a society of volition to a near-feudalism where unthinking obedience is the norm. Into an airless, illegible France Newman brings his passions for boundlessness and clarity. He would storm through the obstacles, and banish all the secrets, of the Old World. When Valentin protests that he does not understand what he is getting into ("You will never understand—you will never know" (p. 162), the hero has his answer ready: "I want to proceed with my eyes open. I will do my best to understand" (pp. 159–60). Claire is a problem he means to solve. "It was the mystery—it was what she was off the stage, as it were—that interested Newman most of all" (pp. 147–48). He assures the heroine that he is "no great mystery" himself but exactly what he seems (p. 168); and she listens to his marriage proposal with "the air of a woman who had stepped across the frontier of friendship and, looking around her, finds the region vast" (p. 172). Later he convinces himself that his fiancée "was a woman for the light, not for the shade," and that he is just the man to rid her of her "mysterious melancholy": "He felt, himself, that he was an antidote to oppressive secrets; what he offered her was, in fact, above all things a vast sunny immunity from the need of having any" (p. 225).

Newman, in other words, will be vulnerable to seduction by the kind of hyperbolic narrative that James, who was shortly to write a critical biography of *Hawthorne* (1879), associated with American fiction. Claire's suitor succumbs to the passion for answers that overtakes so many protagonists of romance. His added misfortune is to enter a lurid plot without having developed the perspective that comes from regularly reading fiction. (James comments early on that his protagonist "had never read a novel!" [p. 63].) The story in which he finds himself, as Richard Poirier pointed out some time ago, begins as a comedy of manners but modulates, with the cancellation of the wedding, into a melodrama.[20] It becomes a sensationalized Gothic fiction from the pen of a romancer—an American romancer who looks at Europe as James has at moments encouraged us to see it but without *his* saving distance and humor. A writer, in other words, who resembles Newman's traveling companion Babcock.

Babcock, a Unitarian minister from Dorchester, Massachusetts, is the comic hyperbole of American fervor to know. He goes too far even for Newman. The clergyman, with his "strikingly candid physiognomy" (p. 105), dislikes European impurity and is troubled, or rather tormented, by whatever he does not comprehend. He decides to part from Newman because, as he says, "We don't understand each other." (The hero's response is, "where's the harm?") The feeling distresses Babcock so much that he fears he will become ill, for as someone who tries "to arrive at the truth about everything," he finds inscrutability unendurable. After they separate, he sends Newman a note reiterating his discomfort and adding as a postscript, "I am greatly perplexed by Luini" (pp. 109–11).

Babcock of course is no Ahab or Roger Chillingworth on the track of a terrible enigma, but once the narrative darkens into treachery and loss, the grimness behind the comedy in his characterization gets displaced onto James's protagonist. Newman catches the minister's fervor, as it were; he contracts romance. And in one respect he has only himself to blame: his insistence on making his impending marriage known to one and all—on "crying it on the housetops," in his words (p. 249)—results in the ball that finally proves too much for the Bellegardes' tolerance. Had the hero been more discreet, he might not have been thrust into a melodrama. As it is, he bumps against the "mystery" of the Bellegarde overture to Lord Deepmere—"Clear it up. I don't like mysteries," he tells the Englishman (p. 287)—and then he stumbles into an intrigue full of family secrets, incriminating letters, wicked nobles, and the labyrinthine interiors of a Catholicism more suited to the paranoid fantasies of nativist Know-Nothings than to a worldly admirer of European art galleries—or to an expatriate novelist like Henry James. "Rue d'Enfer," indeed: it is the sort of street name we expect to encounter in a potboiler by George Lippard, not a work of realism.

The initial effect of the romance narrative on Newman is to blind him. The deceit of the Bellegardes seems "to smite his eyes like the glare of a watchman's lantern" (p. 314). He has the classic American reaction to an ocular blockage: he would retaliate for his temporary sightlessness by expunging the darkness and irradiating everything. Newman alters with the generic alteration: he *does* begin to resemble Ahab and Chillingworth, and Dupin too—all three foes of the insoluble, the first two driven as he is by revenge.

Valentin and Mrs. Bread supply him with the "key" to unlock the "mystery" of Claire's surrender (p. 322). Valentin, fatally wounded in the duel over Noémie, summons Newman to his side. His deathbed scene, like his father's, suggests not so much a Dupin detective story as one of Poe's tales of horror, in which an expiring person seems to die, comes back to life, and finally fades away for good. Claire's younger brother offers Newman "a secret" to use against his family. "It will avenge you," are his last words. The hero's instinctive shock—he thinks of obtaining information in this "illicit way" as tantamount to "listening at a keyhole" (pp. 341–42)—yields to an iron-willed resolve to expose and destroy his enemies. Here Mrs. Bread enters the plot and ratchets up the romantic hyperbole another notch. A Protestant—low Church of England, she announces proudly—she meets with Newman at a ruined Catholic church and, in this hackneyed Gothic setting, tells him of the letter in which the old marquis charged his wife with murder. Of her narration, replete with dramatic sighs and pauses, James remarks: "The most artistic of romancers could not have been more effective" (p. 383). Bread's revelation completes the protagonist's transformation into an "inquisitor" (p. 361). Brandishing his McCarthyite sheet of paper, he calls on the influential duchess planning to "publish" the guilt of the Bellegardes.

But this is the place where Newman's Ahabian monomania begins to melt away. Recognizing "the folly of his errand" (p. 424), he declines to repeat his story to the duchess and renounces the revenge that has consumed him for a hundred pages. "He could close the book," James writes—exit the romance—"and put it away" (p. 446). The Bellegarde crime does *not* have to be made public at any cost; it can join the many veiled things vital to European society and to James's art. Newman, we recollect, abandoned vengeance once before, when an associate from his moneymaking days bilked him of $60,000. The lesson he drew then was prophetic for the present: it entailed accepting the mysterious, not needing to know what was "off the stage" (as he had been determined to know about Claire): "And all this took place quite independent of my will, and I sat watching it as if it were a play at a theatre. I could feel it going on inside of me. You may depend upon it that there are things going on inside of us that we understand mighty little about" (p. 57).

Despite this precedent, Newman's act of renunciation has something European and Catholic about it, an implication urged upon us by the role of a cathedral in aiding him to make his choice. James softens his critique of the church's concealments by allowing the hero to find solace in its otherworldliness. After his visit to the Carmelite convent, Newman enters Notre Dame and sits down in "the splendid dimness." Relief washes over him "because while he was there he was out of the world." At that instant, "the bottom" falls "out of his revenge," and he is overcome with shame for having wanted to inflict hurt by revealing a secret (pp. 445–46).

Aesthetic tact seconds Catholic reserve. Newman's change of heart has an artistic dimension; his burning of the marquis's note says no to writing as inquisition. In effect, the gesture is James's acknowledgment that literature should emulate painting and trade some of its "knowing," its depth, for the visual art's delight in surfaces. From the first chapter of the novel, which occurs in the Louvre, we have been introduced to a Europe where the exquisite appearance is treasured more than what lies behind "the mask." (Newman's role as a proliferator of copies—he engages Noémie to churn them out for him—suggests both his regard for art and the limits of his appreciation.) The Bellegardes are frequently compared to paintings or to unreadable texts: at one moment the marquise looks like "an old lady painted by Vandyke" (p. 273), at another she resembles "a document signed and sealed; a thing of parchment, ink, and ruled lines" (p. 180). And when Newman confronts Madame de Bellegarde and her son with her husband's damning letter, the marquis is said to turn "whiter than Newman had ever seen anyone out of a picture" (p. 412).

James could hardly be more pointed about the opposition of text and image, truth-telling and exterior, American sincerity and French display. (An earlier scene revolves around a similar contrast: Noémie draws two daubs of paint across the canvas she is working on, one vertical and one horizontal, and pronounces the resulting cross [or "t"] "the sign of truth." The painting is spoiled as painting, but Valentin professes to prefer it because it now "tells a story": it has been converted into writing [pp. 198–99].)[21] Newman is in the process of transferring or at least moderating his allegiances; he will eventually destroy not the Bellegardes' lives but the old marquis's letter, and even at this moment of brutal accusation he shows more aesthetic feeling for surfaces than seems compatible with inflexible vengeance. Madame de Bellegarde pretends indifference to the paper, but her son Urbain declares it a forgery. "Your mother does better," Newman observes. "She has done better all along" (p. 415). The hero has no difficulty recognizing the better painting/performance, and we believe him when he admits to admiration for the wicked old woman's sangfroid.

It may seem counterintuitive, despite his voluminous reflections on the fine arts, to think of Henry James as a "visual" writer with a suspicion of linguistic disrobing. He has been acclaimed as the greatest psychological novelist of his time. Yet James's narrator in *The American* clearly shares Newman's sense, by the final chapters, that some things are best left unsaid. (Note, also, James's fondness for painterly titles: *The Portrait of a Lady* [1881], *Transatlantic Sketches* [1875], *Portraits of Places* [1883], etc.) Repeatedly he protests ignorance and will *not* provide us with information—discreetly refuses to escort us behind the stage. "I know not" (p. 46); "I am unable to say . . ." (p. 61); "I am unable to say . . ." (p. 195); "I don't know . . ." (p. 86); "I don't know . . ." (p. 258). These examples of authorial agnosticism could be multiplied. They give the lie to the common view of James as an author relentless (and unrelenting) in his probings of consciousness.

Moreover, when he does venture interpretations of inwardness, the Jamesian narrator often does so with considerable humility. "If this explanation was unsound," he states on a representative occasion, "a deeper analyst than I must give the right one" (p. 175). Such cognitive modesty is not incompatible with civilized knowledge of European manners and art, and the narrator does not hide the fact that he is a more sophisticated observer than his protagonist. But that superior culture does not translate into traffic in secrets. The narrative voice disavows the intention (in Babcock's phrase) "to arrive at the truth about everything" and shows a realist/visual artist's respect for the unknowability of others and of the self. "I don't pretend to say" what caused Newman to relent (p. 446) is the psychological novelist's analogue to Ishmael's admission of defeat about the whale: "I know him not, and never will."

Slavery, James wrote in *The American Scene*, was the South's "monomania."[22] Newman succumbs to an Ahab-like delirium for revenge; but the Bellegardes, too, are guilty of monomaniacal excess. They are fixated on the prestige of birth, an "aristocratic" idea, as Mrs. Tristram says, to which they are so devoted that even Newman's desperately desired wealth cannot persuade them to relinquish it (p. 323). They, not the protagonist, turn out to be the ones in the grip of an obsession. But as James himself rightly points out, ideologies of exclusion have their compensations. Much dignity "may reside in the habit of unquestioned authority and the absoluteness of a social theory favourable to yourself" (p. 217).

Slant the terms a hair, and James could be writing about the post–Civil War South. One might compare the fictional plot of Newman's attempt to breach the enclosed Parisian universe of *The American* with the historical plot being played out below the Mason-Dixon line under Reconstruction (a policy disintegrating, as I have said, at the time of the novel's serialization and abandoned in the year of its book publication, when the Compromise of 1877 restored the white planter class to ascendancy). France is ruled by hierarchy and demarcation, and those who enjoy the privileges of birth are fiercely jealous of their "race." ("Old races have their secrets," Valentin says [p. 163], and later, after his mother breaks faith with Newman, he adds, "When my people—when my race—come to that, it is time for me to withdraw" [p. 340].) A stranger and "democrat" appears on the scene and challenges the status quo, offering the oppressed (Claire de Cintré) the prospect of change. But after initial concessions and promises of cooperation, the entrenched powers go back on their word and set about tightening control over their victim. The text concludes with the visitor/liberator's expulsion and the living burial of the heroine, who faces a lifetime of enforced invisibility and deprivation.

The former Confederacy inherited a social order of racial stratification. All whites benefited from the advantage of skin color, but special status belonged to the old plantation owners who became known as Redeemers. This elite had to accept the Thirteenth Amendment as a condition of rejoining the Union, and they gave, at best, a grudging welcome to the carpetbaggers and Northern bureaucrats who flocked southward to assist the freedmen. Behind the scenes they worked to reclaim their power and to disenfranchise—and, if they could somehow pull it off, effectively reenslave—the Negro. (The KKK was founded as early as 1865.) In the end the white ruling class was to have its way, and a regime of caste was reimposed upon the South. The carpetbaggers, dependent on protection by Northern troops, began leaving before 1877, when the military occupation of the region came to a formal end. Deserted by their allies, the ex-slaves were systemically deprived of autonomy and rights and eventually hounded from visibility.

Was James, an ocean away in Paris, cognizant of these events? He came from a staunchly abolitionist family. Two James brothers had served in the Union army, both in black regiments, Bob in the Massachusetts 55th and Wilky as an adjutant in Colonel Robert Gould Shaw's more famous Massachusetts 54th. Wilky was gravely wounded in the assault on Fort Wagner; it took him over a year to recover. After the war, the two veterans went south, and in 1866, as Louis Menand has summarized their experience, they

> started a farm in Florida using freed blacks as labor, but the racism of local whites and the falling price of cotton brought the enterprise to a disastrous end. Bob bailed out early; Wilky stayed on for six years, long enough to see that the emancipation for which he had fought had only brought a new kind of misery to black people in the South.[23]

I do not mean to propose that James was thinking of Wilky when he created Christopher Newman. But the parallels are certainly arresting, and the fate of his own siblings would have made them hard to miss. James's novel engages the same themes of freedom, inherited condition, and aristocratic abuse that were convulsing his homeland. The defeat of his protagonist, and Claire's "reenslavement" among the Carmelites, took historical form in the triumph of white supremacy and the crushing of Reconstruction's promise. And in the United States, North as well as South, there was little evidence of Newman's generosity of spirit. When, in 1907, James prepared a preface for the New York edition of *The American*, he found, on rereading his book, that "it is as difficult . . . to trace the dividing-line between the real and the romantic as to plant a milestone between north and south."[24] This is of course a misinterpretation of the novel, and of the political climate, of 1876–77. The swerve from realism to romance is palpable with the betrayal of Newman, just as the divisions between North and South needed no milestone to flag them in the tragic last phase of Reconstruction. But thirty years had elapsed since *The American's* publication, and those three decades had made de jure and de facto segregation, as well as class strife and bitterness, pervasive facts throughout the nation. James's statement says more about his present than about the past; and it speaks volumes about the "Bellegardization" or "Southernization" that had overtaken the country since he had imagined a representative American with the hopeful name of "Newman."

CHAPTER 5

Freud and Film Redux

The visual and cognitive extensions represented by the cinema and psychotherapy were renewals, but they were renewals with a twist. They resurrected some of the legibility that seemed to be fading from the American scene as the nation entered the twentieth century. The chaotic growth of cities had extinguished the clarity of the material environment; the influx of millions of strangers from abroad overwhelmed social uniformity; machine politics and corporate oligarchy threatened democratic openness. Alarmed by these changes, so destructive of the coherence of the past, growing numbers of Americans joined a culture-wide movement to stem the spread of disorder. They rallied to Populism and then Progressivism, and in 1912 they elected Woodrow Wilson as twenty-eighth president of the United States. Wilson's book of campaign speeches, *The New Freedom*, compressed their yearnings into a chapter title. "Let There Be Light," he declared, on unwonted (and unwanted) regions of darkness.

Yet the emergent social landscape had its benefits, and these exerted a complicating pull on the quest for renovation. The metropolitan behemoth, though it may have seemed an unambiguous declension to some, offered an exit from the "familiar society" inhabited by most Americans before the last two decades of the nineteenth century.[1] And gemeinschaft, for all its vaunted intimacy and accessibility, can be an oppressive prison, whereas gesellschaft can bring the liberation of anonymity. The novelist Sinclair Lewis, author of *Main Street* (1920) and *Babbitt* (1922), made a successful career out of this recognition.

One benefit brought by the new order was a codifying of the private. The movies and Freudianism occupied an unstable position in this dynamic. In one sense part of a revitalized hunger to know, the two novelties also coalesced with an awareness that—in the words of Warren and Brandeis—"solitude and privacy have become more important to the individual" as a result of civilization's increasing "intensity and complexity." The pair of attorneys introduced the decade of the nineties with their germinal article in the *Harvard Law Review*, "The Right to Privacy." They were the first to formulate a statutory right to protect one's "inviolate personality" from outside intrusion by agencies of scrutiny.

The cinematic and analytic projects had a reflexive sense of the need for safeguards. They threw open new vistas to detection while at the same time providing refuge, in the seclusion of the darkened movie theater and the physician's consulting room, from the prying eyes of others. We might even say that the motion pictures and psychoanalysis contained in their modes of consumption an antidote to their own potential for excess. But it was the excess that impressed Warren and Brandeis. They prominently cited instantaneous photography, the technological forerunner of the cinema, as one of those "modern devices" inflicting invasive injuries on the unsuspecting. The "latest advances in photographic art," by rendering "it possible to take pictures surreptitiously," left innocent parties no redress but through the law of tort.[2]

Wilson's Progressive motto "Let There Be Light," dating from two decades later, suggests in its tardiness that the precedence of politics in setting the agenda for the United States had come to an end with the previous century. The leadership role was passing to mass culture, and to the popular media in particular. This, at least, was the view of Vachel Lindsay, whose classic study *The Art of the Moving Picture* (1915) acclaimed the makers of the movies as the heirs to Benjamin Franklin and Patrick Henry as shapers of the culture. Whereas the official "leaders of the people," according to Lindsay, "scarcely know the photoplay exists," the stars and their vehicle have become as well known to ordinary citizens "as any candidate for president bearing political messages."[3]

Lindsay did not delude himself about the photoplay's backwardness on race. This was one area, he noted regretfully, where civic discourse and cinematic art could not be differentiated. (The caveat applied to American psychoanalysis, too.) While crediting D. W. Griffith with directorial genius, Lindsay complained of the "poisonous" racism infecting Griffith's masterpiece, "which could better be called The Overthrow of Negro Rule." Neither Progressivism nor the two cultural phenomena that developed alongside it escaped the taint of racial exclusion. "Let There Be Light" for some continued to mean enforced disappearance for others. Woodrow Wilson decreed segregation for all employees of the federal government immediately upon taking office in 1913; two years later *The Birth of a Nation*—reportedly with this southern president's blessing—ostracized blacks to the filmic margins. (Photography, let us recall, signifies "writing with light.") And the therapeutic establishment, conflating nonwhites with primitive depth and then pronouncing them, in their very primitiveness, incapable of self-understanding, effectively banned racial minorities as either patients or practitioners. By 1946, at the moment the United States was asserting its psychoanalytic monopoly, the scandal of American medicine was the "total lack" of treatment for Harlem's four hundred thousand residents—this according to Richard Wright. "It is doubtful," the novelist calculated, "if there are eight practicing Negro psychiatrists in the entire nation."[4]

F reud may have seen his first movie in America, but he had no use for either the medium or the country. He refused to collaborate on a plan to make a film about his discovery, W. G. Pabst's *Secrets of a Soul* (1926), and he rebuffed every overture by studio moguls to recruit him as an expert. The science of mind, he was positive, could never be translated into the superficiality of cinematic figuration.[5] And then to add the United States to the mix compounded the absurdity. The cultural upstart across the Atlantic was utterly unsuited as a laboratory for psychoanalysis. Hollywood ruled there, and Hollywood was the enemy of serious thought.

Freud's polarity—the motion pictures (and America) versus the talking cure—has had a long line of supporters from both sides of the equation. Leo Lowenthal, of Frankfurt School fame, recorded what may be the most unforgettable dismissal: "Mass culture is psychoanalysis in reverse."[6] Lowenthal meant that the culture industry, which he identified with the United States as the apotheosis of kitsch, did not advance self-awareness but instead preyed on people's fantasies in order to drug and manipulate them. Celebrants of the present-day information revolution pretty much agree with Lowenthal, while inverting his emphases. They argue that the process begun with the motion pictures and exemplified today by television, videos, computer games, and the Internet has effectively killed off the Freudian legacy. The analyst's high-modernist search for unconscious motivation is an obsolete residue in a postmodern society of surfaces.[7]

Such critiques assume an irreparable disagreement between linguistic and visual representation—an incompatibility, in the terms of this book, between depth and surface.[8] The detractions have more cogency in theory than in historical practice. The movies and psychotherapy were both impure (or mixed) products of modernity. True, early film was silent and included only intertitles as a concession to language (a far from trivial concession, to be sure). But the movies hardly disavowed interiority; on the contrary, they boasted of their superior registration of emotion and thought through the close-up. Cinema and psychoanalysis alike professed an imperialism of ambition that comported with the global thrust of the American century. Returning to Worcester and to Freud's encounter with the New World in 1909 will illuminate the all-encompassing pretensions of both as carriers—or trailblazers—of outward and inward access.

Those who gathered to hear the great man explain his theories included some of the foremost philosophers and psychologists in the United States. G. Stanley Hall, an authority on adolescence and the president of Clark

University, hosted the occasion. The distinguished anthropologist from Columbia University, Franz Boas, attended the conference, as did James Jackson Putnam, America's leading neurologist and a professor at the Harvard Medical School. Also present was the Harvard philosopher William James, whose courage during an angina attack so impressed Freud that he still remembered the episode in 1925, when he described it in his *Autobiographical Study*. James for his part professed to find the Worcester lectures memorable. "The future of psychology belongs to your work," he told an elated Ernest Jones.[9]

The warm tribute concealed a secret history of which Jones was probably unaware. Probably but not definitely, because Jones himself had conducted several colloquia in Boston a year earlier, laying out the principles of psychoanalysis for an audience of local physicians and academics. Among the listeners was a professor of psychology at Harvard, a native-born German whom Jones misidentified as "Werner Munsterberg." Munsterberg had little regard for the new doctrine and made no secret of the fact. When Freud came to the United States to speak—in German, as it happened—Munsterberg showed his disdain by staying away. Among the attentive group of Harvard faculty, he was conspicuous by his absence.

The missing professor was really named Hugo Munsterberg, and he had long been feuding with William James over the future of psychology. James was a student of extreme states of religious ecstasy and distress. Though not a convert to psychoanalysis, he had followed Freud's writings with interest and welcomed the development of depth psychology. Munsterberg considered James's fascination with psychics an unscientific indulgence of quackery. Psychology's true business, he believed, lay in its application to law, education, advertising, and business. As for the unconscious, Munsterberg was blunt. In *Psychotherapy*, a book he published just a few months before Freud's lecture series, he stated: "The story of the subconscious mind can be told in three words: there is none." James, who had lured Munsterberg from Freiburg to Cambridge in the first place, could only shake his head over such pronouncements. He saw Harvard losing ground intellectually while his colleague—American to the core in his entrepreneurialism—bustled about the country selling psychological expertise as an aid to industrial efficiency.[10]

If Munsterberg lagged in his openness to Freudian ideas, in one area he was well ahead of the academic curve: his delight in the motion pictures. He was the first professor to write a scholarly monograph about film, and he did so at a time when the average moviegoer was still working-class, immigrant, and in search of cheap entertainment. In 1916, the year of Munsterberg's *The Photoplay: A Psychological Study*, the cinema seemed to many as disreputable in its way as Freud's discovery of the sexual etiology of the neuroses. The movie industry was dominated by uneducated foreigners who spoke poor English and did not know Ibsen from Oscar Wilde. These parvenus may have been ambitiously eyeing respectability for their medium, but no Harvard professor worth his degree would waste valuable time investigating the phenomenon.

Of course, the absence of native-born Americans among the pioneer generation distinguished both fields. Freud and Munsterberg were representative figures. Both came from eastern Europe, Freud's family from Moravia and Munsterberg's from what is now the Polish city of Danzig. The two were typical in their Jewishness as well, or, to be more specific, in their often ambivalent relation to their Jewishness. Freud, unlike some psychoanalysts, never disguised or disavowed his ethnicity, but he did not attempt to publicize it either. Anxious to downplay the large number of Jews involved in the movement's genesis, he assiduously wooed Christians like Jung in order to dilute the Semitism of his followers. In Munsterberg's case, ambivalence shaded into outright rejection. A number of Hollywood studio heads sought to "pass" as other than Jewish. The Harvard psychologist went further and chose the option more favored by European than American Jewry: he converted to Christianity. In Cambridge he worshiped at a Lutheran church.

(An aside on historical confluence and divergence: Jews as the obverse of African-Americans in the two arenas being considered here had European reaction to "thank" for their good fortune. The pogroms that convulsed Russia in the 1880s created millions of Jewish refugees. Eastern Europe's anti-Semitic outbursts were the equivalent of the post-Reconstruction assault on black rights. Whereas the United States threw open its doors to white newcomers [until the 1920s, at any rate], the nation herded black people ever more tightly into the ghetto of segregation.)

Munsterberg's attraction to film reflected his love of his adopted country and dovetailed at various places with Lindsay's more celebrated analysis. Both authors, for instance, emphasized the new pastime's democratic aspect. (In his writings on American mores, Munsterberg was a loyal follower of Tocqueville and always made much of the determinative influence of equality).[11] The movies cost less than the theater, Munsterberg pointed out, because like other machine-produced goods they could be copied endlessly and watched by many audiences at the same time. They belonged to the universe of the standardized Model T, not to that of the exclusive horse-drawn carriage. Their soundlessness reinforced their leveling effect. Immigrants ignorant of or just beginning to learn the English language could enjoy the picture shows as heartily as native speakers. (Munsterberg wanted to dispense with intertitles, the written cues that sometimes had to be read aloud to immigrant parents by their school-age children.) Images were a universal tongue that needed no priesthood to interpret them. Lindsay had argued a similar point a year earlier: any "cave-man," he wrote, could judge what appeared on the screen for himself. Lindsay favored turning the cinematic occasion into a rehearsal for democracy (the active involvement that Progressivism and, before that, Populism were striving to revitalize) by having the moviegoers vote on the screenplay. "The cards with their answers could be slipped into the ballot-box at the door as the crowd goes out."[12]

Where Munsterberg broke fresh territory was in his effort to marry film and psychology. The cinema demanded such a treatment, in his opinion, because unlike previous cultural inventions it subordinated the outer world to mental processes. The moviegoers, on one level democrats, were on another conquerors; sitting in the darkened auditorium, they had the experience of figurative omnipotence. They could see things in the physical creation never before observed with the naked eye, and they could plumb the consciousness of other human beings without the assistance of language. This proved that the moving pictures were not an offshoot of the drama (or even the novel) but an altogether original art; and despite his title, *The Photoplay*, Munsterberg concentrated on the discontinuities between the two forms of performance.

The theater, he stated, is bound "by the same laws of causality which govern nature."[13] Temporal and spatial limits prevail there just as they do in our everyday lives. An elderly character in a play cannot reverse the course of time and change back into a child. Nor can he or she bid defiance to distance by abruptly materializing in a different location. Such deviations from the real would shatter dramatic credibility. So, too, we see depth and motion on the stage, and they are really there, independent of our activity. Props in the front of the set are nearer to us than those in back, and characters have to raise and lower their legs in order to walk or run. The physical order is undisturbed: "no cause without following effect, no effect without preceding cause" (p. 183).

Stage plays, then, may not give us actuality itself, but they come far closer to capturing the substance of real life than does the cinema. The latter is a subjective medium that glories in its unreality. Film does not observe natural laws but rides roughshod over them, and its ontological insouciance brings it within the purview of the psychologist.

According to *The Photoplay*, the filmic spectator is no passive tabula rasa but an active participant who has to complete what shows on the screen. The picture is flat, but knowing it to be so, we invest it with depth; the static images cannot be animated without our assistance. Munsterberg rejected the notion, stretching back to Goethe's experiments with color and to the studies of Peter Mark Roget on optical deception, that retinal afterimage creates the illusion of motion when we are confronted with a succession of discrete frames. Not our physiology but our psyches supply the deficiency: movement "is superadded, by the action of the mind" (p. 69). These ostensible flaws of the photoplay are in fact its strengths, for they proclaim the intimate bond between the movies and thought. Anything the human mind can devise, the camera can do. Neither temporal sequence nor space is an obstacle to the filmmaker. "Time is left behind. Man becomes boy; today is interwoven with the day before yesterday" (p. 181). A remote mountain range in one shot becomes an inviting bank of wildflowers at our feet in the next. And then to cap the miracles, the wildflower changes into a girl!

Munsterberg gave special weight to the camera's selectiveness in the close-up, the flashback (or cutback, as he called it), and the flash-forward. These mechanically produced marvels—none of them possible on the stage—make visible the mind's capacity for undivided attention, for memory, and for fantasizing and imaginative projection. Take the close-up. Onstage a revolver being fired will attract all eyes to itself. But other objects do not simply dissolve into darkness because we focus on the smoking gun: the characters and the furniture on the set linger on the periphery of our vision. The close-up dispenses with all such visual static. By zooming in on the weapon and the hand clutching it, and emptying the screen of unwanted distractions, the proximity shot reconfigures reality to conform with thought. Whereas matter lords it over the dramatic play, the photoplay bends the cosmos to the structures of human consciousness. It confers absolute "freedom from the bondage of the material world" (p. 183).

Verisimilitude, it will be evident, ranked low among Munsterberg's priorities; indeed, few modernists could equal him in antinaturalism. Failure to approximate external phenomena was, to his mind, a quality to be cherished, not superseded, and he considered it a plus that the movies came equipped with neither color nor speech. Here, to be sure, the author of *The Photoplay* misconceived his medium. Mainstream film, the mass entertainment that was his subject, moved as far away as possible from his visionary ideal of a narrative art speaking "the language of pictures only" (p. 200). American filmmakers in particular were to fetishize representational accuracy and perfect the transparency of story line that became renowned as the Hollywood style. They rushed to embrace the mechanical improvements— sound, color, wide screen—that ratified the genre's mongrel character as both figuration and discourse.

But American movies, and indeed, fictional film in general, excelled at a special brand of realism, or rather hyperrealism, and Munsterberg was entirely right to characterize the medium as a radical departure from lithographic imitation. While he took pleasure in the motion pictures' rendering of surfaces—typically singled out as the screen's forte, its defining aptitude among popular amusements—what entranced him was its double-edged versatility at conveying depth. The cinema flaunted its reach, first, in the tractability of the spectacle. The pictures assume an aggressive and sometimes violent relationship to the actual. They mold, shape, distort, pry apart, and reassemble the physical environment. Penetrating into the invisible that lies buried in the visible, the camera rolls before the viewer prodigies of sight: blood corpuscles, an orchid slowly blossoming, the African jungle glimpsed from the heart of a concrete city. Moreover, film provides access to social and human phenomena we could not ordinarily witness because they are forbidden or reserved: the lovemaking of strangers, an agonizing death, a woman, alone, weeping in a locked bathroom. (Munsterberg, mindful of the negatives of the camera's trespass into the hidden, warned against the glamorizing of "scenes of vice or crime" [p. 227].) The urban masses found in the picture palaces an affordable spectacle in which desire "remodels the world" (p. 144). As they watched the flickering images, they enjoyed a visual and plastic sovereignty that was beyond their daily experience but answered to their dreams.

Or rather, while the cinema's triumphalism appeared magical, feats only slightly less awesome were becoming identified with the hegemony of the United States in industry, warfare, and the international arena. The movies, with their imperialism toward the actual, could boast of a unique affinity with fin de siècle Americans as a people of comparably enterprising scope. If, as Munsterberg's account suggests, the pictures are the expansionist impulse in mass culture, the art form destined more than any other "to overcome outer nature by the free and joyful play of the mind" (p. 233), their provenance in England, France, or even Germany—and all three could lay claim to the honor—was less significant than their migration to the homeland of Hollywood as the nation poised to depose the British as the twentieth century's dominant superpower.

More than this, the cinema's enlargement of optical dominion ties it inextricably to the modern. The movies exemplify the forward-looking spirit of curiosity and technological experimentation that also came to be associated with the United States. Hans Blumenberg, the philosopher of modernity (cited in the introduction), specified rude peering into nature, what has been called the "knowledge drive," as the watershed marking off our world from the Middle Ages. First the telescope and then the microscope precipitated the breach. The two instruments made accessible to the human eye objects formerly "invisible on account of their distance or smallness." They were the signs of man's mastery over the earth.[14] The movies constitute the analogue in popular amusement to Blumenberg's scientific apocalypticism. The close-up and the long shot are the cinematic microscope and telescope, bringing the infinitesimal and faraway into the orbit of mass consumption.

Two more Germans, both Jews and both émigrés from Nazism, were struck much like Munsterberg by film's power to amplify man's perceptual jurisdiction. Walter Benjamin, in his famous essay "The Work of Art in the Age of Mechanical Reproduction," turns to the fine arts instead of the stage for his heuristic counterexample. He contrasts the representation on the canvas to the picture on the screen. "The painter maintains in his work a natural distance from reality, [but] the cameraman penetrates deeply into its web."[15] Siegfried Kracauer offers a related observation in his defense of the movies as "the redemption of physical reality." Cinema, he states, "exposes to view a world never seen before, a world as elusive as Poe's purloined letter, which cannot be found because it is within everybody's reach." Kracauer is especially attentive to the resemblance between cinematic and scientific procedures.[16]

Munsterberg's second crucial insight was to recognize film as a technology of human inwardness. The movies are a psychological art for him because they bare our mental life; the secret of their fascination is that they turn the inside out. Or, to put it in terms that Freud might have appreciated, what is latent in the theater is made manifest on the screen. Although Munsterberg's understanding of depth is neo-Kantian, not Freudian—innate structures of mind, not drives and desires, interest him—he does inch nearer to the father of psychoanalysis when he speaks of the probing of affect in the facial close-up or expatiates on film's power to visualize a character's longings. I quote the following illustration at length:

> There is a girl in her little room, and she opens a letter and reads it. There is no need of showing us in close-up the letter page [recall Munsterberg's dislike of generic alloy] with the male handwriting and the words of love and request for her hand. We see it in her radiant visage, we read it from her fascinated arms and hands; and yet how much more can the photoartist tell us about the storm of emotions in her soul. The walls of her little room fade away. Beautiful hedges of hawthorne blossom around her, rose bushes in wonderful glory arise and the whole ground is alive with exotic flowers. (p. 121)

The change in physical setting communicates, more vividly than the stage play, more effectively than words could, the tenor of the girl's feelings. The reference to her "arms and hands," though Munsterberg discounts it beside the picturing of thought, is a telling addition to his catalogue. Yes, moviegoers can grasp emotional subtlety from a smile or the tremor of a lip. But insight does not stop with these perhaps predictable clues. The screen coaches us in the knowingness of a therapist. Its revelatory intimacy enables the viewer to read seemingly mute parts of the body as symptoms of interior states. As Munsterberg summarizes the photoplay's omniscience, "No shade, no tint, no hue of . . . emotions has escaped us" (p. 122).

Later theorists, for the most part European, have pushed this idea of film's psychological acuity in an even more overtly Freudian direction. Some, stoked by hostility to American cultural imperialism, have totally reversed Munsterberg's argument for the spectator's activism. They compare the flow of dreamlike images on celluloid to the operations of the unconscious and denounce the movies for their power to captivate with narcissistic pleasure. Two prominent members of the psychological school, Jean-Louis Baudry and Christian Metz, assert that "the scopic regime of the cinema" induces a regressive passivity in which the viewer surrenders autonomy to the omnipotent camera eye.[17]

Other critics, more sympathetic, endorse the analogy to the unconscious but find the motion pictures unexcelled as a genre for representing the human psyche. Particularly after the introduction of sound (ca. 1927), film has been held to trump all other media owing to its unique identity as a composite, an aesthetic parallel to the dynamic medley of words and pictures that describes the subliminal associative process itself. The Russian director Sergei Eisenstein has been the most articulate exponent (and practitioner) of this position. He champions montage as a necessary supplement to the "whole arsenal" of surface hints finally deemed "inadequate for the expression of those subtleties of the inner struggle in all its nuances." Citing Joyce's experiments with interior monologue as a textual rival, Eisenstein judges the movies superior not solely because they incorporate the visual but also because they can reproduce the actual rhythm and temporal duration of thought. Stream of consciousness, in his view, "finds full expression . . . only in the cinema."[18]

The movies' credentials as an art of depth or "truth" have been most refined, on the American side, in acting. In the late nineteenth century, middle-class theaters began to promote a "natural" acting technique that eschewed the bombast and hyperbole of melodrama. This understated approach migrated into and matured on the screen, where the intense focus of the camera encouraged thespian minimalism. By 1915, the subdued brand of performance operative in film was being denominated the "American style." It repudiated the stagy excess that classically trained Europeans sometimes carried over into motion pictures. The Canadian-born Hume Cronyn, who starred in both the drama and the cinema, touched all the familiar bases in 1949:

> In "closeup" very little becomes very much; a whole new range of expression is opened to the actor. He can register with a whisper, a glance, a contraction of a muscle, in a manner that would be lost on the stage. The camera will often reflect what a man thinks, without the degree of demonstration required in the theatre.[19]

Cultural laconism as an American idol has been abetted by multiple factors, among them the suspicion of imposture integral to a republican polity and the country's history of immigration (which downplayed verbal facility). But rarely has the cult of the genuine been more evident than in the self-exposing acting style popularized as "the Method." Although it originated with a Russian, Konstantin Stanislavsky, and was first applied to the stage, the Method achieved its American apotheosis in the screen's magnifying of internals. It has been copied by a wide range of actors aspiring to authenticity and spontaneity. As one of them, Jack Nicholson, says, if a style is to be effective, it has to come "from the subconscious."[20] By urging the performer not so much to impersonate someone else as to express his or her own personality, Method acting has contributed to making a visual medium subtly exhibitionistic, a revelatory analogue to the couch.

Film's exhibitionism rests on a paradox, though: self-display on celluloid is conjoined with "the right to be let alone" for the spectator. What tended to impress early observers about moviegoing was its drift toward precisely that "solitude and privacy" that Warren and Brandeis felt had been jeopardized by the camera's intrusive eye. Lindsay as usual invoked the drama as a counterexample, and for him the cinematic experience was at once more individual and more anonymous, a kind of gesellschaft to the theater's gemeinschaft. The stage audience is a "unit" whose members wield communal authority over each other, he wrote. They make known their disapproval of a latecomer by "glaring at" him or her. Movie viewers, on the other hand, arrive singly or "in groups of two or three at no specified hour." Nobody cares, because the spectators constitute a crowd or a "mob" rather than a unified collectivity. And they react as isolated atoms. "The newcomers do not, as in Vaudeville, make themselves part of a jocular army. Strictly as individuals they judge the panorama."[21]

The movies had originated in the peep shows of the kinetoscope parlors, and Lindsay grasped that the medium's beginnings, apparently belied by the nickelodeon and then the palace, were in actuality integral to its identity. The public venues merely disguised the privatization that represented something new in popular entertainment. Analogues proposed in *The Art of the Moving Picture* include "Ali Baba's cave" and "half-lit churches"—apt precursors of the warrenlike screening rooms of today's multiplexes—but the most common comparisons are domestic and studious. The film spectator suggests a reader, and the auditorium, its transfixed isolatoes seated in "half-light," a library. "Book-reading is not done in the direct noon-sunlight," Lindsay reminds us. "We retire to the shaded porch." Here again the parallel is prescient. The VCR and the videotape have taken moviegoing to its apogee as a noncommunal experience, consumable like a book in the sanctuary of the private home.[22]

Munsterberg's approach leads to similar conclusions. His psychological reading of the photoplay gives a theoretical density to the basic insight that the image on the screen is not a reciprocal agent but the stimulus to an intense inner process. Filmgoers can have an intimate communion with the image in part because it *is* insensate. In a sense, they are alone with their own feelings and perceptions, and their absorption can be complete. The spectator's inability to be seen is what connects him or her to that other cultural invention of the period, the analyst. One consumes revelation in a sequestered setting, the other in open assemblage; both are spared the imposition of modern city life, being stared at by multitudes of strangers.

Freud's talks at Clark University in 1909 were published, in English as well as German, a year later as *Five Lectures on Psycho-Analysis*. The alacrity of translation underscored not only the positive response at Worcester to the new ideas but also the wider appetite among Americans for information about the therapeutic revolution. Eager for endorsement by his overwhelmingly Protestant listeners, Freud had the Germanic-looking Jung (a clergyman's son) accompany him on his journey and made frequent mention of Jung's contributions in his speeches. He emphasized the success of his science in bringing order and light into the previously unfathomable workings of the unconscious. (This, of course, he would have said to any audience, although he soft-pedaled his un-American pessimism about the still uncharted [and unchartable] stretches of psychic wilderness.)

The way for Freud's visit had been prepared, in both the long and the short run, by American religion's openness to confessionalism. The Emmanuel Movement, based in an Episcopal church in Boston but with a following among all the city's Protestant denominations, was the latest example of a medical/clerical alliance. Ministers and psychiatrists joined forces to offer counseling to anyone with "moral problems or psychical disorders." The Reverend Elwood Worcester, a founder of the program, expected a handful of the curious to turn out. He reported with disbelief that "one hundred and ninety-eight men and women, suffering from some of the worst diseases known to man," lined up for treatment on the first morning. Over two hundred patients were receiving attention within a month.[23]

Freud, hypersensitive as ever to competing developments, had gotten wind of "this combination of church and psychotherapy"—the quoted words are his—and taken note of its irresistible appeal to the public. At Clark, as a further concession to his Protestant audience, he contrived a rhetorical flourish that would not have played nearly so well in his native (Catholic) Austria. "To-day," he said, "neurosis takes the place of the monasteries which used to be the refuge of all whom life had disappointed or who felt too weak to face it."[24]

Freud's trope got at an important truth about the analytic discipline: it was the antithesis of otherworldliness. Psychotherapy engaged with the most mundane details of human experience. It could emancipate its beneficiaries from the monasticism of mental illness because of its attentiveness to the minutiae and plenitude of everyday life. The analyst reached the depths by making a thorough investigation of the surface: to use the formulation of *Five Lectures*, he grasped the disease through its symptoms.

The speeches at Clark identify three discrete areas of analytic scrutiny. These are hysterical, or more generally neurotic, symptoms; dreams; and seemingly inconsequential actions like slips of the tongue. In each instance, the outward content is a distortion of, and proxy for, an unacknowledged complex or wish, which has been repressed into the unconscious. The physician treats the patient by overcoming his or her resistance to admitting the wish; but in order to do this, he has to be adept enough as a reader of the real to move from the manifest signs of neurosis to the hidden causes of it. And he has to look almost as much as he listens.

Freud's account of the analyst's charge reminds one of Kracauer's description of the cinema as "the redemption of physical reality." His successful therapist is a close-up mechanism zeroing in on the trifles that elude the careless haste of others. For the therapist, "there is nothing trivial, nothing arbitrary or haphazard." Everything human is worthy of notice; everything, no matter how insignificant, can open vistas of discernment: "playing about and fiddling with things, humming tunes, fingering parts of one's own body or one's clothing and so on." These "small things" give away "[a] man's most intimate secrets." Freud's comparison of choice is to a microscope (physical science's close-up), and he likens his technique's adversaries to those who would ignorantly "reject the results of a microscopic examination because it could not be confirmed on the anatomical preparation with the naked eye." The analyst's trained vision, like the moving picture camera, discovers meaning and value where ordinary eyesight is blind.[25]

Elsewhere Freud was frank about the duality of psychoanalysis as an optical as well as an aural method. He characterized the doctor as a human ear who "must adjust himself to the patient as a telephone receiver is adjusted to the transmitting microphone."[26] But the material rising from the patient's unconscious suggested the images recorded by "a compound microscope or a photographic apparatus."[27] Papers on technique foregrounded the role of physical observation in emotional healing. From his privileged position behind the couch, the analyst could spot the telltale sign of a young woman "hurriedly pull[ing] the hem of her skirt over her exposed ankles." He could note the fastidious care with which a self-proclaimed aesthete straightened the crease in his trousers. According to Freud, these gestures were as self-convicting as any utterance. They broadcast the narcissistic exhibitionism that would occupy the female patient's treatment and the "coprophilia," or anal compulsiveness, afflicting the young man.[28]

The psychoanalyst's perceptions were "cinematic," not "theatrical" or reciprocal. The object of study, the reclining analysand, could see nothing of the physician. Freud had abandoned Josef Breuer's hypnosis technique of face-to-face colloquy because it obstructed free association and because, as he admitted, he could not tolerate "being stared at by other people for eight hours a day (or more)."[29] In the security of the consulting room, the therapist and the patient were alone, but the healer did the sufferer one better. He metamorphosed into an ideal type of the privatized modern individual by placing himself outside the circuit of surveillance and, voyeur-like (or moviegoer-like), watching without being observed. Patients who dared to overstep the line of separation paid for it. Those who saved a last thought for the moment when they rose and turned toward Freud were cured of the indiscretion by having their parting words raked over mercilessly at the next session.

The talking cure's alertness to exteriors complements the movies' diving beneath the parade of surfaces. Both projects honor the visible and are at the same time capable, in the phrase of Walter Benjamin, who was attuned to both, of a revolutionary "deepening of apperception."[30] Moreover, like the cinema, the analytic paradigm can be related to the imperial design of the twentieth century. In this case, the target of conquest is internal space, and the United States succeeded to the mantle of a colossus even closer to extinction than the British. America as the therapeutic citadel supplanted the Hapsburg Empire, in whose aging capital city of Vienna—once home to Mesmer and to Gall (the father of phrenology)—Freud devised his treatment for mental illness.

Additionally, in its transportation across the ocean, the Freudian enterprise acquired the democratic coloration of the environment. Freud for certain did not see his creation this way. In public statements if not always in practice, he portrayed the therapeutic relationship as a strict hierarchy. (This is not even to mention the travesty, as he considered it, of conscripting his method to promote "the pursuit of happiness.") And there does appear to be a dissonance between the structure of psychoanalysis, where the troubled individual comes to learn about his emotional makeup from a stranger, and democratic egalitarianism. The analytic dyad, with its priest of consciousness and suffering supplicant, seems galaxies away from the direct apperception of the cinema.

Yet if we take a more historical look, we can see how the therapeutic configuration represents a this-worldly climax of the Protestant sentiment Freud appealed to in his Clark lectures. It culminates the drive toward self-textualization that began with the Reformation. In the seventeenth century, the Bible was known as the "Paper Pope" because reading it enabled believers to bypass the authority of the church and imbibe the Word of God from his text. The believer was to be alone with the Scriptures; that was why the emigrant Puritans gave such importance to literacy. Two centuries later, the New England Transcendentalists, led by Emerson, pressed Protestant anti-institutionalism to a further level. They fired off an attack against books as an impediment between the individual and his encounter with Divinity. One was still a "reader," in Emerson's conceptualization, but the text was no longer a piece of writing: it was God in Nature. Emerson urged his listeners to study this volume directly, not "other men's transcripts of their readings." As he put it in "The American Scholar" (1837), "I had better never see a book than to be warped by its attraction clean out of my own orbit, and made a satellite instead of a system."[31]

The last quotation suggests that Emerson's real subject was the self, and at times he came near to admitting as much. In "The Divinity School Address" (1838), he praised Jesus for teaching the eternal truth, distorted by the Christian churches, that "God incarnates himself in man." Spirit lies within us as well as inhering in Nature, Emerson insisted, and the seeker in the woods is also conning his own biography. "The ancient precept, 'Know thyself,' and the modern precept, 'Study nature,' become at last one maxim."[32]

From the Catholic Church to God's Word in the Scriptures to God in the natural environment to the God within: psychoanalysis at once secularized and added a new self-reflexivity to this Dissenter line of literary-theological development. Is it any wonder that Freud first caught on in the state where the Puritans landed and Emerson made his residence? The "text" to be read, mulled over, deciphered, struggled with, and interpreted this time was the individual self; the analyst, so authoritative in one respect, was in another but the paid coworker, the fellow exegete, in the process of discovery. A search that had been steadily bending homeward had finally completed its journey. It had reached its destination on the couch, where— in Emerson's phrase—it was always "the age of the first person singular."

This spotlight on the self points to another sense in which the analytic hour and the movies are democratic. They annul the determination of the past: the hold of birth and family. Jay Gatsby stated the democratic credo in extremis when, in an exchange with Nick Carraway, he exclaimed, "Can't repeat the past? Why of course you can!" To repeat the past is to have the power to control it, to undo it and remake it. The conviction that one is not the prisoner of one's origins is, of course, what the American dream is all about; it is also the premise of the cinema and of psychoanalysis. Let us re- call Munsterberg's psychology of the photoplay: mind triumphs "over the unalterable law of the outer world," so that "time is left behind" and "man becomes boy" (p. 183). (The technical possibilities of the flashback have been elaborated thematically in films such as *Back to the Future* [1985], *The Terminator* [1984], and *Pleasantville* [1998].) One could even say that the vi- sual bias of film, being spatial rather than temporal, militates against the very idea of a history.[33] It is all the more striking, then, that the talking cure, with its accent on language, shares a similar faith in time's plasticity. The pa- tient on the couch revisits the past in order to escape from bondage to it and to master it. The goal is to live fully in the present without (as Freud wrote of hysterics) "*suffer[ing] from reminiscences.*"[34] Psychological well-being, in the analytic system, emancipates us from the ascriptiveness of emotional feudalism, from the beginnings into which we are born, which constrain us, and which we gain the strength and resourcefulness to leave behind.

I want to end with an excursus on Frank Norris's *McTeague*, a novel that closes out the American nineteenth century. (It was published in 1899, the same year as *The Interpretation of Dreams*.) *McTeague* provides still an- other angle on the sources and convolutions of the country's romance with the cinematic and the psychotherapeutic. This story of an Irish miner turned dentist turned murderer illuminates the transition to a consumer so- ciety that at once traffics in images and abstractions and overheats the needs of the body. Norris plots the action as a rise and fall. His hero, a near "caveman" (Lindsay's epithet for the moviegoing slum dweller), spends the first half of the story advancing into a "civilized," middle-class existence. A fight with his best friend at the exact midpoint halts his upward progress; soon afterward, the protagonist receives a letter informing him that he can no longer practice dentistry without a degree. He loses his job, and the novel's second half chronicles his disintegration into atavism and bestiality.

Norris's fiction has palpable connections to both the photoplay and the Freudian worldview. *McTeague* is constructed as "a series of pictures."[35] Erich von Stroheim, the screen actor and director, was so taken with its filmic potential that he used the book as the basis for his costly and controversial *Greed* (1924), one of the greatest silent movies as well as one of the last. Norris was steeped in late-nineteenth-century psychology, especially the theories of Joseph LeConte, with whom he had studied at Berkeley. In the novel, he presents his subjects as human "animals," prey to inner urges and recidivistic pulls over which they have minimal control. Norris makes only passing reference to film and mentions Freud not at all. But on the evidence of *McTeague*, the age of psychoanalysis could only have been the age of the cinema, because both regimes were erected on a calculus of desire.[36]

The 1890s experienced a prolonged economic downturn, known, in precedence to the crash of 1929, as the "great depression." Observers differed on the causes, but one culprit, all agreed, was the vast overproduction of commodities that, thanks to corporate consolidation and improvements in technology, had been building for a decade. With the recovery of 1897, a consensus began to develop that more effort would have to be paid to consumption as an engine of growth. A revision in societal ethos, a shift from making things as the center of life to a greater emphasis on expending them, held the key to forestalling further depressions. Not that an appetite for goods, or even an embryonic "consumer revolution," had not flourished earlier. What qualified as new was the magnitude of the reorientation, along with the widespread acceptance of its economic rationale. (It was apparent as well that the domestic population could not handle the task alone. "Free-trade" imperialism would have to pry open the world's markets as another emporium for the American products that would otherwise rot in warehouses.)

McTeague alludes to this transition in at least three ways, and the first helps to clarify the change in degree. The story gives an unusually prominent role to Zerkow the junkman. Rag collectors had always existed. But the Polish Jew makes his living from the detritus of consumer society, from the plenitude of "things of iron and cloth and wood . . . that a great city sloughs off in its daily life."[37] Maria Macapa visits his shop with a pillowcase of items to sell: old dental tools and gold fillings, stone jugs, whiskey flasks, a cracked pitcher, half-worn silk shoes, cast-off garments, magazines, sacks, bottles, and bits of iron. Never before has there been such a volume and bewildering array of junk, of quickly used up and discarded objects.

The second piece of evidence is the pivotal event of Trina's winning $5,000 in the lottery. This miraculous news signals the supersession of productionist values. Easy money obtained through luck underscores the fact that hard work and saving have lost their ideological rationale. Finally, the prevalence of consumption reveals itself on the very first page, where McTeague eats his Sunday dinner of "thick, gray soup; heavy, underdone meat, very hot, on a cold plate; two kinds of vegetables; and a sort of suet pudding, full of strong butter and sugar." He washes down the meal with a pitcher of steam beer and drops off to sleep while "smoking his huge porcelain pipe" (p. 5). The hero's tastes will be upgraded a bit by his wife, but this scene sets the tone for the novel: the mouth has moved ahead of the hands as the primary human organ in a social order of incorporation.

Has there ever been a novel in which so many things are thrust into people's mouths and eaten, drunk, smoked, licked, munched, sucked, masticated, and swallowed? Picnics, wedding feasts, stories of gold plate, a gilded tooth—these are the least of it. McTeague, as a dentist, constantly services characters' mouths with his fingers and operating instruments. When he anesthetizes Trina, he is seized by lust for the defenseless girl and leans over to kiss "her grossly, full on the mouth" (p. 28). (In *Greed*, which reproduces this moment cinematically, it looks as though Zasu Pitts is being devoured alive by Gibson Gowland—a prophecy of what is to come.) The hero performs a trick of stuffing a billiard ball into his mouth, and when he and Marcus Schouler have their fight, Marcus takes a bite out of his ear. Later, during his descent, McTeague regularly tortures Trina by chewing on her fingers, and she grows so fond of her gold coins that she puts the smaller ones "in her mouth and jingle[s] them there" (p. 238). *Not* to consume, in this novel, is to die: Marcus and McTeague, their useless hands cuffed together, perish in the desert because they have nothing to drink.

The tale's obsession with ingesting orally contrasts to another function of the mouth that seems on the path to obsolescence: speaking. Or, rather, using language as a tool of communication and truth-telling. "No speech . . . No speech," McTeague mutters at the impromptu party to celebrate the lottery winnings (pp. 95–96); this turns out to be an accurate description of many of Norris's characters. The dentist, whose head is "quite empty of all thought" (p. 18), can scarcely form a coherent sentence. His proposals to Trina consist of a series of repeated importunities: "Will you?" "Will you?" and "Ah, come on!" (pp. 29–30, 69). For most of the novel, Old Grannis and Miss Baker conduct a silent courtship, sitting near each other in their adjoining rooms and never uttering a syllable. Those who are more ambitious linguistically turn words into empty ciphers. Maria's recitals of family riches are pure fantasy, and Marcus gets a reputation as a politician despite (or because of) the disconnect between his "empty phrases" (p. 13) and his actions. The high incidence of first- and second-generation foreigners speaking heavily accented English further diminishes the importance of language in Norris's San Francisco.

As words recede, images move to the forefront. The reason is simple: visual representations are more easily consumed than verbal ones, requiring no education and relatively little intelligence to appreciate them. McTeague, "too hopelessly stupid" to get anything out of his dentistry books (p. 6), has a soft spot for engravings, lithographs, colored prints, and other pictures, and he and Trina move into a photographer's studio when they marry. (The apartment, writes Norris, "was prolific in pictures" [p. 125].) With Trina's family, the hero attends one of the first movie shows in American literature, a kinetoscope exhibition that is part of a vaudeville program and that features a cable car speeding toward the astonished audience. (Mrs. Sieppe, Trina's Swiss-German mother, shrieks in disbelief, "It's all a drick!" [p. 85].)

Significantly, it is a letter regarding his lack of a diploma—pages of writing about a page of writing—that brings McTeague's "visual"-consumerist idyll to an end. (His incomprehension is typical: "I don' know, I don' know," he keeps muttering about the notice, whose meaning has to be explained to him [p. 200].) Once he loses his practice, and with it the possibility of continued indulgence, the protagonist and Trina are forced to give up the photographer's suite and to sell almost all their cherished possessions, including the "framed photograph of McTeague and his wife in their wedding finery, the one that had been taken immediately after the marriage" (pp. 218–19). McTeague slips back into his former habits—drinking steam beer instead of bottled and sleeping off his heavy Sunday dinners—but the erosion of middle-class standards is merely a stage in the gradual relinquishing of consumption itself.

And here is where the psychological dimension of the novel takes over. (LeConte's thesis about reversion to animality may have inspired Norris, but his insights are solidly "Freudian.") Desire, once awakened, does not disappear just because the characters are no longer able to satisfy it through the usual channels. It has to be addressed in other, less normal, ways. As the frustrations endured by the McTeagues accumulate, their unmet desires mutate into pathology and seek ever more perverse outlets. The boundary line between persons and objects or consumable goods—a line never very secure in the text anyway—begins to collapse altogether. The dentist gnaws on his wife's fingers, "crunching and grinding them with his immense teeth," until they become infected and have to be amputated (p. 239). Trina, for her part, develops an erotic attachment to her lottery winnings. She withdraws the gold from her uncle's business and, heaping the coins into a pile, whispers endearments to them: "Ah, the dear money, the dear money, . . . I love you so!" (p. 238). (These are scenes to rival Freud's case studies.) Later she actually spreads the gold pieces between her sheets and climbs into bed with them, and when McTeague manages to steal some of the money, she weeps over the empty bag "as other women would weep over a dead baby's shoe" (p. 273). Note the reductionism at work here: Trina's hoarding is not the antithesis but the summit of consumerism. She commits the category mistake of consuming the gold itself, treating a medium of exchange as a source of bodily pleasure in its own right rather than as a means of acquiring other things to consume.

The couple is reduced to renting the rooms formerly occupied by Maria and Zerkow, the very site where the junkman had stored his debris. The shop is "the last abiding place, the almshouse, of such articles as had outlived their usefulness" (p. 39), and Trina and McTeague have themselves become the junk, the waste product, of urban society. In a curious interlude, the dentist tries to wean himself from consumerist habits, practically from civilization itself. Unemployed and penniless, he goes for walks along the ocean and spends hours fishing for perch, cooking them over an outdoor fire and "eating them without salt or knife or fork" (p. 257). There is no returning to the past, though, and McTeague's experiment in subsistence fails. Starving, he crawls back to Trina for help; when she refuses, he murders her for the gold.

What is often overlooked about the hero's degeneration is that it quickens his intelligence. This might seem an impossibility with a character whose mental shortcomings are so conspicuous. McTeague, Norris says more than once, "never went to the bottom of things" (p. 150). Yet under the duress of his suffering, this creature of limited interiority proves capable of surprising flashes of insight. He starts to speak "with an unwonted rapidity, his wits sharp, his ideas succeeding each other quickly" (p. 230). When he is in flight from the posse, he reveals an intuitive consciousness of danger that is part brute instinct but also part heightened sensitivity, and that "stirred and woke and roweled him to be moving on" (p. 316). He has dreams that warn him to make haste. Not by accident does the protagonist end up back in Placer County, digging into the bowels of the earth as he had as a boy. It is as though, in this "primordial" landscape (as Norris describes it), McTeague has gotten into touch with something deep in his psyche.

The brute thinks. He recognizes the similarity between his boring into the mountains and his aborted career as a dentist:

> Once it even occurred to him that there was a resemblance between his present work and the profession he had been forced to abandon. In the Burly drill he saw a queer counterpart to his old-time dental engine; and what were the drills and chucks but enormous hoe-excavators, hard-bits, and burrs? It was the same work he had so often performed in his Parlors, only magnified, made monstrous, distorted, and grotesqued, the caricature of dentistry. (p. 298)

McTeague now successfully goes to the bottom of things. He befriends the scientifically minded Cribbens, who can tell from the outward signs of a rock formation whether it contains a lode of precious ore. Together the two men hit pay dirt in the ravines of Gold Gulch.

What are we to make of this strange accession of awareness in Norris's dim-witted hero? One way to read the change, ahistorical but highly suggestive for this argument, would be as an omen. Near the end of the novel, as McTeague hurries on through Death Valley with the posse in pursuit, Norris compares "the infinite reaches of dazzling-white alkali" to "an immeasurable scroll unrolled from horizon to horizon" (pp. 326–27). Space and writing page, text and white screen are one here, just as Norris's caveman is both a moviegoer, a consumer of images, and someone suddenly beginning to think about himself, hungry not only for things to eat and drink, to put into his mouth, but also for insight into his existence. The hints of McTeague's mental growth are fragmentary, and they should not be exaggerated. But they are present as an intimation of the popularizing—or is the better word "vulgarizing"?—of therapies among Americans during the next century. (Recall the huge turnout for the Emmanuel Movement's first advertised sessions.) For the system of consumption not only would define all people—men, women, and children, too—as desiring beings; it would also make available to them, as one more object to be purchased and possessed, the self-understanding that Emerson found in nature and Freud in the interaction of patient and physician.

CHAPTER 6

Twentieth-Century Classics and
New Technologies of Legibility

The domestication of film and psychoanalysis as technologies of legibility has haunted the American novel in the twentieth century. The movies in particular have emerged as a rival in narrative vividness, but depth psychology has advanced claims, too, as a competitor in the dissecting of motivation. The three novels considered here all grapple with the imperialism of images as a challenge to literature's cultural authority. They variously seek to incorporate or to contain the new popularity of ocularcentrism. (The novels span the decade of the cinema's Americanization, from *The Birth of a Nation* in 1915 to *The Jazz Singer* in 1927.) A pattern emerges in the three books whereby the image gradually forces its way into the domain of words until, with the breakthrough of Hemingway, language itself evolves into a medium of moving pictures.

My first example, Wharton's *Summer,* is the least known of the three and the most insistent in its distancing from specularity. Wharton deconstructs the visual's seductiveness while she appears to reaffirm language's power of truth-telling. I read Fitzgerald's *The Great Gatsby* as a modernist Western in which the titular hero is identified with the cinematic. Gatsby may be a morally ambiguous protagonist, but his splendor as a kind of disembodied image wins the admiration of even the highly literate Nick Carraway. For Hemingway, in *The Sun Also Rises,* truthfulness is a function of visuality. Writing has ceased to be a technique for getting at hidden layers; it has become a surface medium impatient with the "bilge" of introspection and committed to representing neither more nor less than what the eye beholds.

In none of these works is Freudianism a direct presence, yet all three reveal a disaffection, almost a disgust, with the presumption of the verbal to articulate interiority. In the end, Wharton privileges a reserve that eschews linguistic as well as optical revelation; Fitzgerald's Carraway and to some degree Fitzgerald himself renounce the confidences that have made possible the story of Gatsby's failed quest. Hemingway's effort to craft a sun-drenched narrative of visibility collapses under the pressure of the darkness that his characters have struggled to keep at bay. *The Sun Also Rises* might be described, facilely, as an exercise in the return of the repressed. But it is not the Freudian unconscious that has been repressed; it is the repressed of language that returns, the verbal's penchant for intimating inward depths.

Wharton's *Summer*

S*ummer* was published in 1917, the year the United States reluctantly entered World War I. President Wilson, an advocate of staying out of morally cloudy European conflicts, finally relented and threw American might behind the Allied cause. Three thousand miles separated Edith Wharton, resident in Paris, from her natal land. But as a supporter of the French war effort (and an admirer of Wilson's longtime nemesis, Teddy Roosevelt), she had little regard for the American leader. His moralism, fetish for light, and policy of neutrality all exasperated her. He seemed to stand for everything she disliked about America.

An able case has been made for seeing Wilson as a ghostly presence in *Summer*, his isolationism the model for Lucius Harney's evasiveness with Charity Royall.[1] I want to propose that Wharton may have been thinking of another Wilson as well, the demander of truth and openness who exemplified the most high-minded strain of American legibility. This was the Wilson who declared in *The New Freedom* that "no air [is] so wholesome as the air of utter publicity."[2] This Wilson, already in 1915, was warning against the danger of disloyal "secrets" on the part of hyphenated Americans (meaning Americans of German descent); two years later, he signed into law the witch-hunting Espionage Act.[3]

Wharton of course knew nothing of these paranoid measures when she conceived her novel. But the themes of openness and secrecy, of telling and keeping silent—leitmotivs of Wilson's presidency—are critical to the experience of her heroine, Charity Royall. The themes shape Charity's troubled affair with Harney, the house sketcher and architect from the big city who, though engaged to another woman, takes her as a lover; and they color her relations with her aging guardian and husband-to-be, Lawyer Royall, the man with the "orator's jaw"[4] who has slunk back from that larger world to the claustrophobic village of North Dormer.

Summer shares key concerns with the fiction of Wharton's friend and fellow expatriate, Henry James. The book accepts renunciation and the necessity for "secrets" or discretion, a commitment that is woven into the verbal patterning. Where Wharton differs from James, and strikes a more Hawthornian note, is in her skepticism about the visual and in her striving to extract value from modernity's self-divisions. Wharton, who wrote the novel in France, anticipates some of the anti-American critique of later French intellectuals like Guy Debord. She recognizes that even a relative backwater like Nettleton, the "metropolis" nearest to North Dormer, had evolved by 1917 into an embryonic consumerist society of the spectacle. This awareness prevents her from privileging the image as a check on linguistic violation. She finds shelter instead in a religion-inspired privacy that is the opposite of American confessionalism and that might tempt one to read her novel as a reactionary affirmation of "character" over "personality." (These are Warren I. Susman's well-known terms for the receding and ascendant types of identity that became evident in the early twentieth century.) There is justice in this view, but it is too unnuanced. If Wharton does cast a backward glance in *Summer*, she does so without illusions. The grimness of the narrative's ending does not flinch from the cost of having character in an age of personality, of choosing duty and reserve over glamour and self-expression, and suffering for the choice.[5]

The novel's first paragraph describes Charity coming out of Lawyer's house; its last has the two of them, now married, driving "up to the door of the red house" (p. 205). This return to the beginning suggests entrapment, but it also entails a deepening and subtilizing of the constellation of values Wharton associates with Lawyer Royall. Charity's circular journey is in one sense a theodicy in which she discovers layers of positive meaning in the world she once abhorred. As she leaves Lawyer's house, she is heading for her job at the Hatchard Memorial Library, and the library—and literature and language—are a large part of what she cannot abide about North Dormer.

The Hatchard Library, a "vault-like room" of musty books, is to Charity a "grave" symbolizing the entombment of her life (pp. 5–6). Letters, linked here with authors of the ilk of Washington Irving and Fitz-Greene Halleck, are the past, defunct, unread, and irrelevant. Charity is intensely attracted to the emergent cosmos of images as the cultural antithesis of words. She remembers fondly an exciting trip to Nettleton, with its array of overstocked shop windows, where she heard "an illustrated lecture on the Holy Land." She would have "enjoyed looking" at the pictures had not the "unintelligible" recitation "prevented her from understanding them" (p. 3). Catching sight of Lucius Harney as she ventures out of her front door, Charity performs the characteristic gesture of an image-saturated modernity: she steps back inside for a reassuring glimpse at her reflection in the mirror.

Appropriately, since he awakens Charity sexually, Harney turns out to be an emissary from the metropolis with its seductive visuality: he designs buildings—objects to be looked at—and is in North Dormer hunting up picturesque old houses to sketch. Wharton relentlessly emphasizes this aspect of his appeal to the heroine. (His given name, Lucius, means "light.") To plunder Lacan for a moment, the architect is Charity's "mirror phase": visiting the library in search of books on architecture, he does a double take when he sets eyes on her, and the flattering moment lingers in her consciousness as a turning point in her understanding of self: "She had learned what she was worth when Lucius Harney, looking at her for the first time, had lost the thread of his speech, and leaned reddening on the edge of her desk" (p. 43). This ocular chemistry occurs repeatedly between the two characters and is instrumental in seducing Charity. Harney will suddenly stop listening or speaking and silently study her face, "his impetuous eyes . . . in hers" (p. 119). Charity does more than reciprocate the staring; her eagerness to look transforms her, in a protracted scene, into an archetype of the modern individual or moviegoer. She creeps up on Harney's house at night and watches him intently through the window until he falls asleep, a visual eavesdropper unobserved by the spectacle that glues her to the spot.

To Harney's visuality, Lawyer Royall represents the linguistic. Charity's guardian typically spends his time reading the speeches of Webster and Lincoln. Even before he delivers the crucial address at North Dormer's Old Home Week, Lawyer impresses his ward with his ability to talk well in the presence of "a listener who understood him" (p. 49). But when he has the temerity to propose to her despite the difference in their ages—an act of verbal risk taking that Harney, as Charity learns painfully, is never willing to make—her response skewers the "fatherly old man" as a figure of obsolescence. She scornfully tells him that he has no business competing in an optical universe: "What's come over you, I wonder? How long is it since you've looked at yourself in the glass?" (pp. 21–22).

Charity's involvement with Harney promises an exit from the moribund and constrictive village. North Dormer is the usual New England (or midwestern—see Sinclair Lewis) community where everything is known to everybody. The "harsh code" of small-town life proscribes secrets; "irreverent eyes" allow nothing to remain off limits (p. 170). Charity, despite her caution, has been observed spying on Harney in his rooms. As Lawyer reminds her, "You know there's always eyes watching you" and tongues wagging in slander (p. 80). But chronic surveillance does not cause the heroine to forswear concealment for transparency. On the contrary, her passion for Harney persuades her of the necessity for a modernist "double consciousness," a Hester Prynne–like division between the "public civilities" she exchanges with her lover and "their secret intimacy" (p. 62).

Charity learns to erect a wall of privacy around herself. She grasps instinctively that she must not be seen with the architect, and when they meet in Nettleton, she concocts a story to throw others off the scent. ("Whenever she was with Lucius Harney, she would have liked some impenetrable mountain mist to hide her," Wharton writes [p. 89].) Charity's discovery that she has a hidden identity, a being that is not reducible to the codes and fiats of the social order, brings with it an inquisitiveness about others and an intensified self-awareness. She hungers to know not just about Harney but about Lawyer as well ("now she began to wonder what he was really like" [p. 71]) and, most of all, about her own emotional needs. The reflex of interiority, according to Wharton, is born in sexuality and the illicit: "All that had happened to her within the last few weeks had stirred her to the sleeping depths. She had become absorbingly interesting to herself, and everything that had to do with her past was illuminated by this sudden curiosity" (p. 41).

The flaw in this transformation is its catalyst. Harney, who initiates "the wondrous unfolding of Charity's new self" (p. 128), is a figure of surfaces who has deceived her into believing him unattached. The architect exemplifies the limitations of the ocular as a medium of truth. The day the couple spends together in Nettleton, which has been decked out for the Fourth of July, mobilizes the full splendor of the image to dazzle the heroine while hinting at its mystifications. Shops with "glass doors" and "wide expanses of plate-glass" feature a cornucopia of consumer goods, some arranged on "imitation moss," others presided over by "wax ladies in daring dresses" (p. 93). At a "glittering" movie palace, the heroine is awed by the jumble of exotic sights that passes before her eyes, while the watching audience seems to blend into "the spectacle, and danced on the screen with the rest" (p. 97). The visual climax of the festivities is a gigantic fireworks display on the lake. Charity's rapture is complete as a great golden picture of "Washington crossing the Delaware" lights up the night sky like a man-made constellation (pp. 103–4).

From the vantage of our study, Wharton's choice of July 4 for this incident is rich in meaning. The date and the Declaration it commemorates have signified the American cult of translucence; here Wharton seems to be making a point about the decay of civic culture in the age of spectacle (and Woodrow Wilson). Legibility reconfigured as the image proves shallow and insubstantial. It functions as an engine of mystification. Taking advantage of the "National Hero's" electrifying appearance, Harney bends over to kiss Charity for the first time; and his chronic (if tacit) self-misrepresentation to her now emerges as a central factor in the plot. Not long after their kiss the two characters become lovers, but the architect is no Washington-like truth-teller. Although "he had never said a word to mislead her" (p. 100), neither has he ever uttered a word about his unavailability, and Charity faints after discovering him together with Annabel Balch at Old Home Week. She has to learn of his engagement to this socially better connected rival not from the architect himself but from her friend Ally Hawes.

The "National Hero" also contrasts to Lawyer Royall. Incensed at finding Charity with Harney at Nettleton, Lawyer accuses his ward of being a whore as, in a parody of Washington, he passes before her on a steamboat. This marks the low point in the reader's, and the heroine's, estimate of the older man. Thereafter he begins to reform his behavior toward Charity, and he slowly displaces Harney as the novel's center of male affectivity. Royall grows into a Washingtonian protector by opposing, as it were, the tawdriness of visual legibility with a reversion to Constitution-like linguistic authority. I call this turn "Constitution-like" because Wharton, in the spirit of *The Federalist Papers*, validates language but does not idealize its potential as a tool for seeking out truth. Her narrative implies, instead, in the canonical American grain, that *not* knowing while on earth is the inevitable fate of human beings.

Old Home Week sets the change in motion. The two male principals perform their customary parts in the celebration: Harney prepares a profusion of sketches, and Lawyer is charged with delivering the main address. The speech, a plea to those who have returned in defeat to North Dormer to love "the old homes" and to act for their good (p. 138), is a moral high-water mark in the text. Even Charity is impressed, and the impassioned eloquence of Lawyer's words stirs the Reverend Mr. Miles to exclaim, with Wharton's evident approval, "That was a *man* talking—" (p. 139).

Moreover, it is right after this speech—in which he urges his audience "to look at things as they are" (p. 138)—that Lawyer, with a sudden movement, causes a branch blocking the first row of seats to collapse. The apparent accident enables Charity to see her lover seated beside Annabel Balch and to grasp for the first time "the whole inscrutable mystery of his life" (pp. 139–40). It is not a mystery to her any longer. The heroine has been forced to confront the reality of her situation. Lawyer Royall has staged a "sight" that blossoms into insight, a visual epiphany that uncovers the hidden truth as language might.

Indeed, language, or the avoidance of language, combined with semantic evasiveness, confirms Charity's growing recognition of the architect's weakness. Lawyer shows up at the abandoned house shared by the couple and challenges his ward to "ask him [Harney] when he's going to marry you" (p. 148). The verbal gauntlet proves decisive. Charity cannot get it out of her mind that her lover "had never spoken to her of marriage till Mr. Royall forced the word from his lips" (p. 153). Later, when she insists that Lucius honor his promise to Annabel, he writes back a "beautiful" but equivocal letter that she finds "almost as difficult to understand as the gentleman's explanation of the Bible pictures at Nettleton" (p. 163). Whereas Lawyer has induced the ocular to "speak," Harney has manipulated language as a sleight of hand, using words to obfuscate and confuse rather than to illuminate. Wharton never lets *us* forget that the sight-identified architect is himself literally shortsighted.

Depth and the linguistic reassert themselves at this juncture in the narrative, but they do so under a kind of ban. Wharton enfolds them in a reserve that seems almost French—dare one say Bellegardian? Charity realizes she is pregnant when she experiences a second dizzy spell, this time in the very Hatchard Memorial Library she has always associated with death and obsolescence. The mausoleum of books now becomes the site where new life makes itself felt. This implicit recovery of the verbal's thematic value is followed by a wish on Charity's part to reconnect with her past. She decides to hide her pregnancy by fleeing to "the Mountain," the degraded up-country settlement from which her mother long ago begged Lawyer Royall to rescue her.

The Mountain, she keeps telling herself, is the place she comes from and the place where she "belongs." She must get in touch with her roots, Charity believes, with the parent who, presumably "destitute of all human feeling" (p. 184), sent her away as an infant. But once she gets there, she finds that her mother has passed away and is about to be buried in a cere-mony conducted by the clergyman Miles. "The woman lay on her back, her eyes staring up unblinkingly at the candle that trembled in Mr. Miles's hand" (p. 177). Charity's mother died with her eyes open, and she was right, the heroine now understands, to want something better for her offspring than the Mountain's "savage misery." "What mother," Charity thinks, "would not want to save her child from such a life?" (p. 184).

If revisiting her origins is in some sense an encounter with the primor-dial depths—and the ironically named Mountain is a domain of brute na-ture, immorality, and incest—Charity, like her creator, draws from the ex-perience an anti-Freudian moral. Both face the terrors of inwardness, but they refuse to linger or wallow there. Charity escapes to civilization for a second time with Lawyer Royall. And Wharton indicates that healing does not lie in self-immersion. It comes from sacrifice and self-denial. Least of all, according to *Summer*, are we saved by the rhetoric of self-exposure.

To be sure, Lucius Harney and his superficial visuality lose all hold on the heroine after her harrowing trip up the Mountain and into the "un-conscious" depths. "Even Harney's image had been blurred by that crush-ing experience; she thought of him as so remote from her that he seemed hardly more than a memory" (p. 187). Furthermore, Charity is able to ob-tain from language some of the succor she once derived from the image. At the funeral service for her mother, the Reverend Mr. Miles reads from the Scriptures, and "the mighty words" soothe her horrified spirit, "subduing the tumult, mastering her as they mastered the drink-dazed creatures at her back" (pp. 179–80). Long before, a lecture had inhibited her pleasure in Bible pictures; now the syllables alone, prophesying an eternity beyond images ("in my flesh shall I see God" [p. 179]), bring her necessary strength. When she subsequently marries Lawyer Royall—who will give her child a name and a father—the two of them wait for the minister in "a room full of books." A "looking-glass in a carved frame" hangs from the wall, but this time Charity will not look at her reflection in the mirror (pp. 195–96).

Yet these acknowledgments of language's authority seem less significant than the text's many refusals of articulation. Lawyer Royall, usually so masterful with words, shows the most marked restraint: when he picks Charity up in his buggy on her way down from the Mountain, he respects her silence, not demanding an explanation, "and she felt a softness at her heart which no act of his had ever produced" (p. 189). She struggles to confess her pregnancy, but he calms her by waving off the faltering words and offering his hand and comfort: "You want to be took home and took care of. And I guess that's all there is to say" (p. 192). And after the marriage, when the exhausted heroine crawls into bed, and Lawyer sits fully dressed in the chair beside her, Charity realizes:

> He knew, then . . . he knew . . . it was because he knew that he had married her, and that he sat there in the darkness to show her that she was safe with him. A stir of something deeper than she had ever felt in thinking of him flitted through her tired brain, and cautiously, noiselessly, she let her head sink on the pillow. (p. 200)

Charity herself does not tell Lucius she is pregnant with his child. Nor does she inform Lawyer Royall that she spends the money he gives her for new clothes to retrieve the blue brooch Harney had bought for her in Nettleton.

The point is that secrets are permissible in Wharton's fictional universe; not everything has to be put into language. Wharton explicitly rejects the presumptions of American testifying. In one scene Charity passes a gospel tent and is approached by an unctuous evangelist who exhorts her, "Your Saviour knows everything. Won't you come in and lay your guilt before him?" (p. 114). (The heroine recollects this exchange, with the "fat evangelist's" importunity to confess, while heading up the Mountain [p. 170].) Charity hurries on past the white tent; and Wharton clearly regards such public and pressured unburdening as a desecration of the self. The minister who marries Charity and Mr. Royall, reading from the Scriptures with some of the same "sound of finality" as Mr. Miles, refers to "the dreadful day of judgment when the secrets of all hearts shall be disclosed" (p. 196). Then, not now, shall everything be told, Wharton believes. Then, and only then, shall we see into the hearts of others.

In *Summer*—in fact, in almost all Wharton's later works—this resistance to verbal explicitness, which arguably stems as much from her Episcopal upbringing as from her cosmopolitanism, coalesces into an aesthetic principle. True, a veneration for reserve is present in Wharton's writing from the outset. Even before she became a novelist, her coauthored book (with Ogden Codman Jr.) on interior design, *The Decoration of Houses* (1897), praised moderation and simplicity as the highest artistic virtues. "There is a sense," she writes, "in which works of art may be said to endure by virtue of what is left out of them, and it is this 'tact of omission' that characterizes the master-hand."[6] (Is it relevant, one wonders, that Lucius Harney, as an architect, constructs exteriors, whereas Wharton broke into print with an argument to protect the privacy of internal domestic space?)

"Tact of omission" well expresses the reticence and the emphasis on renunciation that are so common to Wharton's novels after *Ethan Frome* (1911). In our text, the pattern emerges almost as a stylistic tic, in a growing addiction to ellipses. These appear as early as the second chapter and escalate sharply after about the middle of the story. Once the "left-out" starts to supplant the visual and then the verbal as a value, it infiltrates the writing as a check on copiousness and revelation. Conventional enough in dialogue to indicate pauses, the ellipses take over the authorial voice. The following examples are all taken from the last two chapters: "If she had been less exhausted, less burdened with his weight, she would have sprung up then and there and fled away. . . ." (p. 185); "Anything, anything, was better than to add another life to the nest of misery on the Mountain. . . ." (p. 185). "She laid the chemise on the table, and stealing across the floor lifted the latch and went out. . . ." (p. 186); "She shut her eyes, and even these things grew dim to her. . . ." (p. 193); "She understood then that she was married. . . ." (p. 197). These gaps and omissions are Wharton's version of the Jamesian narrator's refrain: "I know not . . . ," "I am unable to say. . . ."

And as with *The American*, there is little to cheer about in the state of unfulfillment. Charity weds, and Lawyer Royall regains the moral compass of antebellum character; but the American future belongs to those like Lucius Harney who have "personality." Confinement as a wife and mother in North Dormer must feel a bit, to the heroine (not to mention the reader), like being interred for good in the village library. Still, we should not forget that even this life is a step up in circumstances for Charity Royall. Moreover, her escape from the Mountain carries an implicit political judgment, not unlike the critique of birthright society in James's novel.

Charity's spurning of her natal community can be read as an advance stricture upon Woodrow Wilson's ostensibly democratic advocacy of national sovereignty. The redrawing of frontiers according to nationalities was a leading principle among the Fourteen Points that the American president imposed on the European combatants during the peace negotiations at Versailles. What the principle was intended to mean in practice was that each European people or ethnic group should have its own homogeneous homeland. So stated, national sovereignty had more in common with segregation and the race riots that erupted between 1917 and 1919, not to mention the ethnic cleansing of our own day, than it did with American pluralism. It was the corollary to Wilson's obsession with border policing and racial and other forms of clarity ("open covenants openly arrived at"). Wharton, who had settled permanently in France, would have appreciated the wisdom of Charity's decision *not* to embrace her origins, a choice similar to the one she had made for herself from the perspective of privilege rather than poverty. Oddly enough, the choice is one that Sigmund Freud would probably have approved of as well. On this point, if on relatively little else, the expatriate novelist and the Viennese physician might have had a meeting of minds.[7] For who was ever more committed to the idea that psychological well-being depends on liberation from one's roots than the father of the talking cure?

Fitzgerald's *The Great Gatsby* as a "Modernist" Western

The Leatherstocking Tales and *The Great Gatsby*. Could any two works by Americans be *less* alike? The first tells the story of a presocial world where hierarchy and class distinction, embodied in stick figures with secondary or tertiary plot importance, linger as obsolete European remnants in a New World of boundless possibility. The second makes class and pedigree absolutely central to the narrative of an adventurer who meets his end at the easternmost tip of the continent, "the old island . . . that flowered once for Dutch sailors' eyes" (p. 227).[8]

I frame the contrast in this way to suggest both its limitations and its undeniable accuracy. From the earliest pages, when Nick Carraway announces himself as "a guide, a pathfinder, an original settler" (p. 7), *The Great Gatsby* asks to be read as a variation on the Western.[9] Nick occupies the traditional role of the "man in the middle," the Natty Bumppo figure who straddles the boundary between the wilderness, with its Indians and outlaws, and the fort or settlement that signifies civilization. The spatial coordinates are reproduced here as West Egg and East Egg: Gatsby's domain of bounders and bootleggers versus the Buchanan enclave of old wealth and antecedents. Nick, as Gatsby's friend—much as Natty is the friend of Chingachgook or, possibly the more relevant example, of Hurry Harry from *The Deerslayer*—and as Daisy's cousin, is the sole character in the novel who can move effortlessly between the two zones. He articulates the pros and cons of "savagery" versus "society" and draws the moral of the action.

The Western is a saga of resolution, however, and *The Great Gatsby* is not. The differences begin, as I have indicated, with the social: with the tribal, restrictive order that has emerged in the 1920s and constitutes the narrative's civilization to Gatsby's lawlessness. It is an order of birthright and obstructions, an anti-America where people like Tom and Daisy hold "membership in a rather distinguished secret society" (p. 24) to which outsiders like Gatsby can never gain admission. The decay extends to the realm of savagery, too. Gatsby, despite Nick's apologia for him, represents among other things social mobility soured into criminality. But Fitzgerald's novel is a "modernist" Western not simply because it takes place in an era when the promise of America seems spent. It is modernist because it replaces the Western's traditional legibility with a chronicle of the opaque. The Nick who begins telling the story believes, as he says, that "I am one of the few honest people I have ever known" (p. 76). By the end he has lost confidence in his own honesty and indeed in the authority or even the possibility of truth-telling. *Not* knowing turns out to be the text's corollary to the corruption of that "fresh green breast of the new world . . . [that] had once pandered in whispers to the last and greatest of all human dreams" (p. 227).

The Western, as we have seen, is a proleptic testing out in literature of the cinema's optical hegemony. As a popular genre it asserts visual mastery over the terrain. The movies do the same, through techniques such as the close-up and the pan shot, and perhaps for this reason the filmic medium has always had a special weakness for tales about the frontier. The first fictional feature film, *The Great Train Robbery*, was a Western that appeared in 1903; the classic narrative and its updated variations—as explorations of space, or battles with extraterrestrials—continue to be perennial cinematic favorites.

The movies are a demotic form, needing no cultural authorities to explicate their meaning for the viewer. They owed their earliest appeal, and their success into the new century, to their egalitarian accessibility. They were cheap, and they told their stories in instantly graspable images rather than language. Immigrants, who arrived in this country in unprecedented numbers until they were choked off by the Johnson-Reed Act of 1924, the year of *Gatsby*'s composition, did not need a thorough command of English in order to enjoy the new art, which quickly established itself as *the* mass entertainment of the twenties. Fitzgerald's novel flags the cinematic medium's importance in almost the same breath that Nick calls himself a pathfinder. The succeeding paragraph compares the expedited "bursting" of leaves on the summer trees to the way "things grow in fast movies" (p. 7).

The disregard of orderly temporal progression in fast-forward associates the motion pictures with Gatsby, who spends the entire novel striving, as he famously vows, to repeat the past. (The association also points us back to the Western, or at least to Cooper's version of it. The Leatherstocking Tales inaugurate the genre as a disruption of chronology. Natty Bumppo goes from being an old man of seventy or so in the first installment of the series, *The Pioneers* [1823], to a young man in his twenties in the last, *The Deerslayer* [1841]. He inverts temporal sequence and succeeds in doing precisely what Fitzgerald's protagonist wants: he reenters the past.) Gatsby's parties teem with movie actors, directors, and producers. Daisy, transfixed, watches a famous movie star at one of the gatherings, but she is otherwise "appalled" by the vulgar assemblage her lover hosts in West Egg, "this unprecedented 'place' that Broadway had begotten upon a Long Island fishing village" (p. 136). Paramount Pictures maintained a studio complex at the Long Island suburb of Astoria into the 1920s, but the film industry had all but completed its migration westward, anticipating Nick's decision to return home at the novel's end.

If Gatsby is a figure of the cinematic, Tom and Daisy, oddly enough, are linked to writing and language. The association is curious because the Buchanans, as a couple, could hardly be more philistine. And yet, although he allows for some suggestive spillage at the edges, Fitzgerald generally identifies his "Eastern" characters with a kind of mystified textuality in contrast to the imagistic presentation of his "Westerners."[10] (Tom and Daisy, of course, are technically from the West [or, rather, the Midwest]. But they not only reside in East Egg and embody its values; unlike Nick, they elect to remain on the East Coast after Gatsby's death.) Fitzgerald does this not so much because language is an instrument of depth or truth seeking—though it is for Nick—as because it is exclusionary. It is a register of cultural hierarchy. Literacy was a touchstone of the campaign for immigrant restriction that began in the 1890s, when the first upsurge in newcomers from the "hinterlands" of Europe occurred. Nativists tried to stem the foreign tide by demanding proof of ability to read and write from the uneducated and supposedly unassimilable Jews and Catholics pouring in from Italy, Poland, and Russia. Whereas Tom and Daisy naturalize the verbal—her "voice" is her most salient quality—Gatsby is alienated from language. His educational credentials are at the center of the story's most important scene, the decisive confrontation at the Plaza Hotel.

So it is Jay Gatsby, the glamorous current avatar of James Gatz of North Dakota, in whom the Western, the outsider, and the cinematic converge. The narrative, Nick comes to realize, "has been a story of the West, after all" (p. 221), and the "elegant young roughneck" (p. 62) who is his West Egg neighbor stands for the uncivilized energies emanating from the frontier. The ambiguities in Gatsby's characterization, at once outlaw and hero, are consistent with the often double position of the Western protagonist. There is a fair amount of Natty in him, too, the Natty of *The Pioneers*, perhaps, who finds himself in close proximity to the spreading settlements and reacts by deliberately breaking the law.

Gatsby's "gonnegtions" with Dan Cody and Meyer Wolfsheim flesh out his portrayal as desperado. Cody, Gatsby's first "mentor," was a ruthless participant in every Western metal rush who "brought back to the Eastern seaboard the savage violence of the frontier brothel and saloon" (p. 127). His name evokes Daniel Boone and William F. "Buffalo Bill" Cody. Gatsby's subsequent sponsor, Wolfsheim, fixed the 1919 World Series "with the single-mindedness of a burglar blowing a safe" (p. 93). Wolfsheim, a short Jew (as Nick describes him), apparently set up the eponymous hero in the bootlegging and fraudulent bond businesses. He tells Nick proudly that he was the man who "made" Gatsby (p. 215).

Along with his obscure origins, Fitzgerald's hero has a talent for self-invention or renomination. This suggests, once again, that he has a literary forerunner in Natty Bumppo. Natty, let us recall, is illiterate, and with his peculiar surname, which sounds vaguely ethnic, he probably would have been kept out of the country by nativists of the 1920s. Few readers have a clear recollection of his given last name, but none ever forgets his nicknames, the titles bestowed on him by admiring friends and foes: Hawkeye, Pathfinder, Deerslayer, Leatherstocking. Gatsby renames himself with equal relish: he has changed his unfortunate birth name for the more aristocratic-sounding one he is known by in the novel. Their assumed, not their natal, names supply the titles for the books that chronicle the exploits of the two men. Gatsby's youthful reading has been about a Natty-like hero; the volume in which he inscribed his daily schedule was *Hopalong Cassidy*. But Gatsby's death, unlike that of the classic hero, is ignominious. His end is more like that of a villain. He is sneaked up on and shot to death by Wilson, in a climax that echoes countless tales of frontier violence.

In Fitzgerald's version of the Western, automobiles have taken over the place of horses. They are the principal means of transportation in the text and as much a topic of conversation as the animals in, say, Cormac McCarthy's *All the Pretty Horses* (1992). Fitzgerald's novel features automotive accidents, disagreements and mistakes about ownership, and arguments over prices and value. A modern "corral," Wilson's garage, is a thematically portentous location, a halfway point between Gatsby's garish mansion and the East Egg home of the Buchanans. And the fatal collision that precipitates the denouement is caused by Gatsby's car while Daisy is driving it.

Hawkeye sees; Gatsby, another ocularcentric being, is seen. Consider his first appearance in the book. Nick spots him, standing under the stars, as though on a stage, and stretching out his arms toward the green light on Daisy's dock. He says nothing, and although Nick at first intends to call to him, the moment passes in silence. Critics sometimes describe such scenes as photographic, but that is too static. According to Nick, restlessness defines Gatsby, and he is constantly in motion. The nighttime scene on his lawn, like so many others, is cinematic, and the silence reminds us that the moving pictures did not incorporate sound until 1927, with *The Jazz Singer*, two years after the novel was published. The early movies compensated for their speechlessness with musical accompaniment. Gatsby's parties always have orchestras, and he is surrounded by music. He even keeps a permanent houseguest, a young man named Klipspringer, whose sole function in the story is to play the piano.

But speech is a problem for Fitzgerald's hero. His first communication in the text is an invitation to Nick to attend one of his parties, "a surprisingly formal note" that hints, in its lack of ease, at his verbal awkwardness (p. 53). And a volley of clues confirms the suspicion even before we hear his initial words. Nick sits down at a table with three men, each of whom introduces himself as "Mr. Mumble"; he then wanders into the library, where the books are "absolutely real" but the pages uncut. A man whom Nick calls "Owl Eyes" acclaims the host as "a regular Belasco" for his realism in using genuine "printed matter" but knowing when to stop (pp. 58–59).

Gatsby's conversion of a linguistic medium into a prop or ornament, a pure performance of surfaces, is characteristic of his distancing from language. When he finally introduces himself, Nick has the impression "that he was picking his words with care." His "elaborate formality of speech just missed being absurd" (p. 62). Nick in general finds that his neighbor "had little to say" (p. 81), and when the two of them finally go on a drive together, Gatsby's lies are so transparent—he claims to be from San Francisco in the Middle West—that Carraway can barely restrain himself from laughing. Chatting with Gatsby, he remarks in a phrase that recalls the unread books in the library, "was like skimming hastily through a dozen magazines" (p. 84). Nick briefly accepts that the stories of wartime valor and family wealth are true only because Gatsby produces visual confirmation, a snapshot of himself at Oxford.

These encounters set the pattern. They specify the protagonist as visually alluring and verbally impoverished, which is how the reader experiences him. He has "little to say" in our presence. We do hear him talk, and on occasion he gets off a memorable phrase, but his forays into direct speech are far less common than one would expect from the central character. Fitzgerald organizes the narrative so that Gatsby's accounts of his life are commonly received at second or third hand, filtered through the voices or written redactions of others. Our first history of the Daisy-Gatsby romance comes from neither one of the principals but from Jordan Baker, whose words Nick reproduces verbatim. Nick, in his own language this time, also tells (or rather writes down) the story of Gatsby's youthful dreams—said to be "unutterable" and "uncommunicable" (p. 141)—and his adventures with Dan Cody. On the night of the accident Nick fills in further details of the story, and in both instances the principal actor appears before us not as "I" but as "he." A narrative full of reflections on people's voices gives scant evidence of Gatsby's. And when the time comes for effective speech, not surprisingly he cannot deliver it. During the climactic quarrel at the Plaza, Gatsby is unable to mount a convincing reply to Tom's charges. He is out of his element: "He began to talk excitedly to Daisy, denying everything, defending his name against accusations that had not been made. But with every word she was drawing further and further into herself, and so he gave that up" (p. 170).

Gatsby's narrative, as Fitzgerald himself said, is structured as a series of scenes,[11] like a motion picture. The cinematic resonances may account in part for the frequent allusions to a dreamlike imaginary world—a world with some of that curious double quality of presence and absence, physicality and immateriality, we associate with the ghostly but animated figures on the screen. Nick speaks of the "unreality of reality" in Gatsby's reveries (p. 125); and when Wilson glides up on the hero in his pool, we read of "a new world, material without being real, where poor ghosts, breathing dreams like air, drifted fortuitously about . . ." (p. 203; ellipsis in original).

An exchange at the Buchanan home in chapter 7, just before the party heads for the Plaza, crystallizes this imagistic quality of Gatsby's, his seeming to be there without being embodied. The day is intensely hot, and the characters perspire profusely—all except the hero, who appears to lack a physical dimension, and of whom Daisy says, "You look so cool," adding, "You resemble the advertisement of the man" (pp. 149–50). Gatsby's power is to impart to the ghostly, the similitude, a greater reality than the actual. He comes by this talent honestly; his father, as we learn on the day of his funeral, has it, too. Mr. Gatz shows Nick a photograph of his dead son's house while the two of them are standing in the hall. "He had shown it so often that I think it was more real to him now than the house itself" (p. 217).

Gatsby as the pictorial, I have suggested, is antipathetic to chronological coherence. The visual image of course is spatial rather than temporal, and the movies, although they narrate stories, typically do so with cavalier disdain for chronological sequence, employing flashbacks as well as fast-forward and prolonging or contracting time to build suspense or speed up the action. Gatsby's war on time dominates the text.[12] Fitzgerald packs in a multitude of references to defunct or run-down timepieces; mentions and quotes snatches of songs about time ("In the meantime, / In between time" [p. 121], "Three O'Clock in the Morning," [p. 138], etc.); lists the names of Gatsby's guests in a train schedule; and shifts from the past to the present tense and back again to the past when describing Nick's first visit to Gatsby's house in chapter 3. The temporal fractures are also an expression of the hero's attempt to rewrite his ancestors and pass himself off as something other than "Mr. Nobody from Nowhere" (p. 163), the contemptuous epithet Tom hurls at him.[13]

The Buchanans are the thematic obverse of Gatsby, an East Egg upper crust that has calcified into racial and class permanence. Tom has none of the elegance but much of the investment in birthright privilege that Henry James imputed to the Bellegardes, who rejected Christopher Newman because his "antecedents" failed to measure up to their aristocratic standards. For James, such obsession with pedigree was "un-American"; in Fitzgerald's novel, it has become a societal norm. The contrast between Europe and America has reconfigured itself as the Western's split into civilization and savagery, with both sides pushed to corrupted extremes: Gatsby as the criminalization of the outsider dream of opportunity, and the 1920s United States as the antidemocratic and Europeanized half of the formula. The terms "secret society" and "conspiracy," which Fitzgerald uses to describe the Buchanans (Nick, seeing them together at the kitchen table after the automobile accident, writes: "Anybody would have said that they were conspiring together" [p. 183]), extend to the social order as a whole and convey its exclusive, nonparticipatory character.

Language or writing supplies an integral part of Tom and Daisy's portrait. Daisy is practically reduced to her voice—it is "full of money," Gatsby unforgettably remarks (p. 151), and no one can doubt that the money in question is old—but Tom, too, is known by his "speaking voice," which has "a touch of paternal contempt in it" and is second only to his hulking body in the inventory of traits cited by Nick. Tom's voice carries a message, Carraway adds: "'Now don't think my opinion on these matters is final,' he seemed to say, 'just because I'm stronger and more of a man than you are'" (p. 11). As both examples confirm, the verbal for the Buchanans serves to discriminate, to rank, and to categorize on the crudest possible basis. Theirs is a language vulgarized and debased.

This is evidenced in the very first chapter by Tom's reading. Much to Nick's amusement, Buchanan *is* a reader, and a voracious one at that. As Daisy says, "He reads deep books with long words in them," and at the dinner table he bursts out with a garbled account of "*The Rise of the Colored Empires* by this man Goddard," raving about the "scientific" evidence that supposedly proves the superiority of Nordics to other races (pp. 18–19). Later the same evening Jordan reads aloud to him from the *Saturday Evening Post*, the words "murmurous" and "soothing" (p. 39).

When the venue switches from East Egg to the New York City apartment Tom keeps for his mistress, the reading material grows more crass still. Myrtle Wilson unwittingly satirizes her paramour's intellectual and class pretensions. She favors gossip and scandal magazines, and she parrots Tom's "scientific" views about racial and social stratification. Her husband, George, she snorts, appeared to "know something about breeding, but he wasn't fit to lick my shoe" (p. 45). Nick, left alone while Buchanan and Myrtle have sex in the bedroom, distracts himself by reading a chapter from *Simon Called Peter*, a trashy popular novel he finds on the coffee table. This degrading of the linguistic through illicit sexuality follows the Buchanans to the party they attend at Gatsby's. When Tom goes in search of available women, Daisy offers him her "little gold pencil" to take down names and addresses (p. 134).

The importance of words, for the Buchanans, applies especially to names. To Gatsby, we know, names are insubstantial and mutable. At his West Egg parties, everyone is a stranger, and there are enthusiastic greetings between men and women "who never knew each other's names" (p. 52). To Tom and Daisy, on the other hand, names—given names and surnames, the names one is born with—have some of the perdurability, the weightiness, of real objects. Among people who cherish bloodlines and credentials, "Mr. Nobody from Nowhere," that is, Mr. No Name from No Place, is about as stinging a denunciation as can be imagined. Tom, a prig when he is not a philanderer, speaks indignantly of modern people "sneering at family life and family institutions" (p. 163). He has a territorial sense of Daisy's name. He tells his mistress that she has no right even to mention it. When Mrs. Wilson persists in shouting "Daisy" at him, Tom responds by breaking her nose. And the scene at the Plaza, which begins with a telephone book—a book of names—falling heavily to the floor, gets going with an argument about "[a] man named Biloxi" (p. 160) who crashed Tom and Daisy's wedding by pretending he was a classmate of Tom's from Yale. By the end of this scene, Daisy, repelled by Gatsby's illegal activities, has been emptied of any identity save the power of speech. She is nothing more than her voice: "The voice begged again to go" (p. 170).

Tom and Daisy's "regressiveness," their association with hoary technologies and value systems, is congealed in that massive "cruel body" (p. 11)

Fitzgerald makes so much of when writing about Tom. Daisy's husband is solid physicality to Gatsby's cool image—Nick imagines the butler roaring, "The master's body!" (p. 144) on the stifling day when Daisy compares her lover to an advertisement—and the hero's dreams shatter "like glass against Tom's hard malice" (p. 185). Buchanan has even taken a step back toward the authentic Western past. An accomplished polo player, he has purchased a garage and turned it into a stable for his collection of ponies.

The special role of Nick Carraway as *The Great Gatsby's* pathfinder is to negotiate between the novel's discordant worlds. He stands "within and without" (p. 46), as he puts it, somewhere between the lineage and scripturalism of the Buchanans and the fresh start and ocularcentrism of West Egg. He not only is a Yale classmate of Tom's and a cousin of Daisy's, but also claims on the third page of his narrative to be descended from "the Dukes of Buccleuch." (There is even an echo of "Buchanan" in that title, although the Carraway family got its American start in the wholesale hardware business, which sounds rather more like Gatsby's chain of "drugstores" than Tom's enormous ancestral wealth.) Gatsby, he tells us, "represented everything for which I have an unaffected scorn" (p. 4). Even when he pays the hero the supreme compliment of saying he is "worth the whole damn bunch put together," he cannot resist adding that he, Nick, disapproved of Gatsby "from beginning to end" (p. 193). Nick, too, comes from a place where names matter, a midwestern city "where dwellings are still called through decades by a family's name" (p. 221), and at times his discriminations seem only a little less invidious than those upheld by Tom Buchanan. One long-ago night Gatsby possessed Daisy, Carraway says, because, being penniless and without connections, "he had no real right to touch her hand" (p. 186).

But on balance Nick's sympathies lie with his neighbor, with the Gatsby for whom he at first acts as a go-between, arranging a tryst with Daisy, and then gradually comes to admire as a noble if misguided dreamer. He "had an extraordinary gift for hope," Nick says of the hero, "a romantic readiness such as I have never found in any other person and which it is not likely I shall ever find again" (p. 5). Nick's involvement with Jordan Baker, another "middle" character, though one who finally sides with the Buchanans, underlines his strategic position in the text. Jordan is an old friend of Daisy's from Louisville, and she looks down her nose at West Egg. She is also an athlete like Tom. But it is precisely her celebrity status as a golf champion that suggests affinities with Gatsby, who collects famous guests the way Tom collects polo ponies. The protagonist, perhaps sensing an ally, chooses Jordan to confide in about Daisy. Gatsby's favorite expression, "old sport," hints at other affinities. Nick recognizes Jordan from "rotogravure pictures of the sporting life" (p. 25), and it turns out that she has a trace in her of Meyer Wolfsheim, the Series fixer who is Gatsby's business associate. She is "incurably dishonest" (p. 75), according to Nick. Her cheating in a golf tournament just missed becoming a major scandal.

Nick's narration, like his persona, mediates between the novel's polarized settings and characters. We know him right off the bat as a writer, and thus by implication as a kindred spirit to the Buchanans. (A bona fide college graduate, he passes evenings boning up on securities at the Yale Club library, whereas Gatsby spent only five months at Oxford.) Nick is a man who invites confidences, he says by way of introduction; not because he is a deliberate seeker of secrets but owing, rather, to his nonjudgmental manner, which inspires trust and "has opened many curious natures to me." Thanks to this quality, which has made him the recipient of Gatsby's "intimate revelations," we have the book we are reading (pp. 3–4). He informs us more than once that he has been "reading over" or jotting down his impressions of that fateful summer, and he reminds us, too, of the temporal dimension of textuality. The process of composition has consumed about twelve months, because when Nick began writing, Gatsby had been dead a year, and he says in the last chapter, "After two years I remember the rest of that day" (p. 205).

Nick the writer pays a kind of homage to his friend's vivid imagination by compiling the story in an unusually pictorial style. His account is arranged as a succession of discrete incidents, each like a scene in a movie, and he often describes physical objects as though they were props on a colossal stage. A moon rises gloriously over Gatsby's first party, "produced like the supper, no doubt, out of a caterer's basket" (p. 55). Nick is exceptionally sensitive to lighting and color. In chapter 1 the sunshine fades from Daisy's face, "each light deserting her with lingering regret, like children leaving a pleasant street at dusk," and Tom and Jordan stroll into the library "with several feet of twilight between them" (pp. 20, 22). Then there are those remarkable shirts of Gatsby's, "piled like bricks in stacks a dozen high": apple green, coral, lavender, and faint orange, "with monograms of Indian blue" (p. 117). On the morning of the murder, as Nick prepares to catch a train for the city, Gatsby's "gorgeous pink rag of a suit" is said to stand out like "a bright spot of color against the white steps" (p. 193). Complementing this cornucopia of images is Carraway's own chronological insouciance. Like the hero, he plays fast and loose with time, for example, placing the visit to Myrtle's Manhattan apartment in chapter 2 when strict order dictates that it should come after chapter 3. And he sets a pair of eyes to brood ominously over the whole narrative, the gigantic blue painted "eyes of Doctor T. J. Eckleburg" that gaze across the valley of ashes from an oculist's billboard. (Here Nick is indistinguishable from Fitzgerald, a point to which I will return.)

The Great Gatsby is written in a highly figurative style, and one mannerism in particular gives Nick's prose an ocular cast. He is addicted to "as though" and "as if" formulations, metaphoric equations that immerse the reader in images. Consider, again, from the first chapter, the dinner party at the Buchanans': Daisy and Jordan sitting on the couch are "buoyed up as though upon an anchored balloon" (p. 12); their dresses ripple and flutter "as if they had just been blown back in after a short flight around the house" (p. 12); Jordan has her chin raised "as if she were balancing something on it which was quite likely to fall" (p. 13); Tom hooks his arm under Nick's and escorts him into the dining room "as though he were moving a checker to another square" (p. 15); and Jordan sits down at the table with a yawn "as if she were getting into bed" (p. 16). The pattern persists throughout the novel and flavors the characters' speech as well. On the drive to the Plaza, to cite just one example, Jordan pronounces New York in summer "overripe, as if all sorts of funny fruits were going to fall into your hands" (p. 157).

One might conclude from these illustrations that Nick's prose style has been infected by the "overripe" (to use Jordan's word) gorgeousness he sees everywhere around him, and I will in fact propose something like this argument momentarily. But his intention is plainly otherwise. What Nick wants is to purify textuality of Buchanan carelessness and vulgarization, to impart to it a bit of Gatsby's romantic splendor. He strives to create a cinematic visuality in words, an updated Western that would renew the genre's traditional legibility.

Nick means his narrative as a memorial to the hero's "greatness." But more than that, he is writing to get to the bottom of things, to clear up the rumors that have swirled around the protagonist from the instant of his arrival in West Egg, when people first began speculating wildly that Gatsby was a relative of Kaiser Wilhelm's, or a German spy, or that he had killed a man.

Carraway, we recall, prides himself on his honesty. He is also someone who does not "like mysteries," as he says to Gatsby when the latter uses Jordan as an intermediary (p. 90). Whereas most of Gatsby's guests pay him the "subtle tribute of knowing nothing whatever about him" (p. 90), Nick differentiates himself from the crowd of spongers by resolving to learn the truth. As he writes in chapter 4, after the first long digression on Gatsby's past:

> He told me all this very much later, but I've put it down here with the idea of exploding those first wild rumors about his antecedents, which weren't even faintly true. Moreover he told it to me at a time of confusion, when I had reached the point of believing everything and nothing about him. So I take advantage of this short halt, while Gatsby, so to speak, caught his breath, to clear this set of misconceptions away. (p. 128)

For the Nick who pens these words, language is a means of knowledge and illumination. He will share with the reader his hard-won discoveries about the protagonist, and he will conceal nothing about the summer of Gatsby's death, not letting the Buchanans off the hook for their cruelty and self-absorption and not even sparing Jordan for her chronic falsehoods.

But these commendable aspirations, which tip the Western in the direction of the detective story, cannot withstand the "foul dust" (p. 5) that seems to have settled over Fitzgerald's America. The goal of seeking the truth about Gatsby is tainted from the second Tom conceives an antipathy for him and makes up his mind to "investigate" the hero. "I'd like to know who he is and what he does," Buchanan insists at their first meeting. "And I think I'll make a point of finding out" (p. 138). At the Plaza, Tom uses the information he has uncovered from his friend Walter Chase like a weapon with which to bludgeon Gatsby. He denounces his would-be rival as a bogus Oxford man and then, more devastatingly, as a bootlegger whose "drugstores" sell grain alcohol and who, along with Wolfsheim, has gotten into something so bad that everybody is afraid to talk about it. The words that Gatsby has always viewed with discomfort and suspicion catch up with him here. They undermine Daisy's infatuation and destroy his dreams.

Indeed, language, with its promise of penetrating beneath appearance to reach the truth, proves lethal and unreliable as the novel races toward its conclusion. Tom finishes the wreckage he began by giving Gatsby's name to George Wilson as the owner (and presumably the driver) of the yellow car that killed his wife. Although the last inference turns out to be inaccurate, from his point of view Tom technically tells the truth—only omitting the relevant fact he, Tom, and not Gatsby, was Myrtle Wilson's secret lover. This selective disclosure is the "verbal" clue that sends Wilson searching for Gatsby's West Egg residence and produces the "holocaust" at the pool. When we last see the Buchanans together, Tom and Daisy are talking "intimately" and "earnestly" to each other across the kitchen table. To Nick, they look like "conspirators," plotting to purge Gatsby from their lives as they retreat into their moneyed security. The shoddiness of language has reasserted its sovereignty over language's potential for revelation.

As confusions multiply in these final pages, words seem to have less and less purchase on reality. A striking feature is the way characters collapse into each other once the pace picks up in chapter 7. Identities and names become progressively more difficult to tell apart. Jordan is mistaken for Daisy by Myrtle Wilson; Tom drives Gatsby's car and tells Wilson it is his; Myrtle, thinking the yellow car is Tom's, mistakes Gatsby for her lover and shouts Tom's name at him as she rushes into the path of the oncoming vehicle; Wilson thinks Gatsby is having an affair with his wife; Tom believes Gatsby ran over Myrtle and tells Wilson as much when in actuality the driver was Daisy; and so on.

Meanwhile, Nick tampers with our trust in him as a narrator. Until now he has been scrupulous about relaying only what he knows. In chapter 8, though, he describes a scene between Michaelis and Wilson that he could not possibly have witnessed. Moreover, he does not recount the scene as though he got it from another person, as he does with Jordan's and Gatsby's stories. Michaelis must have been his source, but the point is never clarified, and Nick includes minor details and firsthand dialogue that have the feel of omniscience. Is he making it up? For the first time, we entertain doubts about his reliability.

The proliferation of sound bites and half-truths is another oddity of the final sections. In part this linguistic debasement can be traced to the arrival of the media on the scene. In the hands of the press, Gatsby's yellow roadster is renamed the "death car" (p. 173), and this is but the first of many sensationalized distortions—"grotesque, circumstantial, eager, and untrue," according to Nick (p. 205)—circulated by the newspapers. An anonymous individual applies the term "madman" to Wilson, and the reporters seize on the expression with enthusiasm. They give it so much currency that Wolfsheim recycles it in his letter to Nick, and Mr. Gatz, having read the papers halfway across the country in Chicago, declares that the killer "must have been mad" (p. 210). Little wonder that the last thing Nick sees at Gatsby's deserted house is "an obscene word," scrawled on the steps "by some boy with a piece of brick" (p. 227). He erases the word with his shoe, but the gesture seems too late to arrest the verbal pollution.

The use of language to obfuscate, to dazzle or awe but fail to penetrate to the core of things, is, interestingly enough, a charge that *The Great Gatsby's* early reviewers brought against Fitzgerald. The *Milwaukee Journal* felt that the novel read too much like a "newspaper story" and was all "on the surface." No less a figure than H. L. Mencken concurred with this estimate, using almost the identical terms. The book has "gusto," he wrote, but it "does not go below the surface."[14] Even Fitzgerald spoke at times as though he deployed words to cover up the narrative's shortcomings. The absence of detail about Gatsby and Daisy's relationship after their reunion was, he told Edmund Wilson, a serious flaw in the structure. "However," he went on, "the lack is so astutely concealed by the retrospect of Gatsby's past and by blankets of excellent prose that no one has noticed it."[15]

Fitzgerald's defense is a questionable one, and his words say more about the text's mystifications than about its success. Even admirers of the book—and I emphatically include myself in that number—will have to admit that there are patches of overwriting where the "ineffable gaudiness" spun out of Gatsby's brain seems to swamp Fitzgerald's prose (p. 125). The "blankets" of glitter can sound positively embarrassing when taken out of context:

> He knew that when he kissed this girl, and forever wed his unutterable visions to her perishable breath, his mind would never romp again like the mind of God. So he waited, listening for a moment longer to the tuning-fork that had been struck upon a star. Then he kissed her. At his lips' touch she blossomed for him like a flower and the incarnation was complete. (p. 141)

Such passages, purporting to unpack Gatsby's history and motivations, are highly burnished surfaces with some of that very "unutterable"—untranslatable, illegible—quality Fitzgerald ascribes to the hero's fantasies. (Does Fitzgerald really mean to imply that Daisy was a kind of Christ figure to Gatsby? Or is Gatsby himself the Christ figure? Earlier he was said to be "a son of God" [p. 124].) The passage is "overripe" (to quote Jordan again) and suggestive but balks depth. And many of the novel's legendary exchanges have a comparable pairing of profundity and superficiality: "'Her voice is full of money'" (p. 151); "'You can't repeat the past.'" "'Can't repeat the past? . . . Why of course you can!'" (p. 140); "'it was just personal'" (p. 191); "'God sees everything. . . .'" "'That's an advertisement'" (p. 201). These portentous moments are unforgettable in the way effective sound bites are. They constitute a high literary equivalent to "madman" and "death car."

Perhaps it is to be expected, then, that Nick, in looking back on the whole sordid business, feels revulsion from all verbal interchange. The man who presented himself to us as a natural confessor confesses that after Gatsby he wants no more "privileged glimpses into the human heart." He cares neither to hear nor to relate confidences about "the abortive sorrows and short-winded elations of men" (pp. 4–5). Nick states, as well, that his pride and even his belief in his honesty have not survived the passage of time. He turns thirty in the course of the narrative, on the same day, as it happens, that Tom exposes Gatsby at the Plaza. That day pretty much extinguishes his faith in the power of truth. In parting from Jordan, who thought him "rather an honest, straightforward person," he admits that he "is five years too old to lie to myself and call it honor" (p. 224). A last meeting with Tom practically concludes the novel. Buchanan angrily accuses Gatsby of having run over Myrtle like a dog. "There was nothing I could say," Nick comments, "except the one unutterable fact that it wasn't true" (p. 225). The "truth" that Daisy was behind the wheel is, once again, "unutterable," and Nick does not bother to speak it. It would make no difference anyway. Defeated, and rid of his "provincial squeamishness forever," he ends the scene by swallowing his disgust and consenting to shake Buchanan's hand (p. 226).

F. Scott Fitzgerald is not reducible to Nick Carraway, of course, but it may be pertinent to mention that almost a full decade elapsed before he published another novel. *Tender Is the Night* appeared in 1934; it was the last book-length work of fiction he completed. It tells the story of an American psychiatrist, the significantly named Dick Diver, who believes that the truth about "the human heart" can be put into words. But in seeking to get to the source of his wealthy patient's psychological problems, to understand and articulate her interior, he succeeds only in plummeting to his own destruction.

Hemingway's *The Sun Also Rises*

Contemporary reviewers of *The Great Gatsby* judged the novel a work of external notation, like a story in the newspapers. The description applies equally well, perhaps more so, to a book published a year later by Fitzgerald's friend Ernest Hemingway: *The Sun Also Rises*. Unlike Fitzgerald, Hemingway *was* a journalist, and the narrator of *The Sun Also Rises* is a

working newspaperman. Despite the prominence of writing as an occupation in the text, however, Hemingway's fiction is generally dismissive of language, and his proxy, Jake Barnes, is skeptical about narrative consistency.
Jake mistrusts "all frank and simple people" like Robert Cohn, "especially
when their stories hold together."[16]

The statement is curious because Hemingway could expatiate as vol-
ubly as Herman Melville about the importance of "truth." "A writer's job,"
he liked to say, "is to tell the truth," and who can ever forget his admonition
to himself as an author, "Write the truest sentence that you know"? Paradoxically, Hemingway's notion of truth, of the true sentence, is nonverbal
or antiverbal. It seeks to hone language to a minimalism that approximates
the clarity of vision—the unconsciousness of visual images. Hemingway
was acutely mindful of the competition of the early cinema, and at the time
he was perfecting his style, the movies were soundless. He felt that he could
trump them by fashioning speaking or talking pictures in prose. *These* pictures would restore literature to its primacy as an unsentimental and unde-
ceptive cultural medium.

Literature would regain its preeminence, moreover, by maintaining a
stoicism about emotions. The "manly" silences of Hemingway's prose—
"What is it men feel about quiet?" wonders Brett Ashley (p. 61)—culminate
an American tradition of reticence.[17] His forerunners as practitioners of ellipsis include his seeming opposites, James and Wharton; his craft of omission is not the antithesis of their fastidious decorum but the analogue to it.
This commitment to quiet stamps Hemingway's work as resolutely anti-
Freudian. The talking cure clashes with his characters' doubts about the
value of verbalization. There is even something "Catholic" about his aversion to the parading of interiority. The novelist, who was raised as a Con-
gregationalist, apparently converted to Catholicism after he was wounded
in 1918, and his narrator Jake volunteers, "It was a grand religion" (p. 97).
One thing Hemingway must have cherished about the faith was the public
taciturnity it imposed on the congregant.[18]

The Sun Also Rises does not fit the pattern of canonical works we have
examined, in that it is not structured around a secret or a conundrum. Yet
Hemingway's novel, which occupies a single summer in the 1920s, does
have a stake in the triumph of the "sun." It aspires to visibility and truthfulness, to flooding areas of darkness and dishonesty with light. We might wish
to take Don Manuel Orquito, "the fireworks king," as a sort of stand-in for
the writer. Don Manuel's charge during the San Fermin festival is to light
up the night sky by launching a collection of "globos illuminados"
(pp. 178–79). A crowd gathers to watch the spectacle. The fire balloons get
caught in the wind, flare, and sputter to the ground. It is as though Hemingway were acknowledging the limitations of his own project, offering up,
in the failure of the "pirotecnico of esta ciudad," a figure for the opacity that
in the end engulfs his narrative.

The novel is at once obsessed and disgusted with the verbal. The loathing is impossible to miss because, unavoidably, it gets put into words. Talking, the characters state over and over again (in a fiction packed with dialogue), is something to be shunned at all costs. Talk gives expression to things better left undisclosed; it is embarrassing, or self-indulgent, or misleading, or positively harmful. "Talking's all bilge," says Brett Ashley (p. 55); it's "a lot of rot" (p. 181). Brett is emphatic on the folly of speech, inverting the usual identification of women with gossip and sentimentalism (a cliché recycled in the novel by Count Mippipopolous, who claims that women prefer "noise" to the quiet of men [p. 61]). When Brett summons Jake to Madrid at the end, to tell him about her breakup with Pedro Romero, she cannot stop repeating: "Let's not talk about it," "Don't let's ever talk about it. Please don't let's ever talk about it" (pp. 242–43).

Jake pretty much agrees. "Only I'd a hell of a lot rather not talk about it" (p. 124), he says when Bill asks him about his feelings for Brett, and later he declares, "You'll lose it if you talk about it" (p. 245). At times he seems to want to disavow nomination altogether, surely a strange longing for a man who earns his livelihood at the typewriter. He makes the admiring remark, "There is no Spanish word for bull-fight" (p. 173), and he professes respect for the "English spoken language"—among "the upper classes, anyway"—because of the paucity of its vocabulary. The English use "one phrase to mean everything," according to our narrator; they have "fewer words" than the Eskimo or the Cherokee (p. 149).

Writing does not fare much better in Jake's estimation, a lot, perhaps most of it, being similarly unreliable. Cohn, we learn early on, has absorbed foolishly romantic ideas about South America from a book by W. H. Hudson; he does not care for Paris because of something he read in a second book. *That* book, we are later told, is probably by H. L. Mencken, another source of erroneous impressions. "So many young men get their likes and dislikes from Mencken" (p. 42), Jake complains.

Some of this impatience with language can be attributed, of course, to Hemingway's famous exasperation with the overblown rhetoric of warfare—with words like "glory" and "honor" that were bandied about, to a generation's revulsion, by the architects of World War I. In *The Sun Also Rises*, Jake mentions a solemn speech about his war wound, delivered by a humorless Italian colonel, that he can hardly recall without laughing. But the resistance to articulation seems directed not just at insincere or inflated affect; more generally, the recoil is from speech's entanglement with inwardness itself—from language's power, commonly taken to be its special virtue, to convey emotional depth.

Nighttime comes under suspicion in Jake's narrative because the darkness is so conducive to excesses of feeling and verbiage. One quality the narrator cannot abide about Cohn is the latter's addiction to tiresome discourse during the night. In Paris Cohn has been losing sleep "talking" into the early hours with Frances, the woman he is planning to abandon, and the thought depresses Jake, who pictures "the bedroom scenes" of the couple verbally lacerating each other (p. 13). Jake is not immune, though, to emotional outpouring in the darkness. When one cannot see, one is thrown back on one's inner state, and he finds himself sampling all sorts of "large statements" that amount—as Brett would put it—to "a lot of bilge" (p. 149). Jake even cries at night, a weakness he deplores in others (notably Cohn, who cannot seem to stop bawling). Once, he confides, he went six whole months without turning off the lights while he slept.

As a Catholic, the hero regularly attends confession—another darkened site of self-exposure. But this venue is proscribed both to the other characters and to the reader. Brett wants to accompany Jake to the confessional, "but I told her that not only was it impossible but it was not as interesting as it sounded, and, besides, it would be in a language she did not know" (p. 151). One's innermost thoughts should always be in a tongue that would-be eavesdroppers cannot understand and have no right to listen in on. One cannot, perhaps, help reflecting on painful things—Jake admits he's unable to follow the church's teaching "not to think about [them]" (p. 31)—but at least one can avoid spilling them in words. And there is always the certainty of the light's return. "It is awfully easy to be hard-boiled about everything in the daytime," Jake sums up the dark's collusion with every sort of seepage, "but at night it is another thing" (p. 34). The narrative's title memorializes, with a sigh of relief, the sun's diurnal rising; its rays can be counted on to banish the provocation to linguistic intemperance.

Hemingway's wariness toward words has to be set against the profusion of writers and foregrounding of speech in his text. Jake's status as a journalist actually ranks him rather low in the novel's literary pecking order. His good friend Bill Gorton is not only a novelist but also a great talker whose spontaneous wit charms Brett (although when Jake introduces him to Romero, Bill exclaims, "Tell him I'm ashamed of being a writer" [p. 175]). Cohn has written a novel, too, "and it was not really such a bad novel as the critics later called it" (pp. 5–6). Moreover, characters are constantly communicating by telegram and exchanging letters with each other. Even Mike Campbell, who lacks the patience to read correspondence, is said to "write a damned amusing letter" and wishes he "were one of these literary chaps" (p. 144). And one should mention the many pages of sheer dialogue without a line of descriptive narration, more like a stage play or a screenplay than a novel, that give *The Sun Also Rises* its fast-paced, colloquial quality.

The affinity is really with the screen or photoplay, and this is the clue to the book's self-conception, and to Hemingway's "revision" of the linguistic. His goal is to shed the falsity of language by turning prose fiction into a vivid skimming of surfaces, a sun-drenched medium that like the motion pictures does its best work outdoors and in the light of day. He builds on the pre-talkie movies by using words as kinetic visual units, and he surpasses the silent pictures by integrating the ocular with the spoken, punctuating exposition and description with direct verbal exchanges. But even in his use of dialogue, Hemingway follows—or rather predicts—the cinematic. He seldom elaborates the affect behind the colloquy. One senses the psychic activity beneath the verbal give-and-take, but Hemingway leaves it to his readers to guess at its content; he almost never names it. (The rivalry with the motion pictures was to evolve, with the advent of sound a year later, into a lucrative symbiosis. Within a decade, Hemingway was able to live comfortably on the money he earned from regularly selling his novels and short stories to Hollywood. The contrast to Fitzgerald is instructive. Fitzgerald had to support himself by writing screenplays; Hemingway never did. His writings were *already* cinematic, which is one reason—bestsellerdom and his notoriety being the others—that the studios paid such high sums for the film rights.)

Consider Hemingway's much-remarked-on touristic imagination, perhaps his clearest link to those earlier American authors, Mark Twain and Henry James, who introduced their compatriots to foreign cultures. When Cohn speaks of wanting to go to South America, Jake's response is telling: "All countries look just like the moving pictures" (p. 10). To the tourist, other nations resemble movies because one never knows them in depth; one "sightsees" as one passes through, picking up as much information as one can from enlightened looking. *The Sun Also Rises* is a fictional Baedeker offering not a native's view of Paris, or Burguete, or Pamplona, but the discoveries and impressions of a seasoned traveler. It is a guidebook for those who want to be knowledgeable about the most interesting places to visit, how to get from one location to another, and what to pay for food, drinks, and services.

For example, we learn among other details the shortest taxi route from the Rue de la Montagne Sainte Geneviève to the Parc Montsouris (take the street behind St. Étienne du Mont, go past the Place de la Contrescarpe, follow the cobbled Rue Mouffetard, etc. [p. 25]); the names of the trendiest bars in Paris (Wetzel's gets a special plug for "good hors d'oeuvres" [p. 37]); what it costs to hire a motorcar and driver from Bayonne in France to Pamplona in Spain (400 francs [p. 91]); where to fish for trout in the Irati River; an "insider's" view of the fiesta at Pamplona (which the novel enveloped in so much glamour that it became a major tourist stop); and what to order for a luxurious lunch at Botin's in Madrid, "one of the best restaurants in the world" (Jake, much depressed by this point, gets the suckling pig and washes it down with "three bottles of *rioja alta*" [pp. 245–46]).

These bits of information complement a descriptive prose that often seems to confine itself exclusively to what the moving eye beholds. Feelings and reactions are barely mentioned, and the language strives to empty itself of anything but the ocular and generic. In Paris, walking or riding in a taxi, Jake relates the names of the streets, whether they are deserted or crowded, the lighted bars, the tables stacked on the pavement, the statues under the trees. He tells us what he observes from the rented car as he, Bill, and Cohn journey from France to Spain; these descriptions in particular are filmic, not painterly or static, suggesting a mobile camera lens and recalling the early association of the movies with the railroad. The sights pass so rapidly before the narrator-spectator that the brain scarcely has time to register specifics:

> [The car] started up the white dusty road into Spain. For a while the country was much as it had been; then, climbing all the time, we crossed the top of a Col, the road winding back and forth on itself, and then it was really Spain. There were long brown mountains and a few pines and far-off forests of beech-trees on some of the mountainsides. The road went along the summit of the Col and then dropped down, and the driver had to honk, and slow up, and turn out to avoid running into two donkeys that were sleeping in the road. We came down out of the mountains and through an oak forest, and there were white cattle grazing in the forest. Down below there were grassy plains and clear streams . . . [W]e saw a whole new range of mountains off to the south, all brown and baked-looking and furrowed in strange shapes. (p. 93)

The drive to Pamplona covers four pages of visualized prose narration, relentlessly pruned of affect.

The experience of being a tourist, which involves a constant expenditure of money for goods and services, supplies Jake with a philosophy. At the inn in Burguete, the rooms are expensive (twelve pesetas), but the meals come with unlimited wine. "We did not lose money on the wine" (p. 111), Jakes reports with satisfaction, and he, Bill, and the other characters convert the idea of "a simple exchange of values"—the phrase is Gorton's (p. 72)—into a governing principle, a lesson for life. "Don't we pay for all the things we do, though?" (p. 26) asks Brett, who interprets Jake's impotence, as well as her later crush on Romero, as the payback for all the pain she has caused men. And Jake's nighttime reveries—"Enjoying living was learning to get your money's worth and knowing when you had it"—revolve around the same standard. "The bill always came," he reflects. "That was one of the swell things you could count on" (p. 148). It reads like *Europe on Five Dollars a Day* repackaged as metaphysics.

The prominence of bodies and sports in Hemingway's tale reinforces its insistent ocularcentrism. Bodies, unlike thoughts and feelings, are accessible to vision; they exist in space, like that dusty white road snaking its way into the Basque country, and their motions can be witnessed and described. The materiality of bodies stands out sharply in the narrative. One might almost say that the human in Hemingway is constituted by its physicality, a reductionism that allies the novelist with the Freudian emphasis on drives or instinct. (Bill cracks at one point, "Sex explains it all" [p. 116].) Jake Barnes lingers in most readers' memories because of the war wound that renders him impotent; the Count shows off the scars from the arrows that pierced his chest in Abyssinia (exhibiting bodily injuries is far more acceptable than speaking of emotional ones); Brett attracts all eyes with her beauty and "curves like the hull of a racing yacht" (p. 22), plus the close-cropped hair that so troubles Romero; and the torero himself, as Jake informs us, is "the best-looking boy I have ever seen" (p. 163).

Bodies require extensive ministration in *The Sun Also Rises*, and their needs range from the trivial to the overpowering. We watch Jake and Bill shave, and Cohn gets his hair cut. Characters are constantly eating and drinking, often to excess. Brett takes innumerable baths, and she and Mike need their sleep, seldom rising before noon. Brett as a victim and agent of sexuality seems at times almost reducible to her body. She solicits Jake's kiss and then recoils from him because his touch arouses her; she refuses to live with him because she cannot survive without physical contact ("It's the way I'm made" [p. 55]); and she trembles and her hand shakes with desire for Romero. Brett has the power to reduce others to animality, too, to their physical identities. Robert Cohn compares her to Circe, the sorceress adept at transforming men into swine, and she has this degrading effect on a string of male characters, including Mike, Jake, Cohn, and even, some would say, Pedro Romero.

Sport is a close second to sex—or possibly it is ahead of sex (and here Hemingway is more American than Freudian)—as an occasion for bodily display, expression, and gratification. The novel's celebrated first sentence announces that "Robert Cohn was once middleweight boxing champion of Princeton," and his skill at the sport comes in handy when, at various times, he flattens Jake, Mike, and Romero ("It was quite a thing to watch," remarks the minor character named Edna. "He must be a boxer" [p. 191]). Jake is fond of swimming and goes fishing in Spain with Bill and the Englishman Harris. Bullfighting occupies the entire middle section of the story. At the end, before he joins Brett in Madrid, Jake spends time catching up on the Tour de France.

One reason bodies matter in Hemingway is that they are so luminous. Bodies speak volumes without literally speaking, rather like those silent film stars who could communicate subtleties of thought and feeling through posture, gait, facial expressions, and gestures. Brett's trembling hand would give away her passion for Romero even if she did not tell Jake about it, and the physical signs are more expressive than any words could be. (This is where Brett, for all her toughness, betrays her "womanly" side; she usually talks right through her vows not to talk about it.) Sport, again, is more eloquent than sex. Above all, fishing and bullfighting initiate the attentive reader into the domain of professional "secrets," including self-reflexive revelations about the art of writing—which, Hemingway's descriptions suggest, is best understood as a visual discipline.

The passages will be familiar to every student of the novel: Jake's account of hooking the fish at Burguete until "in a little while I had six. They were all about the same size. I laid them out, side by side, all their heads pointing the same way, and looked at them. They were beautifully colored and firm and hard from the cold water" (p. 119). The parallel to the use of concise, non-Latinate words in the construction of sentences is unmistakable; equally noteworthy is the implicit stress on the sentence's appearance on the page, its clarity and crispness figured in the row of fish.

And then there is the bullfight, where Romero functions as the artist and Brett as the avid spectator or "reader," riveted by the purity of his performance and unwilling to avert her sight from even the bloodiest moments of the "show" (p. 166). (Brett's eyes, Jakes observes early in the story, are fearless and consumed by curiosity; they "would look on and on after every one else's eyes in the world had stopped looking" [p. 27].) Under Jake's tutelage, the heroine learns to detect and appreciate the many nuances of Romero's unfaked technique (which is contrasted to the decadence of Belmonte and Marcial). Jake explains that the young torero has "a left and a right just like a boxer," and Brett, fascinated, exclaims, "I saw it. . . . I saw him shift from his left to his right horn" (p. 140). She learns to read the spectacle visually, much as we, Hemingway's readers, are educated in his athletic, transparent prose; and the bullfighter's mastery merges seamlessly with the novelist's:

> Romero went on. It was like a course in bull-fighting. All the passes he linked up, all completed, all slow, templed and smooth. There were no tricks and no mystifications. There was no brusqueness. And each pass as it reached the summit gave you a sudden ache inside. The crowd did not want it ever to be finished. (pp. 219–20)

I have suggested that Hemingway's novel is a product of the sun, like the motion pictures. But darkness is never far from the text's field of vision. The movies cannot be seen in sunlight; they are typically watched at night, or at the very least in darkened auditoriums that prevent the day's glare from erasing the images on the screen. Cinematically, darkness is the condition that enables seeing to occur. Moreover, the sun sets; the night follows the day with the same regularity that "the sun also rises." The inextricability of the two phenomena weighs on Hemingway's cult of vision. Darkness merges with writing to cast a shadow over the adventures of Jake Barnes and his friends.

Death, by critical consensus, throws the longest shadow. The fish at Burguete are dead, and the bull at Pamplona will be, once Romero has his way. If the bullfighter is careless, he may be the one who bleeds to death before an audience of thousands. The running of the bulls through the town's streets takes its toll on the audience as well. Jake witnesses a man on the runway being caught by a horn and jerked into the air before he is dropped senseless in the mud. A waiter later tells him that the gored man has died, leaving a wife and two children. The waiter can only shake his head over such self-destructive risk taking. "All for fun," he comments sardonically. "Fun, you understand" (p. 197).

The Spanish waiter is the Starbuck of *The Sun Also Rises*, appalled by lethal games with "brute animals," and no more than the *Pequod*'s first mate does he speak for the author. But he has a point about the allure of extinction in the Hemingway universe. Corpses, imitation corpses, and insentient bundles of flesh litter the plot, and their prevalence seems to be connected to the very verbal ethic that the novel strives to disavow.

Boxing and bullfighting are unequaled at piling up unconscious and deceased bodies, some of them human, others bestial. Outside the ring, the state of being defunct is a source of endless repartee, humor, and art. Bill dotes on jokes about dead animals. He recommends that Jake buy a stuffed dog to beautify his flat and wonders if Brett and Mike would like "a couple of stuffed racehorses" for their wedding (p. 76). Jake introduces his friend as a taxidermist, but "that was in another country," Bill amends. "And besides all the animals were dead" (p. 75). In the Spanish inn, pictures of dead creatures line the walls. "There was one panel of rabbits, dead, one of pheasants, also dead, and one panel of dead ducks" (p. 110). Human characters, like stuffed animals, are said to be inanimate under their lifelike masquerade. Brett tells the Count, "You're dead, that's all" (p. 61). And when Cohn gets drunk and passes out—a fate shared at one time or another by all Hemingway's characters—Bill and Mike have an argument about whether he is dead or asleep.

These many moments of fixation with nothingness take over the text. Knowing the values, being "one of us" (as Brett observes of the Count [p. 60]), cannot in the end compete with the taxidermy motif, the deadness under the superficial appearance of life. Mike and Brett turn out to be freeloaders who default on Hemingway's touristic philosophy; they borrow recklessly and try to get by without paying for value. Jake does the procuring for Brett that compromises him in the eyes of Montoya and the other aficionados; and his self-revulsion overwhelms the novel's final pages, which culminate in the famous (and cynical) words "Isn't it pretty to think so?" The eruptions of morbidity, doubleness, and self-betrayal have been construed as evidence of a "death wish" on Hemingway's part.[19] But they are less manifestations of psychological disorder than an index to the repressed dimension of writing. They represent the retribution of textuality on the fetishizing of the depthless visual, language's ultimate loyalty to language and a prophecy of the imminent intrusion of the verbal into the motion pictures themselves (which occurred a year later, with *The Jazz Singer*).

Writing has been associated throughout the American tradition with inaccessibility and disappearance. Hemingway's attempt to clear away these inherent properties of script is eroded by his own descriptions of the literary process. The fish at Burguete, laid out on the ground in a neat row like words on a page, are lifeless; the bullfighting scene in which Romero's clarity of line evokes authorial grace results in the slaying of the animal. Even flight to the optical cannot annul the linkage of writing with extinction.

The ghosts of the canon insinuate themselves into Hemingway's novel as the love affair of the printed word with absence and the unknowable. Grammatology returns, as it were, to glamorize death; to sour interpersonal relations with moral decay; and to topple *The Sun Also Rises* from its sunlit perch into an abyss of night. Hemingway, who meant, like Don Manuel, the fireworks king, to illuminate the heavens, leaves us with writing's indeterminacy, a confounding and unintelligible blankness at the core of his narrative.

But blankness, or the ghostly, has its redeeming value, and this may be nowhere more true than in the writings by and about American blacks that we will look at next. A snapshot of a black boxer from *The Sun Also Rises* makes a good bridge to our discussion, among other reasons because the figure of the physical fighter—a boxer in Ellison and Roth, a wrestler in Douglass—has such a prominent place in the African-American tradition. Bill Gorton describes a prizefight he attended in Vienna where a "noble-looking nigger" thrashed a local favorite. As the hometown crowd roared its disapproval, the victorious black tried "to make a speech" to the angry whites. The result was a full-fledged riot. "Can't knock out Vienna boy in Vienna," Bill explains (p. 71). It is a lesson African-American literature has always known. If, as a black, you fight to win, you had better be prepared either to put your life on the line (Douglass); or to disappear by becoming invisible (Ellison); or to pass as a white man (Roth). And if you insist on delivering a speech to your enraged audience, it had better be one that emulates the absence and indirection of writing.[20]

CHAPTER 7

Race/Erasure:
Douglass to Roth

"Trust no man."[1] So counsels Frederick Douglass in the founding document of the black literary canon. Douglass's words denominate *illegibility* as the originary impetus of this countertradition. Survival trumps candor, and survival necessitates silence and dissimulation. African-American texts are always already in what I have called the "Constitution" mode: they contest a hegemonic transparency by adopting the rhetorical strategies of the federal compact (reticence, disguise, obscurity). Many minority works, like Douglass's, self-consciously embrace the protection of a disembodied scriptability. The founding father subtitles his narrative of the life of an American slave *Written by Himself,* and he recognizes that the sentence of disappearance imposed on his people as an affliction can be, in its very severity, a strength and a refuge. In the hands of white writers, too, the presence of "blackness" can operate aesthetically as an obstruction, a collapsed passageway, an insoluble riddle. It has worked its disruptive magic on popular forms, such as the detective story, which are structurally dedicated to dispelling the unknown.

The ironies are so multiple that even a partial cataloguing feels presumptuous. One might cite, for example, the apparent oddity that the most rarefied artworks of the culture share with some of the most disadvantaged a refusal of accessibility. Or that the white canon's discovery of writing's seclusion, in "The Revelation of the Scarlet Letter," has never had to be learned by a people habituated by law, custom, and endurance to hiding in plain sight. Or that those who take heart from the Declaration's faith in self-evident equality find sanctuary in documentary ambiguities more suggestive of the Constitution. But rather than compile a list, and in the confidence that further ironies will accumulate throughout this chapter, I will simply state my goal for a greatly abbreviated overview: to trace black resistance—and white resistance through blackface—to the oppression of being known. My subjects will include, besides Douglass, Mark Twain's mystery of race, *Pudd'nhead Wilson*, and the great exemplar of black illegibility, Ralph Ellison's *Invisible Man*, as well as Philip Roth's meditation on Ellison's classic in *The Human Stain*. A few remarks on the ideological construction of race, as opposed to class, as *the* American failing, will conclude the chapter.

Two first paragraphs establish the tenor of Douglass's autobiography. Paragraph "A," by William Lloyd Garrison, prefaces the text as a whole. It begins with the phrase "In the month of August, 1841" (p. 33), and it goes on to describe how the two men, ex-bondsman and renowned abolitionist, met at an antislavery convention in Nantucket. Garrison's assurance about the date of this first encounter forms a stark contrast to paragraph "B," the dozen or so sentences with which Douglass begins to narrate his life. The former slave does not know his birthday, he confesses immediately, "never having seen any authentic record containing it." Ignorant of his age, he can offer no more than a rough guess: he is somewhere between twenty-seven and twenty-eight years old. His father's identity is also a mystery to him, and although he knew his mother, he never set eyes on her "by the light of day. She was with me in the night" only (pp. 41–42).

The slave is excluded from the clarities and knowledges that define human (and American) experience. Douglass registers time not as a system of coherent numbers and dates but as an animal knows it, according to the imprecise succession of the seasons. The darkness in which he lies down beside his mother is an emblem of his relegation to eternal benightedness. On one level, the purpose of the *Narrative* is to secure for the freedman the same legibility that whites take for granted. Douglass reports with pride that he fled his chains for good "on the third day of September, 1838" (p. 143): the birthdate of his freedom. The last words of the book reaffirm his entrance into numerical certitude. Douglass emulates the Founders who affixed their signatures to the Declaration of Independence on July 4, 1776, a date remembered with gratitude by every American: "I subscribe myself, FREDERICK DOUGLASS. Lynn, Mass., April 28, 1845."

Literacy, as in signing his name, is Douglass's redemption in the *Narrative*. Nicely capturing its spatial implications, he calls literacy "the pathway from slavery to freedom" (p. 78). It is the potent technology monopolized by the master class and proscribed to the enslaved. In Douglass's introductory remarks on age, written records get the better of oral memory; they are a repository of truth and accuracy. I want to focus on a trio of moments in the *Narrative* that elucidate additional meanings of literacy for Douglass and that map, as it were, the modifying, if not indeed the dethroning, of reading and writing's identification with legibility. The three incidents, which I will take up in the order that they appear, direct us to literacy as a spur to consciousness; as a defense for the body; and as a mechanism of ambiguity. The last meaning in particular suggests the Constitution, not the Declaration, as a cultural precedent (and the authors of the government charter also took the step of signing or "subscribing" their names).

In the first passage, Douglass describes the songs in which the bondsmen express the ineradicable sadness of their lot. The account can be interpreted—with Douglass's encouragement—as a near parable of literacy's nurturing of reflection. The wild sounds, he writes, reveal more about the evils of slavery "than the reading of whole volumes of philosophy on the subject would do." The oral appears to reassert itself against the cogency of texts; but Douglass swiftly undercuts this impression by pointing out that when he was a slave, he had no grasp of "the deep meaning of those rude and apparently incoherent songs. I was myself within the circle; so that I neither saw nor heard as those without might see and hear. They told a tale of woe which was then altogether beyond my feeble comprehension" (p. 57).

Like Hester Prynne listening from the marketplace to Dimmesdale's sermon, and intuiting the undercurrent of guilt that eludes the congregation, Douglass needs to stand back to appreciate the message of the songs. Proximity does not yield the subtext. (The plantation owners misconstrue the chants as proof of the blacks' contentment.) Douglass achieves full understanding only as "I am writing these lines," at a temporal and spatial distance, and the memory overwhelms him with sympathy for his still-suffering brethren. Anyone curious about "the soul-killing effects of slavery" should consult the songs, but as Douglass now does, with the advantage of mediation. He (or she) should become a kind of reader, as Douglass is now a writer, and listen at a remove, with the perspective necessary for enlightened comprehension. He should "place himself in the deep pine woods, and there . . . in silence, analyze the sounds that shall pass through the chambers of his soul" (p. 58).

For slavery itself does not awaken Douglass to the injustice of his plight. Consciousness comes to him from reading a book. That work, *The Columbian Orator*—the very title of which records the translation of speech into writing—enables him to pierce the fog of convention and recognize the seemingly superior race of masters for what they really are, nothing but "a band of successful robbers" (p. 84). Moreover, literacy is the cause around which Douglass rallies his fellow blacks. Teaching them how to read forges a sense of community among the slaves that defies their scattered, dehumanized condition and emboldens them to plot their flight from bondage.

But incitement to reflection, the most important gift of literacy, may not be its most strategic contribution to black survival. To be "without the circle" is to be invisible or incorporeal, to inhabit the state of absence that demarcates communication in writing from oral interchange. Truthful speech can be lethal to the defenseless slave. When the master asks how he is treated, the slave dare not reply honestly for fear of being sold into more terrible servitude, stolen from his family "by a hand more unrelenting than death. This is the penalty of telling the truth, of telling the simple truth, in answer to a series of plain questions." Douglass invokes the maxim "A still tongue makes a wise head" (p. 62). There are times, though, when utterance is unavoidable, when the tongue must break its silence. And if the slave is to speak frankly without exposing himself to physical retaliation, he must do so through the medium of script.

Our second passage, in documenting the helplessness of the slave, hints at the protection writing offers to the vulnerable flesh. As a youngster on the plantation, Douglass often went without adequate food, but he suffered most from the cold, having no shoes or jacket to wear, and no bed to sleep in at night. He would have died from the winter's freezing temperatures, he believes (this was in Maryland), had he not crawled into an empty corn bag and covered his head while leaving his feet exposed. "My feet have been so cracked with the frost, that the pen with which I am writing might be laid in the gashes" (p. 72). The pen, figure of literacy, is placed in the brittle and damaged flesh, almost an act of incorporation. (Our next episode will entail the actual ingestion of a piece of paper with words inscribed on it.) Writing, Douglass seems to be suggesting, has the power to heal the body, to safe-guard and nurse it back to health after the deprivations of enslavement. This is true, literally, in that the bondsman could not complain in person about the cold; he can protest through the writtenness of his autobiography at the remove, and the relative safety, of a thousand miles from the South. But the merger of writing implement with "cracked feet" implies a symbolic use of script, too, a subversive intervention in the regime of presence.

Our last episode develops the implications of writing "within the circle." Douglass has joined a number of other slaves in planning an escape, and as the most literate he is entrusted with forging the passes they will need in case they are spotted by patrols. But the conspiracy is betrayed, and the would-be runaways are seized before they can put their scheme into opera-tion. A mistress denounces Douglass as the ringleader, and an enraged con-stable demands a search "for the protections which he had understood Fred-erick had written for himself and the rest." At this point, with Douglass in mortal danger, "Henry [a fellow captive] inquired of me what he should do with his pass. I told him to eat it with the biscuit, and own nothing; and we passed the word around, '*Own nothing*,' and '*Own nothing!*' said we all" (p. 128). The captured slaves swallow their passes and maintain a unified front under examination; all deny ever intending to run away. Douglass is returned to Baltimore, learns the trade of caulking, and within a few years effects his final escape to the North

Why label this resistance "writing inspired" when on its face it is noth-ing more than lying in self-defense? Because Douglass himself insists on the connection; because he represents "owning nothing," or misowning or disowning, as inextricable from the absorption of writing by the body. For Douglass, obfuscation is an act of informed consciousness, not a simple un-reflexive prevarication but a willful, calculated, and "scripted" gesture of de-fiance. It is "writing" with the mouth, being within and without the circle at the same time. Douglass commented earlier on how the slaves routinely "suppress the truth rather than take the consequences of telling it" (p. 62). But speech modeled on writing is not simply falsifying or withholding in-formation. It is one element in a unified strategy, a single skirmish in an all-consuming struggle for emancipation. Let us not forget that the textuality devoured with the biscuit, and metabolized into the eater's bloodstream, is a pass (or "pathway from slavery to freedom"). With the act of incorpora-tion, the bondsman figuratively internalizes intellectual liberty; he converts his ignorance about himself, about his age and parentage, into the inability of others to possess his mind. No longer an object of knowledge, he be-comes the subject who refuses to be known.

The injunction to "trust no man" extends beyond the South. Its re-quirement of obscurity sharply differentiates Douglass's testifying on behalf of the slaves from the appeals of white abolitionists, who exalt truth-telling without qualification and even admit to their participation in the Under-ground Railroad. Douglass deplores such candor as effectively transforming the subterranean pathway to freedom into "the *upperground railroad*" and so giving aid to those who would intercept it. (Douglass's defense of the "underground" as an essential dimension of black experience anticipates Ellison's unnamed narrator writing *his* autobiography from a basement "hole" where he is invisible.) He himself will say nothing about the railroad, either in the *Narrative* or in his public lectures, but instead will "keep the merciless slaveholder profoundly ignorant of the means of flight adopted by the slave" (p. 138).

Douglass's appreciation of reserve led him to a second break with Gar-risonian abolitionism: over the relevance of the Constitution to the anti-slavery struggle. In this, too, in his fealty to the government compact, the author of the *Narrative* stands at the fountainhead of the African-American tradition. (He again foreshadows Ellison, whose protagonist's grandfather learned the entire document by heart.) To Garrison, the Constitution was fatally tainted by its compromises with slavery (such as the provision for re-turning fugitives). Garrison appealed to the moral absolutism, the higher law, of the Declaration against the Constitution, which he excoriated as a covenant with hell. Douglass refused to follow his mentor here. He became a convert to the views of Lysander Spooner, an antebellum thinker who in-sisted that the spirit of the Constitution was firmly emancipatory, as indi-cated by its preamble. The former runaway, steeping himself in legal theory, wrote a concurring pamphlet titled *The Constitution of the United States: Is It Pro-Slavery or Anti-Slavery?* (1860).[2]

Douglass's endorsement of the polity's blueprint expressed his com-mitment to action in the public or civic sphere. But his embrace of the

Constitution can also be understood as a reaffirmation of multivocal complexity. It is consistent with Douglass's digesting of the principle of script, his resolution not to expose all but instead to see "in every white man an enemy, and in almost every coloured man cause for distrust" (p. 144). Douglass takes suspicion of others and unremitting self-concealment as the givens of African-American life. He thus intimates a view of the self as permanently divided and fundamentally opaque, a presumption of interior depth that at once prefigures and problematizes the Americanization of Freudian thought.

M ark Twain was Freud's favorite American writer. The fondness had many causes, and *Pudd'nhead Wilson* puts a good number on display: the irreverent wit; the dark view of human nature in Wilson's calendar; the addiction to doubling (Freud wrote extensively on the doppelganger). Freud may also have savored Twain's debunking of the mystery form. *Pudd'nhead Wilson*, as all readers know, solves the riddle of Judge Driscoll's murderer by exposing his nephew Tom as a black man, switched in the cradle with the rightful heir; in doing so, the novel sows more confusion and unhappiness than illumination. Some puzzles, it would appear—and they are the most intriguing ones—lie outside the expertise of the police, or even the percipient private eye. They call for a specialist in human motivation equipped with the insights of psychoanalysis. Freud did not hesitate to compare his method—to his advantage—with that of the crime solver.

Before pursuing these psychological themes in fuller detail, I want to look at Twain's meditation on, and quarrel with, American legibility. *"October 12, the Discovery,"* reads one of the late entries in Wilson's calendar. "It was wonderful to find America, but it would have been more wonderful to miss it."[3] This is one of just two entries with a date, a conspicuous omission in a calendar, and the absence hints at the dismantling of certainties, numerical and otherwise, in Twain's revision of the detective story. (The other entry is April 1, "the day upon which we are reminded of what we are on the other three hundred and sixty-four" [p. 153].) *Pudd'nhead Wilson* takes place in the 1830s and 1840s, the era of slavery, and it depicts the antebellum South as a "blood" society where birthright counts as much as or more than it does in the Old World. But Twain composed the novel in 1893, and the persistence of obsession with lineage and birth—terms Twain invokes repeatedly in the preface and postscript—suggests an ongoing Southernization (or Bellegardization, to recall *The American*) that by the fin de siècle was turning the entire country into a carbon copy of Europe. What gives the book its radical edge, though, is not Twain's defense of democratic merit against pedigree; it is his questioning of mobility as an improvement over quasi-feudal stasis.

As emphasized previously, the 1890s formalized division between the races. The decade completed the unmaking of Reconstruction. *Plessy v. Ferguson*, the infamous segregation decision of 1896, was a capstone, but the processes of disenfranchisement and Jim Crowism had been gathering speed since 1877, when federal troops abandoned the South. "New" immigration, breakneck urbanization, and the hectic pace of industrial change engulfed the country in disorder; but black and white at least no longer commingled but were once again inhabiting separate zones. Standards of legibility patrolled racial boundaries, keeping the lines clear and distinct, even if—or, more probably, because—the principle was under pressure everywhere else.

Twain's novel looks back in time in order to expose contemporaneous efforts at caste precisionism. At first blush, the text and its eponymous hero appear to bear out the pretensions of a reinvigorated racism, as Pudd'nhead Wilson employs the most recent scientific techniques, in this case fingerprints, to prove the reliability of "one-droppism." But the disastrous results of Wilson's "revelation"—Tom is sold down the river, and Chambers, restored to his white patrimony, can neither read nor write, "and his speech was the basest dialect of the Negro quarter" (p. 166)—suggest that policing the racial dyad brings no more clarity (or happiness) than does the intermixture of races. In his concluding "Author's Note," Twain describes his original manuscript as an analogous "tangling" of lines, the story of Roxy, Wilson, Tom, and Chambers and the unrelated story of the Italian twins being mixed up with each other. He claims to have separated the two tales for publication with "a kind of literary Caesarian operation" (p. 169)—an act of violence that afflicted both fictions with numerous incoherences and lacunae and that parrots the radically opposite fates available to European immigrants and African-Americans. The two narratives, which Twain brought out as a single volume in 1894, are discrete yet inextricable, much as they were in the larger culture: *The Tragedy of Pudd'nhead Wilson and the Comedy of Those Extraordinary Twins.* As the age was a tragedy for blacks, so it was a comedy in the formal sense for white foreigners: it had a happy ending. Even new immigrants were "allowed" to assimilate and enjoy the fruits of a social mobility forbidden to the freedmen.

Wilson's miraculous rise from town dunce to the serenaded hero of Dawson's Landing could be construed as a celebration, however qualified, of opportunity. In actuality, the eponymous hero's vindication both suggests the ethnic narrowness of Horatio Algerism and reaffirms the infrangible tie between white advancement and black subordination. In the 1890s, the unaccustomed diversity among whites elicited theories of ranking *within* the race, with Nordics and Anglo-Saxons "scientifically" classified as superior to Slavs, "Hebrews," Italians, "Celts," and other groups.[4] Wilson, Twain tells us, "was a young fellow of Scotch parentage" (p. 24), and his success marks the limits and not the enlargement of ethnic opportunity. The Scotsman's social trajectory contrasts with the near lynching of Luigi and Angelo Capello, who encounter as much bigotry as adulation in the New World. Judge Driscoll variously belittles the twins as riffraff, "peanut peddlers," and "organ-grinders bereft of their brother monkey" (p. 126). By the tale's end, it is no wonder that they have had their fill of America and returned to Europe.

Moreover, Wilson's elevation is predicated on Tom's plunge. The former "pudd'nhead" becomes "a made man for good" (p. 165) by cracking the puzzle of the racial impersonator's identity and thus consigning the "falsely called Thomas à Becket Driscoll" (p. 163) to permanent enslavement—an almost unprecedented fall from white pseudo-aristocrat to subhuman piece of property. *Almost* unprecedented, because a curious bit of doubling is at work in Twain's text. Tom himself could not thrive in Dawson's Landing without having caused another person, the unfortunate Chambers, to enact precisely the descent from white privilege to black chattel that he suffers at the hands of Wilson, who replicates his victim's "theft" of status. Judge Driscoll, let us recall, lectured Tom on the "sacredness" of a secret: "A man's secret is still his own property, and sacred, when it has been surprised out of him" (p. 120). But Wilson shows no scruples about surprising Tom's secret out of him and robbing another man of his property.[5] The white "comedy" always necessitates the black "tragedy."

It is a significant detail that Wilson *dreams* the solution to the murder mystery. The fact that the "revelation" of Tom's race emerges from the detective's "unconsciousness" (p. 153) points to layers of interiority that confound the very idea of a stable identity. Beyond the structural doubling—his repetition of Tom's theft and displacement—Wilson's dream raises the possibility, even the likelihood, of an unacknowledged identification with the thief/murderer as the man whose rise he covets. He intuits Tom's usurpation because he wants to do a version of the same thing himself.

Fingerprinting purports to be an infallible science that can tell who a person is from his or her "natal autograph." Every human being supposedly carries this "sure identifier" from "birth to death" (p. 159). Wilson's dreamed discovery invites us to think of "natal autograph" as referring not exclusively to biological continuity, as in fingerprints, but also to the unconscious desires that define each individual and are constitutive of his or her uniqueness. That these desires make us who we are does not mean, of course, that we can command or comprehend them. While Freud sometimes thought the desires were accessible to insight, Twain on the whole did not. He saw them as a permanent enigma within the self. (So did Freud as time went on.) And both men tended to associate these inner drives churning just below consciousness and never quite entering that state with black people—or, more precisely, with the products of miscegenation.

I will cite a Freudian example from his essay "The Unconscious" (1915). Freud compares the most "highly organized" of instinctual impulses "with individuals of mixed race who, taken all round, resemble white men, but who betray their coloured descent by some striking feature or other, and on that account are excluded from society, and enjoy none of the privileges of white people."[6] In this passage, Freud uncannily echoes Roxy, who, reminding Tom that he is thirty-one parts white and one part black, attributes his cowardice at the prospect of a duel with Luigi to the minute fraction that is "de nigger in you!" (p. 109).

Twain agrees with Roxy and Freud to the extent that he equates his "passer" with primitive desires insistently demanding to be met. Tom, with his addictions to gambling, thieving, drinking, and other forms of dissolution, represents the "id" in the text. As a toddler, he motions at things and bawls "Awnt it!" (want it) at the top of his lungs (p. 40). (Is the near anagram of "Twain" deliberate?) As a boy, he commandeers Chambers as his proxy to fight and steal for him. And as a young man, he prowls about in disguise, at one moment a young girl, at another an old woman, in order to carry out his crimes with relative impunity—just as, according to the Freudian system, unacceptable, instinctual urges must cloak themselves in mufti in order to obtain a measure of satisfaction.

Pudd'nhead Wilson leaves ambiguous the question of whether this id-like behavior stems from Tom's drop of black blood or his spoiled upbringing as a "First Family of Virginia" scion. And that unknowability is Twain's crucial difference from Roxy and Freud: Tom, one-thirty-second part black, is above all else a question mark, a principle of illegibility, in Dawson's Landing. His function is to put into doubt every imaginable dogmatism about birth, race, and identity, including the supposition that one can gain and profit from knowledge about one's self. When Tom learns from Roxy that he is a "nigger," changed at birth with the real Driscoll, he takes the disclosure as a warning that he had better amend his conduct to avoid suspicion. He vows to change: "I take no more risks. I'll gamble no more. I'll drink no more. . . . It's the sure way, and the only sure way; I might have thought of that sooner—well, yes, if I had wanted to. But now, dear me, I've had a scare this time, and I'll take no more chances. Not a single chance more!" (p. 107). This pledge and subsequent ones are swiftly broken, and Tom's altered character proves a chimera. The reason is simple, according to Twain: "He did not know himself" (p. 76).

In the end it is that self-ignorance, the ineluctable mystery at the core of his being, that does in Tom Driscoll. Not even Wilson's science of fingerprints rivals the "unconsciousness" as a force for bringing down the impostor. Indeed, Tom would never have been found out had his own inner demons not compelled him to expose himself. Having committed the murder in a woman's dress, he burns the clothes and discards the ashes to eliminate any possibility of detection. "Nearly always in cases like this," he reflects, "there is some little detail or other overlooked, some wee little track or trace left behind, and the detection follows; but here there's not even the faintest suggestion of a trace left." The sole evidence is an unknown woman who does not even exist; only someone who could "track a bird through the air in the dark" has a chance of pinning the crime on Tom (p. 150).

But Driscoll is the clairvoyant who convicts himself. We are told early on that he is "ironical of speech, and given to gently touching people on the raw" (p. 47). As the narrative progresses, the "gentleness" of Tom's taunting evolves into outright sarcasm at the expense of others. His relish for irony looks increasingly self-destructive as it tempts him into situation after situation that threatens his safety. For example, Tom baits Constable Blake about his inability to catch the "old woman" who has been conducting raids on the town's houses. "Has anything gone wrong with the detective business?" he asks, causing Blake to redden with anger. He then turns on Wilson and makes the lawyer wince with jibes about his "revolutionary" method for apprehending criminals (pp. 115–16). And the evening before the trial, he insanely visits Wilson in search of "good entertainment." Just a few hours away from being completely in the clear, his act of homicide another of the world's "permanent mysteries" (p. 142), Tom cannot help himself from goading Wilson "with an exasperating word or two of sympathy and commiseration now and then" (p. 151). He picks up the lawyer's strips of glass and leaves the prints that condemn him.

All of which is to say that Tom Driscoll *wants* to be discovered. ("Awnt it!") When he faints at Wilson's courtroom summation, the lawyer exclaims, "He has confessed" (p. 163). In actuality, the murderer has been confessing for some time without knowing it. For whatever reason—guilt over having killed his uncle or perhaps a wish to acknowledge his true identity—Tom has incautiously strewn clues in the path of those most intent on finding the criminal. His "Imp of the Perverse," Poe's term for the compulsion, has driven him to betray the very secret his conscious mind had every reason to hide.

We are all figures of "mixed race," Twain seems to suggest, beings of multiple lineage who are "separated" at birth by socialization from our most objectionable impulses. Yet the urges persist, and they continue to shape us even as we labor to disavow them. We are irrevocably "twain," creatures of illicit desire: Clemens and Twain, Chambers and Tom, white and black, consciousness and unconsciousness, ego and id. The classic Freudian categories belong on the list because Twain's novel so thoroughly imbricates the conundrum of race with the predicament of selfhood. The classic Freudian confidence in the therapeutic benefits of unearthing is another matter, however. *Pudd'nhead Wilson* does not believe in a solution to either of its quandaries. Tom's wordless confession of his hidden identity is the narrative's culminating catastrophe. No healing ensues from the electrifying revelation of guilt. Pudd'nhead's truth, his light, is darkness.

I *nvisible Man* is an act of illumination. On the most literal level, Ellison's unnamed narrator strives to banish the darkness by irradiating his basement quarters with electricity siphoned from Monopolated Light and Power. More ambitiously, the text is a coming into sight of the occluded race. Published in 1952, two years before *Brown v. Board of Education*, the Warren Court decision mandating school desegregation, the novel participates in the midcentury struggle to extend the rights of legibility to black Americans. It narrates the life of a young intellectual as he journeys from the

South to Harlem, flirts with the Communist Party, and eventually elects to "hibernate" underground. The final pages promise that Ellison's protagonist will emerge from the depths to publish his story to the world.

Ellison's goal was to fashion an African-American hero who was not a criminal or a primitive, and who, like his pale-skinned countrymen, "could think as well as act" (p. xxi). In the novel's second sentence, this character declares that he is "not a spook like those who haunted Edgar Allan Poe."[7] A resonant moment: the phrasing looks back to the nineteenth-century canon and ahead to Roth's *The Human Stain*, where the passer Coleman Silk loses his teaching post for inadvertently referring to blacks as "spooks"; and it strongly evokes the context of the book's appearance at the height of the Korean War, when Senator Joe McCarthy loosed his paranoid campaign to root out Communist spies or spooks from the government. Invisible man's grandfather brings the several meanings of "spook" together on his deathbed: since the end of Reconstruction, he says, he has been "a spy in the enemy's country" (p. 16). A spook is a ghost is a spy is a black is invisible.

It would be possible to elaborate at length on the ways that communism, which figures in Ellison's narrative as the autonomy-denying Brotherhood, acted as a catalyst for black visibility or integration (or representation as a thinking being). As the ideology of class, communism has a not-so-disguised connection to race, and its appeal as a universalist doctrine persuaded many Americans that the country had to improve its record on minorities to prevail in the global competition.[8] (Roth's novel, which includes a Vietnam War veteran as an important character, implies a similar recognition. The civil rights legislation of 1964 and 1965 passed Congress as involvement in Southeast Asia escalated.) But another historical confluence may be more relevant for this discussion: the fact that the 1950s, the beginnings of black emergence from behind the veil, were the heyday in the United States for Freudian psychoanalysis. In *Invisible Man*, psychological themes often seem as bound up with racial ones as they do in Twain's deformation of the detective genre. And Ellison follows Frederick Douglass, whose portrait his narrator cherishes, in relating those themes to the "disembodied voice" of literature (p. xiv).

Ellison, who worked for a time as an assistant to the celebrated analyst Harry Stack Sullivan, appears initially to accept the equation of negritude with the id—or if not negritude at least that (substantial) portion of the black masses who qualify, in the veteran's view, as a peasantry. They know "things about life," the veteran tells Mr. Norton. "Such things as most peasants and folk peoples almost always know through experience, though seldom through conscious thought" (p. 91). Trueblood is a notorious case in point: he not only knows without thinking but seems scarcely distinguishable from the unconscious, having committed the "dream-sin" (p. 62) of incest with his daughter. To Norton, the white benefactor whom invisible man has been chauffering around the countryside, Trueblood's act is doubly monstrous because it fulfills his inadmissible longings for his own daughter.

"You did it and are unharmed," he exclaims with a mixture of horror and envy. "You have looked upon chaos and are not destroyed" (p. 51). At the Golden Day, the always-astute vet labels Norton a "trustee of consciousness" (p. 89). Ellison's point, clearly, is that figures like Trueblood have been assigned the societal task of personifying the white man's forbidden desires, the chaos that consciousness would disavow.

Blackness as instinct has a salutary function in *Invisible Man* insofar as it brings repressed energies into the open (much as Roxy, in *Pudd'nhead Wilson*, is a wellspring of creative energy). Trueblood's perverse family arrangement is an astonishment to Norton and a source of shame to respectable blacks. But while Ellison hardly shares the embarrassed denial, neither does he uncritically endorse the alignment of dark skin color with the id. He shows the trope, which crops up again in the wild scene at the Golden Day, where the mental patients overthrow their attendant (the Supercargo/superego, in the text's pun),[9] to be a construct that blots out complexity and is in need of revision. Under the pressure of Ellison's art, the minority character metamorphoses from a surrogate for irrational urges into a sign of the inscrutable. Blackness comes to be linked with unfathomable complexity and depth.

The prevalence of dreams in the book underscores the association—and makes it impossible to overlook the danger for white Americans who refuse to perceive otherness in society and, figuratively, within themselves. Again, Ellison folds race into psyche, "dreams" being one of the hallmarks of black aspiration, as well as the domain of the unconscious. (Martin Luther King's "I Have a Dream" speech is an imperishable installment on the dream motif.) The Reverend Barbee, preacher at Founders' Day, hails the black college attended by invisible man as a "dream" "made flesh" and instilled "in the hearts of the people" (pp. 120, 124). More commonly, the recurrent dreams bristle with peril. (Trueblood committed his "dream-sin" while dreaming of another sin, sex with "a white lady" [p. 57].) Climactic turns in the plot regularly leave the protagonist with the impression that he inhabits a waking dream. On the night of the riot, Ras the Destroyer appears a "figure more out of a dream than out of Harlem, . . . yet real, alive, alarming" (p. 556). At the end of his adventures, free of illusions, invisible man dreams his own castration/blinding. And at the beginning of his narrative, he—or rather an anonymous white man—has the nightmare that sets the agenda of lethal mysteries rising from the depths. The white person bumps into invisible man and, believing himself "in the midst of a waking nightmare," spits out a curse. The narrator brutally retaliates, reducing the insolent white to a bloody mass on the pavement. A dream "made flesh" indeed: "Something in this man's thick head had sprung out and beaten him within an inch of his life" (p. 5).

But immediate physical response is not the hero's mètier. Thought defines him more than action, and growing comfort with elusiveness, including his own, causes him to shift his loyalties from speech to script. Orality, as in Douglass's memoir, simplifies multiplicity. As the discourse of presence, the oral too often places the narrator in harm's way. He delivers five speeches in the course of the novel—the first follows the blindfolded "battle royal," suggesting the propinquity of direct utterance and action—and by the end he has renounced them all as provocations to senseless violence.

As an orator for the Brotherhood, "chief spokesman of the Harlem District" (p. 359), invisible man realizes that he has been "a tool" (p. 533) of the Party, inciting his fellow blacks to suicidal riot. Mind and reflection have nothing to do with the outbreak. The gathering crowd emits an inhuman "sound" like a "river at floodtide" (p. 535). Ras the Exhorter/Destroyer—and the conflation of verbal arousal with demolition could not be more explicit—eggs on the mob to "get guns and ammunition" (p. 556). Invisible man asserts his independence from such reductive oratory by hurling a spear that rips through Ras's cheeks and "locked his jaw" (p. 560). (Ellison is so determined for the reader not to miss his point that he belabors the symbolism.) Henceforth language at a distance will be the hero's only medium. He will become a speaker from the underground who communicates in print and not in person. A collaborator with the "disembodied" voice, he resolves "to put invisibility down in black in white" (p. 14). His famous concluding words continue the theme of incorporeality through a more modernized radio metaphor: "Who knows but that, on the lower frequencies, I speak for you?" (p. 581).

Rather like Arthur Dimmesdale, the preacher turned figurative writer whose ordeal initiates the canon, Ellison's protagonist learns to hide in plain sight. The lesson has been pressed on him from the outset by his grandfather's counsel of defiance within accommodation; but five hundred pages are required for him to master it. The veteran, too, understood the uses of concealment: "You're hidden right out in the open," he says to invisible man when they meet for the final time at the train station, "that is, you would be if only you realized it" (p. 154). *Invisible Man* is the evidence of the narrator's realization, his enactment of inaccessibility, or invisibility, in a work of prose fiction—in what Ellison, in his introduction, described as "the novel's capacity for telling the truth while actually telling a 'lie,' which is the Afro-American folk term for an improvised story" (p. xxii). To tell the truth in a lie is to acknowledge one's "twinness," to make script's duality as revelation and absence an integral part of one's personality. It is to "digest" the principle of writing.

Ellison's protagonist does just that. Early in the text he states, "When I discover who I am, I'll be free" (p. 243); but his confidence drains away as he recognizes the extent to which he has been used by others, and by blind men at that. No longer disclaiming his invisibility, the hero distances himself from all totalizing ideologies, the fantasy of a unitary, comprehensible identity included. One can no more know for certain who one is in Ellison's cosmos than consciousness can plumb the unconscious, white canvass black, Norton appropriate Trueblood. (Predictably, when invisible man reencounters Norton in a subway station at the end of the novel, the "trustee of consciousness" is baffled—and offended—by the narrator's claim to be his "destiny" [p. 578].) Invisible man writes, he puts it all down, because the medium allows him to "approach" the "nightmare" of his experience "through division. So I denounce and I defend and I hate and I love" (p. 580). "Only in division," he sums up what he has learned, "is there true health" (p. 576). True health: it is therapy, from Sullivan's quondam amanuensis, for a nation of sleepwalkers.

It is also a reaffirmation of the Constitution as a governing model. In the novel's epilogue, the hero decides that his grandfather's duplicitous advice "*must*" have meant "the principle on which the country was built." At first the language seems ambiguous: Is "the principle" in question the Declaration's "all men are created equal"? The narrator writes of the progenitors who "dreamed" the ideal "into being out of the chaos and darkness of the feudal past." Presumably the quoted phrase refers to the renunciation of human hierarchy, the underpinning of European feudalism, and indeed the narrator goes on to suggest that the Founders then "violated and compromised" their democratic faith by perpetuating slavery. Yet an instant later the Declaration's principle of equality—if that is what is meant here—has evolved into the body of foundational precepts enshrined in the government contract. His grandfather, continues the narrator, must have wanted him to affirm "the plan"—no longer the solitary principle but the whole plan—"in whose name we had been brutalized and sacrificed" (p. 574). An earlier remark about the grandfather corroborates this enlargement of reference. After Reconstruction the old man had been required to memorize "the entire United States Constitution as a test of his fitness to vote. He had confounded them all by passing the test, although they still refused him the ballot" (p. 315).[10]

I propose that the epilogue's apparent shift from the Declaration to the Constitution be read as emblematic, as a corollary to the hero's movement from being "an orator, a rabble rouser" (p. 14) to becoming a writer. Constitutional complication, for invisible man, is the political equivalent to his retailing of diversity in himself and others. The text-as-camouflage unites the legacy of the Founders—white as well as black, the federal charter as well as Douglass's *Narrative*—with the hero's conversion to the philosophy of his family patriarch. He lives as a spy or spook "in the enemy's country" because he preserves his experience in a book of literature.

Invisible Man marks the cultural formalization of a defining American difference, one anchored in the dearth of far-flung colonies and the presence at home of a large nonwhite population. Against sociologists who blamed the plight of blacks on their "high visibility" (p. xv), Ellison was one of the first to crystallize in language the genuine exceptionalism of the American racial experience. Because people of African descent were everywhere in the United States, they had to be made to disappear in thought if not in fact; their very pervasiveness was the precondition for their nonperception. The European powers, in contrast, had colonies in Asia and Africa peopled with racial others; but those alien beings seldom settled in the metropole, or they did so in relatively minor numbers. Nonwhites stood out in the European epicenters because there were so few of them, and they could be perceived, admitted into vision, because the great majority of their brethren were safely ensconced in foreign lands. The situations were the mirror images, the optical reversals, of each other.

Just as Ellison's book is in some respects the inversion of Frantz Fanon's *Black Skin, White Masks*, a classic psychological study of French colonialism published in the same year as *Invisible Man*. One could bracket the disagreements and marshal an array of common interests. Fanon, born in Martinique, trained in France, was a psychiatrist who sought in the *socius* causes for the high incidence of mental illness among blacks. He found the answer in the imposed sense of inferiority bred by colonial status. The Negro, Fanon argued, is always identified with "the lowest values." For whites, he or she serves to symbolize the "base and inferior" desires seething within the unconscious. The black person who buys into this paradigm equates his or her skin color with "ugliness, sin, darkness, immorality." "Hence a Negro is forever in combat with his own image," forever torn apart by loathing for what he represents.[11]

So far, a measure of common ground, although Ellison is more willing to construe the illicit power of blackness as a tonic. *Black Skin, White Masks* diverges most sharply from the American novel when Fanon's colonial finally makes his long-awaited journey to Europe. There he has no hiding place from "the burden of . . . corporeal malediction." His *visibility* damns him. Fanon relates the humiliation of his own encounter with chromatic objecthood:

> "Look, a Negro!" It was an external stimulus that flicked over me as I passed by. I made a tight smile.
>
>   "Look, a Negro!" It was true. It amused me.
>
>   "Look, a Negro!" The circle was drawing a bit tighter. I made no secret of my amusement.
>
>   "Mama, see the Negro! I'm frightened!" Frightened! Frightened! Now they were beginning to be afraid of me. I made up my mind to laugh myself to tears, but laughter had become impossible.[12]

The Negro in Europe is too conspicuous not to see. Vanishing is not a condition he would flee but a state he hungers for, as a relief from white contempt and from his own shame at his skin color. "I slip into corners," Fanon writes, ". . . I strive for anonymity, for invisibility. I will accept the lot, as long as no one notices me!"[13] An ocean away, Ellison agrees that "it is sometimes advantageous to be unseen." But as a black American, he cannot forget that invisibility as a lifetime sentence "is more often rather wearing on the nerves" (p. 3).

Fanon's book hardly acknowledges the United States. His principal contrast is between blacks and Jews, not between blacks in Europe and those in America.[14] From Jean-Paul Sartre and Marie Bonaparte, he takes the observation that whereas in the Old World the Jew is singled out as an exemplar of the demonic, the Negro fulfills much the same purpose in the New. But Fanon wishes to modify the contrast. Even the Holocaust—"a little family quarrel," as he sarcastically calls it—cannot equalize the fate of the two peoples, because the Jew always enjoys a "chance" not permitted to the black person. He "can be unknown in his Jewishness. . . . He is a white man, and, apart from some rather debatable characteristics, he can sometimes go unnoticed." The Negro, on the other hand, is the prisoner of his appearance; he can never really blend in. This biological determination produces a crippling reductionism: the black is identified with the body, the Jew with greed, cunning, intelligence. "In the case of the Jew," concludes Fanon, "one thinks of money and its cognates. In that of the Negro, one thinks of sex."[15]

Fanon's generalizing continues to slight the American exception, where racial passing has been a much-debated cultural phenomenon for three centuries. And while Jews and blacks have followed dissimilar paths in the United States, their fates have not infrequently been intertwined in ways indicating a commonality of experience and outlook. Roth's *The Human Stain*, issued in 2000, is a millennial commemoration of that kinship. The central character, Coleman Silk, is a light-skinned African-American from Newark who masquerades not simply as a white man but as a Jew. He makes himself into a signifier of mind by teaching classics at Athena College, marries a Jewish woman, and fathers a son who graduates from Brandeis! Meanwhile, Philip Roth, who also comes from Newark, performs a masquerade of his own. As a writer who has always wanted to put "the Id back in Yid," and who has spent his career resisting efforts to pigeonhole him, Roth merges into his protagonist: the Jew in blackface in Jewface. And like Ellison, whose novel he self-consciously builds on, Roth interprets the id to mean both raw, uncensored energies and, even more important, the impossibility of decoding others and one's self.

E veryone Knows." So Roth titles the first section of his book, giving a sinister and oppressive inflection to the American hostility to secrets. *The Human Stain* is a tale of knowing and not knowing, and a brief for the limits of what can be known. It takes place during its own moment of McCarthyite excess, Kenneth Starr's Chillingworth-like pursuit of President Clinton as a perjurious adulterer. (And we should bear in mind that Clinton, according to Toni Morrison's well-known quip, was our first "black" president.) Its debts to the canon are no less extensive than its gestures to the present. An incriminating letter (the one in which Delphine Roux charges Silk with erotic transgressions, as well as a follow-up e-mail), a tale of Massachusetts "adultery," a preoccupation with sex and detection: *The Scarlet Letter* is second only to *Invisible Man* among Roth's acknowledged predecessors. The nod to Ellison's book includes an African-American who boxes and who is literally invisible in his blackness, no one in his chosen life, including his wife and children, having any idea of his true racial lineage. Roth adds the tribute of a meditation on the meanings of "spooks"—the title Silk plans to give his unwritten memoir of his firing—as a word connoting blacks, ghosts, spies, and sleuths or spy catchers. Nathan Zuckerman, Roth's alter ego, volunteers for the last role. He dedicates himself to getting to the bottom of Silk's identity and proving that his friend and Faunia Farley were not the innocent victims of an automobile accident but the targets of a murder carried out by Faunia's ex-husband, Les.

Faunia, as her name suggests, is the text's icon for forbidden desires, for id-like animality, for the stain or "contaminant of sex."[16] She has no interest in the sentimentality of love, she tells the seventy-year-old Coleman: she craves only physical coupling. Zuckerman first sets eyes on her when she is milking cows, and she delivers several affectionate speeches to crows, including one to the bird with whom she leaves the ring given to her by her human lover.

When Delphine Roux gets wind of the affair between Silk and Faunia, she rushes to denounce it as the exploitation, by an elderly and immoral professor, of a defenseless female worker. To Roth, Roux's campaign exemplifies American prudery and "id-baiting" (to mint a phrase) at their worst. Roux is a product of European high cultural hauteur transported to the American academy. Her inveterate sanctimony and disdain for Silk evoke the surveillance of sexual McCarthyism, as well as Roth's own quarrel with the literary police who have denounced him for indecency ever since he published *Portnoy's Complaint* in 1969. Identity politics hovers behind this blast at academic culture. Reducing the individual to a single trait, the politics of identity is a left version of ascriptive transparency, the bête noire of Roth's oeuvre. (Roux, perhaps as a critique of her flattening of others, is the least rounded characterization in the novel, and Roth comes uncomfortably close to ascribing her witch-hunting to sexual frustration.)

The Human Stain begins with an epigraph from Sophocles' *Oedipus the King*, and Roth's novel imitates the Greek tragedy in locating its sexual violations at the center of a mystery story. No word gets more reiterated in the book than "secret." Silk's passing is of course the main piece of concealment. Roth refuses to render judgment on his protagonist's racial "betrayal," viewing it instead as another act in the classic American drama to "become a new being. To bifurcate" (p. 342). Coleman's talent at impersonation is a *gift*, according to the narrative voice, "like being fluent in another language—it's being somewhere that is constantly fresh to you" (p. 136). Coleman's brother Walt is allotted the voice of condemnation, and honesty compels Roth/Zuckerman not to scant the pain of "upping and leaving— and the energy and cruelty that rapturous drive demands" (p. 342). But on balance, and it is really no contest, we are asked to take Coleman's deception as legitimate and his secret as justified, not solely, perhaps not principally, because a black raised in the 1950s had as much right as anyone else to succeed and could only do so in whiteface but because identity is a riddle beyond solution, and certainly beyond the power of others to apprehend. As with the previous works considered in this chapter, dark skin pigment is the color of indeterminacy.

Roth lets Zuckerman declaim this thesis in the scene where he sees Faunia and Coleman at a concert rehearsal at Tanglewood. To Delphine Roux's certainty that "everyone knows," Zuckerman's response is unequivocal: "*Nobody* knows."

> What we know is that, in an unclichéd way, nobody knows anything. You *can't* know anything. The things you *know* you don't know. Intention? Motive? Consequence? Meaning? All that we don't know is astonishing. Even more astonishing is what passes for knowing. (p. 209)

What "passes" for knowing in this fiction is no more reliable than what passes for white or passes for black. The mild genuflection to the detective form—"it's the secret that's his magnetism," Zuckerman announces when he embarks on his quest to "solve" Coleman (p. 213)—deconstructs itself. Confidence in enlightenment cannot survive the narrative's own success at detection. Zuckerman realizes that his dead friend is no more accessible to him as a part African-American posing as a white man than he was as a Jewish classics professor sacked for a racial slur he did not intend. When Coleman's sister, Ernestine, finishes her "torrent of disclosure," Zuckerman supposedly has the answers he has been searching for. In actuality, the "facts" merely intensify his perplexity: "I couldn't imagine anything that could have made Coleman more of a mystery to me than this unmasking. Now that I knew everything, it was as though I knew nothing" (p. 333). Passing is the human condition, and to strip away the "false" identities under which people hide is to bring us no closer to the secret of who they (and we) are. For we are all bifurcated, as the creator of Tom Driscoll knew, all "twain."

The Facts (1988) is the title of a book in which Roth professes to lay before his readers the autobiographical origins of his fiction. Here at last, fed up with masks, he will bare the truth behind the many personae, self-portraits, and alter egos of "Philip Roth." But like so much else Roth has written, the book makes a mockery of the notion that literature of any kind can provide unvarnished revelation. One hundred fifty pages of unbosoming concludes with a long letter from Roth's fictional character Zuckerman, who charges his creator with indulging in "the disguises of autobiography." It can never be otherwise, the character says: "We always tell in order also not to tell."[17] He adds that Roth does a better job of explaining himself when he poses as Portnoy or Tarnopol or Zuckerman and tells the truth in a work of acknowledged falsehood.

The Human Stain marks a further stage in this process of occultation within disclosure, and for our purposes it is a culminating phase. Roth, secreting himself in Coleman Silk, integrates the white canon with the African-American logic of illegibility and brings the two traditions to a temporary summit. The climax is only temporary because the theme is sure to have future permutations. The American compulsion to expose will continue to beget a countervailing obstinacy to conceal, and Roth, writing at the height of the Clinton impeachment, has no illusions about the resilience of either pressure.

"America." It is the last word of Roth's novel and of the trilogy that also includes *American Pastoral* (1997) and *I Married a Communist* (1998).

I have argued throughout this book that race has historically been the great fault line of American visibility. In the final pages of this chapter, my aim is to complicate the argument by proposing that class, while not as salient a concern as it has been in European society and thought, has nevertheless been a persistent thread of continuity in the American fabric, and one as seldom brought into the light as racial otherness. Indeed, one could make the claim that race has obstructed the perception of social class, not just because, as in Tom Watson's Georgia, appeals to race prejudice have often served to paper over economic antagonisms between whites (a fact that Frederick Douglass found to be true on the Baltimore docks fifty years before the Populists); or even because blacks have been disproportionately represented among America's poor, so that efforts to regulate the largest racial minority have also had the effect of disciplining the labor supply.[18] Rather, a third, related, process of eclipsing has been more thoroughgoing and less manifest. It has constructed race and class as mutually exclusive yet integrally related phenomena, and it has calibrated their significance with the United States and with Europe. What makes the ideological formation of special interest here is that the biggest best-seller in American literary history was instrumental in diffusing and consolidating it for the nineteenth-century chattering classes.

The work I am referring to is Harriet Beecher Stowe's *Uncle Tom's Cabin* (1852), whose influence may have been as relevant for political history as it was for literature and the Civil War. The construct Stowe helped to naturalize is stated explicitly in chapter 19, about halfway through the novel; but it permeates the entire text and blinds the author, as well as the social group she speaks for, to the class coordinates of their abolitionism. I do not intend to pillory *Uncle Tom's Cabin*, as does so much contemporary criticism, for being insufficiently enlightened on the issue of race. It is quite enough for any book, in my opinion, to have helped galvanize a reluctant nation to excise the cancer of slavery. Contrary to the critical consensus, I am proposing that Stowe's championing of the oppressed is suspect in terms of class. Her racial progressivism harbors a thoroughgoing conservatism. The text's humanitarian program rests on social attitudes redolent of Old World hierarchy and inextricable from an ascendant industrial capitalism.

Which is to say that Stowe's novel can stand as a kind of test case for the thesis of racism's inextricability from democratic egalitarianism. Stowe inverts the usual problematic. She is not a believer in equality who sneaks back caste in the form of race, but an advocate of black emancipation who clings to stratification among whites. Parity (of Africans with Caucasians) and subordination (of social inferiors who do not know their place) go together for her as well, but in her reversal of the more familiar pattern she seems less American than European. This impression may need some revising in light of the cultural work Stowe performs. *Uncle Tom's Cabin* shows her evolving a point of view—relative tolerance toward racial others combined with haughtiness toward aspirants—that may be a minority position among her countrymen but has had a long history in American politics.

The normative paradigm emerges out of a dialogue between Augustine St. Clare and Miss Ophelia. Or perhaps the exchange should be called a "trialogue," since St. Clare relates at second hand the reasoning of his brother Alfred, as a third party to the discussion. What makes the class-Europe/race-America formula appear so irrefutable is that although St. Clare is himself appalled by slavery, he ends up ceding most of the argumentative ground to his brother, an unabashed racist and proponent of the strong devouring the weak. According to Alfred, every civilization deserving of the name must have a higher and a lower tier. It must have those who enjoy the wealth, education, leisure, and taste to appreciate art and culture, and to set a moral and polished tone for society as a whole. In Europe, and especially in Great Britain, this position is occupied by the aristocracy, along with other big landowners, manufacturers, and merchants (Alfred refers to the last three collectively as capitalists). In the United States, and especially in the slaveholding South, the upper echelon is formed by white people.[19]

At the lower end of the scale are the masses, those who carry out the backbreaking labor necessary to maintain the higher class in privileged circumstances. The workers are appropriated "body and bone, soul and spirit," to the "use and convenience" of their masters (p. 228). They are bereft of volition, stupefied by endless physical toil, and scarcely removed from a state of animality. In England and on the Continent, this condition describes the white laboring classes. (In France, Alfred later says approvingly, the inferior orders are known without euphemism as the *"canaille"* or the *"sans culottes"* [pp. 266–67].) And in America, the bottom tier is represented by the black bondsmen.

But surely, objects Miss Ophelia (a New Englander), Alfred's comparison discounts crucial differences. The English worker, unlike the slave, is free; he can quit and move away from his place of employment if he so desires. Nor can he be physically abused or parted from his family. The professedly democratic St. Clare sides with Alfred here, going so far as to agree that the great majority of slaves are actually better off than the typical English workingman.

> He is as much at the will of his employer as if he were sold to him [Augustine observes about the white laborer]. The slave-owner can whip his refractory slave to death,—the capitalist can starve him to death. As to

family security, it is hard to say which is the worst,—to have one's children sold, or to see them starve to death at home. (p. 228)

St. Clare cannot see his way around Alfred's social binary. The main revision he offers to his brother's formulation is that the degrading of the black slave is more painful, and potentially more harmful, to the planter class because the slaveholders, unlike English aristocrats and capitalists, live in such close proximity to their dependents.

Stowe both dissents from the analysis mapped out by St. Clare and endorses it. She considers it true that race is the American dilemma, but as an abolitionist, she favors emancipation of the oppressed Africans. Moreover, as a supporter of the ascendant Republican Party (and eventual backer of Lincoln), she can imagine a "third way" that Alfred's theory has no room for. Opponents of slavery, put on the defensive by apologetics like George Fitzhugh's *Cannibals All; or, Slaves without Masters* (1857), increasingly emphasized social mobility as the distinctive American alternative to either English hierarchy or Southern enslavement. Lincoln's famous rise from impoverished backwoodsman to national prominence and finally to the White House was the rallying cry of those who insisted that, at least in the North and West, the European model of class stasis did not apply. The energetic American workingman could acquire education and property and transform himself from a paid employee into an entrepreneur or professional. According to Stowe, the reality of mobility could override even the disadvantage of race. At the end of her novel, she supplies a list of some half dozen freedmen who have learned profitable trades such as furniture maker and dealer in real estate and accumulated fortunes worth as much as $30,000. The complement to Uncle's Tom cabin was the Kentucky log cabin in which the man who became the sixteenth president had been born.

With this amendment, one might propose the following generalization, still in the spirit of Alfred's thesis: whereas race has haunted American history, class is a European problem that has little relevance here. The Stowe-Lincoln consensus almost has it that class, understood as a fixed place in the social order, does not exist in the United States. There are rich and poor, to be sure, but no one is condemned to occupy a particular condition forever. The poor can better themselves, the affluent can lose their wealth. Class troubles the republic only as a kind of aftereffect of race, only insofar as dark skin pigment can stigmatize a group of persons as permanently as birth into a prescribed social rank governs people's lives in Europe.

We have encountered this position before, in Beaumont, in James, even to some degree in Roth. It is an ideologically laden bipolarism that contains a measure of truth but that *Uncle Tom's Cabin* exposes as flawed. In Stowe's case, the bipolarism conceals an elitist revulsion at odds with her own commitment to mobility. As early as the novel's first page, its second paragraph, Stowe communicates an antipathy to those who rise that is commensurate, by her own logic, with English mores rather than American ones. Change the setting from Kentucky, and the second paragraph would be perfectly at home in an English fiction of the 1840s or 1850s. In it, Stowe levels a diatribe against the slave trader Haley as an ill-bred parvenu lacking in the graces of civilization. Having already introduced Haley as a gentleman in the first paragraph, she now retracts the designation by belittling his fondness for gaudy colors in dress, his profusion of rings and gold chains, and his neglect of "Murray's Grammar," as well as his unselfconscious bursts of profanity. But what especially rankles Stowe are the trader's physicality and manner. She describes him as "a short, thick-set man, with coarse, common-place features" and "large and coarse hands." He has the "swaggering air of pretension which marks a low man who is trying to elbow his way upward in the world."

The phrase "low man" reverberates powerfully in a reformist narrative subtitled *Life among the Lowly*. For Stowe, justice demands that members of the African race, her prime example of a subordinate group, be lifted from the depths to which white greed and inhumanity have consigned them; but overdressed and badly mannered upstarts scaling the social ladder are another matter. *That* is one category of the "lowly" Stowe wants to lock into inferior status eternally. The drive to get ahead at any price, including through trafficking in human beings—and Mr. Shelby claims that Haley would "sell his own mother at a good percentage" (p. 34)—is a principle of darkness in the text, and the reader of that second paragraph might be excused for suspecting that avidity to succeed incites Stowe's indignation as much as or more than collusion with the "peculiar institution." Indeed, Stowe often speaks generously of individual slaveholders, many of whom she has no hesitation pronouncing authentic gentleman. Shelby is one, Augustine St. Clare is another, and the unnamed "gentleman of opulence and taste" (p. 342) from whose estate Simon Legree acquires his Red River plantation is a third.

Legree himself dwarfs Haley as a target of Stowe's dislike, and for many of the same reasons. This villain's vaguely ethnic surname evokes Beecher family nativism and hints at a century of anti-immigrant feeling among Republicans. (Harriet's father, Lyman Beecher, was the author of an anti-Catholic tract titled *A Plea for the West* [1835].) Crass, dissolute, uncultured, and tyrannical, Legree is emphatically not a gentleman: he began life as a common sailor and clawed his way into the affluence of plantation owner. His lofty station gives the lie to Alfred's slaveholder as guardian of civilized values. Legree and those like him—Haley the trader, Marks the catcher— are midcentury freaks of mobility, and they are becoming more common by the moment. If the Fugitive Slave Law prevails, according to Stowe, and "all the broad land between the Mississippi and the Pacific becomes one great market for bodies and souls, . . . the trader and the catcher may yet be among our aristocracy" (pp. 68–69). But such undeserved ascents are a grotesque disordering of natural hierarchy. There is something positively cross-species about their merger of laboring-class—no, subhuman—physiognomy and manners with substantial wealth. Stowe writes scornfully of the slave catcher Tom Loker: "Could our readers fancy a bull-dog come unto man's estate, and walking about in a hat and coat, they would have no unapt idea of the general style and effect of his physique" (p. 61). As for Legree, canine is too mild an epithet. Uncle Tom's murderer is short, "of gigantic strength," with a "round, bullet head," and stiff, wiry hair. His immense hands are "hairy, sun-burned, freckled, and very dirty, and garnished with long nails." He is less human being than beast, and Stowe likens him to an alligator and a rhinoceros (p. 379).

Here is the abhorrent side of mobility, as seen by one strand in the Republican coalition: it permits the unworthy to rise, to muscle or slither out of their rightful place. And this social mongrelism is not just an unfortunate side effect of slavery; it is a widespread phenomenon of the nineteenth century, with its "locomotive tendencies," rapid social change, and economic turbulence (p. 69).[20] It is impossible to ignore the class contempt in Stowe's picture of her evil characters, whose very bodies telegraph their "low" origins. Arguably, these aggressive individuals are *more* typed by genetic inheritance than are blacks; their animality is the essentialism of class.[21] Stowe, the daughter and sister of ministers, and the wife of a college professor, not surprisingly shared the biases of her middle-class, professional milieu, right down to a preference for tall, slender physiques and hands uncallused by manual labor. (Her milieu was prophetic of today's academy, which has tirelessly recycled Stowe's outlook, reproaching her for racial obtuseness but ignoring her condescension toward bounders.)

Stowe's prejudices, which the class-Europe/race-America binary cannot accommodate, were those not only of her social stratum but also of her political party, or of an influential segment of it. Neither Stowe nor Lincoln could foresee the large-scale industrialization of the postwar period, of course. Neither would have welcomed a society of rich and poor, Alfred St. Clare's upper-class capitalists and the mass of unskilled laborers, which the United States came more and more to resemble. But Republicans in the 1850s had already identified their Democratic adversaries (many of them, anyway) as pro-slavery, foreign-born, and lower class, and they had anointed themselves, in contrast, as the headquarters of business, gentility, and moral righteousness.

For the next hundred years, that opposition continued more or less to characterize the two parties. The Republicans allied themselves with established wealth, lent a small measure of support to blacks, opposed immigration from the European hinterlands, and tended to look down their noses at ambitious upstarts. The Democrats, on the other hand, were the party of immigrants, workers, and rising "new men"; and they were dominated by Southerners with no liking for blacks. Not until the 1960s and afterward, with the ascension of Richard Nixon, Ronald Reagan, and Newt Gingrich, did the two parties reverse their profiles, and the southeasterner Haley change his affiliation to the Republicans. Perhaps some things never change. Bill Clinton, to his Republican critics, was immoral white trailer-park trash; George W. Bush is the scion of a prominent "old wealth" family and the first case of a father-son presidency since the Federalist-Whig Adamses. But, then again, to get elected, Bush had to sweep the once-Democratic "solid South" and successfully position himself as a Texas soul mate of Simon Legree.

One antebellum writer who did view race and class as comparable areas of erasure was Herman Melville. In two great stories of the 1850s, Melville pondered the affinities in America's treatment of the newly form-ing white-collar proletariat and the enslaved Africans. The titular hero of "Bartleby, the Scrivener: A Story of Wall Street" (1853) is an impoverished law copyist whose brain-numbing work eventually produces the rebellion of refusing to copy. At least we assume this is the reason; we cannot know for certain because Bartleby's thoughts and feelings remain a mystery. Melville never provides access to his mind or allows him utterance beyond the repetition of "I would prefer not to." Individuals such as the scrivener, sighs the lawyer who narrates the story, are not ordinarily heard or seen by the "good-natured gentlemen" and "sentimental souls" who constitute the reading public. They form a blank in our understanding of the world: "I be-lieve that no materials exist, for a full and satisfactory biography of this man. It is an irreparable loss to literature."

The second story, "Benito Cereno" (1855), prefigures *Pudd'nhead Wil-son* as an ironizing of the detective form. It concerns a rebellion aboard a Spanish slave ship and features an American captain, Amassa Delano, who tries to figure out what is happening; American sailors ultimately play the central role in restoring the rebels to bondage. The text gives us every per-spective on the uprising except that of the slaves themselves. They speak in code to avoid arousing white suspicion, and neither in the narrative (which is told from Delano's point of view) nor before the tribunal do they get to relate the injustices that goaded them to violence and bloodshed. Melville writes of the black ringleader Babo in the spirit of Douglass, Twain, Ellison, and Roth: "Seeing all was over, he uttered no sound, and could not be forced to. His aspect seemed to say, since I cannot do deeds, I will not speak words."

The slave's "voiceless end," the silent scrivener who wants "nothing to say to you": they are the question marks that punctuate "America."

Total Visibility in Utopia
and Dystopia

It is a simple object, a glass paperweight with a fragment of coral, and the hero has the impression that he "was inside it. . . . The paperweight was the room he was in, and the coral was Julia's life and his own, fixed in a sort of eternity at the heart of the crystal." Everything is visible inside that tiny world "as transparent as air"; nothing can be hidden, nothing kept from the eyes of the observer peering through the glass.[1] The paperweight is a metaphor for life in Oceania, George Orwell's dystopian society of the future where "Big Brother" is always watching and telescreens operated by the Party transmit and receive simultaneously, so that "every sound you made was overheard and, except in darkness, every movement scrutinized" (p. 7).

The leitmotiv of Orwell's text is ocularity. Winston Smith struggles to carve out a space of private freedom for himself and his lover, Julia, a location where they *cannot* be seen. When he is betrayed by his apparent ally and fellow dissident, O'Brien, the Thought Police consigns him to a special chamber in the Ministry of Love known as "the place where there is no darkness" (p. 17). This site of absolute illumination is a sinister prefigurement of the afterlife, a torture room where everything is known and judged. Under interrogation, a prisoner's worst and most secret fears are laid bare; the Party exploits the knowledge to crush his or her spirit of resistance. In Smith's case, the innermost terror is of rats, and O'Brien gets him to inform on Julia to save himself from being attacked by them.

By now the paradox should be evident: the totalitarian regime of *1984* has multiple points of agreement with the United States as the ultimate "open society," in Karl Popper's term, the adversary and antithesis of the "closed society" of Communist Russia or Nazi Germany. The comparison, to be sure, is hyperbolic. Popper would be the first to object, and rightly so, that American legibility is not statist and authoritarian, and I will return in a moment to this essential distinction. But even hyperbolic comparisons can be instructive, and it would not be difficult to compile a list of parallels between the American glasshouse society and Orwell's negative utopia. Winston Smith's paperweight, for example, brings to mind Henry James's observations on New York's cityscape of "glass towers," where "window upon window" allow the casual spectator unimpeded access to the interior. New Yorkers, James relates, swelled with pride over their skyline. But James himself winced at the "inordinate" exposure of Manhattan's architecture, "as positively serving you up for inspection, under a clear glass cover."[2]

Or consider those all-seeing telescreens, which evoke both American leadership in telecommunications and contemporary anxieties over the threat to privacy in the "computer state."[3] Or, unexpectedly, the ruling Party's campaign to purge language of confusion and ornament. This may surprise readers who remember only such deceptive slogans in doublespeak as "WAR IS PEACE" and "FREEDOM IS SLAVERY" (p. 17). The Party, one would think, favors language as obfuscation in order to mask its intentions and inhibit the circulation of discontent. But, in a kind of perversion of Hemingway, Oceania's rulers recognize that a more effective strategy is to minimize language, "cutting . . . [it] down to the bone" and abolishing the shadings and ambiguities of adjectives, adverbs, synonyms, and figures of speech. The goal, by "destroying" words, is to "narrow the range of thought." Eventually thinking itself will be eradicated, and Jake Barnes's dream of endless sunlight without the introspection of darkness will be realized in a perfection of unconsciousness (pp. 45–47).

The pellucid homogeneity superintended by Big Brother travesties the durable American dream of a city on a hill, a community of total translucence where, as John Winthrop would have it, words and actions are inseparable. The Thought Police ensure that no one entertains heretical ideas. Surveillance is so relentless that not even the contents of one's mind can escape discovery, and unacceptable modes of thought have become "literally unthinkable, at least so far as thought is dependent on words" (p. 246). Reflection is orthodoxy internalized; behavior is orthodoxy externalized. The Puritans may have dreamed of such a state; not for an instant did they achieve it. The maverick like Roger Williams could always lay his hands on some unconventional treatise or find an outlet for his doctrines among English or Continental publishers. In Oceania, however, the Party accompanies its policing of language and thought with absolute control over every channel of communication, and dissent expires before it can be born. "The possibility of enforcing not only complete obedience to the will of the State, but complete uniformity of opinion on all subjects now existed for the first time" (p. 170).

I want to pry apart the two halves of Orwell's sentence, because the comma-hinge establishes the dividing line between American knowing at its worst and totalitarian methods of control. The one-sidedness of the Party/State's vigilance sets it apart decisively from a democratic polity. Whereas the ordinary inhabitant of Oceania can conceal nothing, the government and its workings remain opaque and unobtainable. The notorious Ministry of Love has not a single window. It is "a place impossible to enter except on official business, and then only by penetrating through a maze of barbed-wire entanglements, steel doors, and hidden machine-gun nests" (p. 8). Even whether Big Brother exists or not is a closely guarded secret. This, for Orwell, is the quintessence of tyranny: the state can access every detail about every citizen at any time but is itself an enigma or blank screen about which nothing can be known. In the United States, by contrast, publicity encompasses the government and has generally continued doing so through the excesses of the Cold War and its aftermath.

Indeed, in this country attempts to monitor the citizenry have tended to recoil upon their architects and to subject government leaders to a comparable level of scrutiny. Orwell's novel was published just as the Truman administration was laying the foundations for the national security state. The National Security Act had created the Central Intelligence Agency in 1947, and the tensions of the Cold War—the Soviets exploded their atomic bomb in 1949—led Truman to institute loyalty tests for federal employees. But the gravest danger to civil liberties, and the most frantic calls for total exposure, came from outside the administration: from the House Committee on Un-American Activities, which began probing the film industry in 1947, and from Joe McCarthy, who initially directed his charges of Communist infiltration against employees of the executive branch, the State Department in particular.

McCarthyite attacks took the form of a war on official secrets. If the red scare orchestrated by the senator from Wisconsin contributed to the conformism of the Eisenhower period, another consequence was to reinvigorate the suspiciousness of government that has characterized American politics since the era of Paine and Jefferson. The corollary to "BIG BROTHER IS WATCHING YOU" has been the watching of Big Brother. McCarthy's legacy includes the Watergate downfall of President Nixon in 1974 and the impeachment of Clinton a quarter century later.

Let us return to Orwell's sentence about the strangling of dissent. Excise the first half this time, and his words might be a description of the United States as seen by Tocqueville in the 1830s. An even more topical reference would be to an American blueprint for utopia from the same era as Orwell's grim prophecy, practically from the same year: B. F. Skinner's *Walden Two*, published in 1948. Skinner's book has been immensely popular; a recent paperback reissue marks the thirty-second printing. *Walden Two* elaborates a vision of a small-scale experiment, limited to one thousand volunteers, that seeks through "behavioral engineering" to realize a community of absolute harmony and happiness.[4] The modest size indicates a determination to vanquish the anomie of modernity. In an introduction from 1976, Skinner explains that urban anonymity is fatal to behavior modification. People can disappear into the multitude and evade communal pressure. And full-time oversight is an integral component of the Walden Two paradise.

What is nightmare in the Englishman's dystopia is sublimity in the American's rewriting of Thoreau. Freedom, another name for the unpredictable and the unknown, has been banished from the settlement, and the members, who retain a subjective illusion of free choice, would not have it otherwise. They have come together voluntarily and agreed to delegate planning and management to experts. There is no state in Walden Two, no ascriptive or elected elite monopolizing power. Psychologists are the new society's "priests" (p. 186), and they endeavor through positive reinforcement to shape human activity so that it can be predicted. All is training and education, yet far from being the robotlike victims of a totalitarian government, the residents, according to Skinner's proxy Frazier, enjoy the only "freedom" worth possessing. They do what they want to do, and they have been programmed to "want to do precisely the things that are best for themselves and for the community. Their behavior is determined, yet they're free" (p. 279). "Give me the specifications," Frazier exclaims, distilling the experiment's guiding principles into an axiom, "and I'll give you the man!" (p. 274).

Walden Two makes an easy target, and Skinner's "improvement upon Genesis" (p. 280), his Eden of predictable human beings, is more a parody of American transparency than a meaningful analogue to it. The much-maligned Skinner box—actually a baby tender with a safety-glass front—hardly warrants being mentioned in the same breath (or study) with Orwell's glass paperweight. (Critics of Walden Two labeled the community a "*box populi*.")[5] Skinner's ideal tests the limits of American conformity; and my point has been that for all its oppressive elements, its approximation of Oceania, the would-be utopia is qualitatively different from the rule of Big Brother, just as the United States, for all *its* majoritarian intrusiveness, differs fundamentally from a totalitarian polity.

Nothing illustrates this point more clearly than the divergent fates of privacy in the two futuristic novels. The most harrowing aspect of Oceania is the absence of any harbor proscribed to bureaucratic jurisdiction. As a result of the "constant surveillance," Orwell says, "private life came to an end" (p. 169). The Party/State—and the two are identical—administers the assault on the inexplicit, and thus the State as public sphere has colonized the entire society. We could say that Oceania marks a perverted return to (and exaggeration of) the absolutist regimes of the seventeenth century, before the private sphere or civil society had been separated out from the prerogatives of government. Orwell's fictional dictatorship culminates a reactionary European phenomenon that the power sharing of modernity had been steadily eclipsing since the Puritan civil war of the 1640s. But the degree of governmental dominance over the social order associated with absolutism never successfully transplanted itself to the New World.

In America, the agencies of visibility were more pandemic and subjective. Access was not just a privilege of state authority; it was an abiding feature of religious practice, of environmental planning, and of interpersonal discourse. Publicity permeated every aspect of social life; as Tocqueville emphasized, the "public sphere" was diffused throughout the culture. The state could actually provide a sanctuary from the inexorable march of ocularity. Instead of intruding its tentacles into hidden recesses, the government could pass legislation, or its judiciary could hand down judgments, to secure the right of ordinary citizens to be let alone. Even in his behaviorist utopia, where the reign of knowing seems to leave no quarter undisturbed, Skinner follows Tocqueville in identifying areas of personal inviolability. In *Democracy in America*, the domestic realm allowed a refuge from consensual pacification; in *Walden Two*, where family life has yielded to the group, the space shrinks to the confines of four walls. The "advisability of separate rooms for husband and wife," a policy devised by the Managers, ensures a greater measure of "personal privacy than is likely to be found in the world at large. You may be alone here whenever you wish. A man's room is his castle. And a woman's, too" (p. 128).

What thoughts occur to one in that solitary chamber? Are they thoughts, perhaps, that have not been sculpted into one's interiority by Skinner's Managers or Tocqueville's majority? Reflections about things the culture does *not* want to see or hear: melancholy, or the noninstrumental, or loss without reparation, all the proscribed subjects that Freud, for one, felt Americans refused to entertain. A room reserved for oneself has historically been a place to write, which should remind us that the enclave most secure from encroachment may well be the word on the page. Skinner's self-designation as the successor to Thoreau calls for a final comment here. *Walden Two* repeatedly invokes its textual forerunner, and Skinner "doubles" the earlier memoir by writing his book in thirty-six chapters; the original *Walden* has eighteen. It is safe to say that Thoreau would not have welcomed the compliment. *Walden*'s emblematic artifact is not a crystalline object but a phenomenon of nature. Thoreau's goal being to "have attained to obscurity," he wishes his pages to emulate the Pond's ice: "Southern customers objected to its blue color, which is the evidence of its purity, as if it were muddy, and preferred the Cambridge ice, which is white, but tastes of weeds. The purity men love is like the mists which envelop the earth, and not like the azure ether beyond."[6] The surface that withholds its depth: is it only coincidence that the ice is a dark color, like ostracized "dark" people, and has layers unsuspected by those who prefer the white ice of Cambridge? In any event, Walden's winter coat can stand for the literary tradition I have traced from Hawthorne to Roth. It is Thoreau's rejoinder to the glass paperweight, a perfect figure of resistance to the utopia and dystopia combined that is American legibility.

NOTES

Introduction

1. Karl Marx, *The Communist Manifesto*, ed. Frederic L. Bender (New York: Norton, 1988), pp. 57–58.

2. Hans Blumenberg, *The Legitimacy of the Modern Age* (1966), trans. Robert M. Wallace (Cambridge, Mass.: MIT Press, 1983), pp. 361–64.

3. Walter Bagehot, *The English Constitution*, 2d ed. (London: Kegan Paul, Trench, Trubner, 1922), p. 59; Jeremy Bentham, "Of Publicity," in *An Essay on Political Tactics*, vol. 2, *The Works of Jeremy Bentham*, ed. John Bowring (Edinburgh, 1843), pp. 310–17.

4. The definition of modernity as the "tacit made explicit" is developed by Michael McKeon in his forthcoming study, *The Secret History of Domesticity: Public, Private, and the Division of Knowledge.* I am grateful to Professor McKeon for allowing me to read parts of his manuscript. On the crucial differences between American and British understandings of privacy and publicity, see Edward A. Shils, *The Torment of Secrecy: The Background and Consequences of American Security Policies* (Glencoe, Ill.: Free Press, 1956).

5. Vachel Lindsay, *The Art of the Moving Picture*, rev. ed. (1922; repr., New York: Modern Library, 2000), pp. 43–49.

6. Sigmund Freud, *Dora: An Analysis of a Case of Hysteria* (1905; repr., New York: Collier, 1963), p. 96.

7. A great deal has been written about the adoption and supposed simplifying of Freudian ideas in America. Some examples are Hendrik M. Ruitenbeek, *Freud and America* (New York: Macmillan, 1966); Robert C. Fuller, *Americans and the Unconscious* (New York: Oxford University Press, 1986); two books by Nathan G. Hale Jr., *Freud and the Americans: The Beginnings of Psychoanalysis in the United States, 1876–1917* (New York: Oxford University Press, 1971), and *The Rise and Crisis of Psychoanalysis in the United States: Freud and the Americans, 1917–1985* (New York: Oxford University Press, 1995); and Joseph Schwartz, *Cassandra's Daughter: A History of Psychoanalysis* (New York: Viking, 1999), pp. 144–92. I discuss Lacan more fully in my treatment of Poe's detective stories.

8. See the essays collected in Werner Sollors, *Interracialism: Black-White Intermarriage in American History, Literature, and Law* (New York: Oxford University Press, 2000), especially the introduction by Sollors, pp. 3–16.

9. The classic study here is Edmund S. Morgan, *American Slavery—American Freedom: The Ordeal of Colonial Virginia* (New York: Norton, 1975). Also relevant is David R. Roediger, *The Wages of Whiteness: Race and the Making of the American Working Class* (London: Verso, 1991). Controversial, though indispensable, on the nexus between egalitarianism and racial hierarchy is Louis Dumont, *Homo Hierarchicus: The Caste System and Its Implications*, trans. Mark Sainsbury, Louis Dumont, and Basia Gulati (1966; repr., Chicago: University of Chicago Press, 1980).

10. A standard work on pornography is Walter Kendrick, *The Secret Museum: Pornography in Modern Culture* (1987; repr., Berkeley: University of California Press, 1996). William Dean Howells pointed out in the late nineteenth century that young Americans, especially girls, had the freedom to read what they wanted, whereas their French counterparts were comparatively sheltered and had their reading monitored. Hence pornography was permissible in France but not in America. See Larzer Ziff, *The American 1890s: Life and Times of a Lost Generation* (New York: Viking Compass, 1968), pp. 41–43.

Prologue

1. Ernest Jones, *Years of Maturity 1901–1919*, vol. 2 of *The Life and Work of Sigmund Freud* (New York: Basic Books, 1955), p. 56.

Chapter 1

1. It would be instructive, but beyond the scope of this project, to situate the New World's settlement in relation to the twin movements of modernity: the Age of Exploration and the Protestant Reformation. The opening and exploration of new territories, climaxing in the voyages of Columbus, marked an unprecedented expansion of knowledge over the world's surfaces; the emergence of Protestantism, with its emphasis on inward faith rather than sacraments and tradition, initiated a comparable plumbing of the human interior. Columbus might lay claim to instigating the American passion for accessibility. He was stirred by the lust to observe (and appropriate) things never before beheld by Western eyes. "My eyes never weary of looking," he wrote in a typical statement. "I wish to see and discover as much as I can." Columbus quoted in Mary B. Campbell, *The Witness and the Other World: Exotic European Travel Writing, 400–1600* (Ithaca, N.Y.: Cornell University Press, 1988), pp. 196–97. Also see Stephen Greenblatt, *Marvellous Possessions: The Wonder of the New World* (Chicago: University of Chicago Press, 1991). The Pilgrims and then the Puritans were motivated to cross the Atlantic by the Reformation dream of a church purified of Catholic corruptions.

I might also note here the calibration of "surface" and "depth" with the suppositions of postmodernism and modernism. Postmodern discourse disavows depth for a preoccupation with externals; modernism aims to uncover the deep motivation beneath the visible. In chapter 5, I attempt to unsettle this stark opposition, at least with respect to film and psychoanalysis; but insofar as the contrast has validity, American attentiveness to both surfaces and depths gives the United States some right to the title of first "postmodern" society as well as first modern one. For spirited reflections on these matters, see Slavoj Žižek, *Looking Awry: An Intoduction to Jacques Lacan through Popular Culture* (Cambridge, Mass.: MIT Press, 1992).

2. I will use the readily available reprint of Winthrop's speech in Alan Heimert and Andrew Delbanco, eds., *The Puritans in America: A Narrative Anthology* (Cambridge, Mass.: Harvard University Press, 1985), pp. 82–92; page numbers are given in the text. Much has been written about "A Model." Emory Elliott briefly summarizes the scholarly debates in *The Cambridge History of American Literature*, ed. Sacvan Bercovitch (New York: Cambridge University Press, 1994), 1:193–95. A reading I have found particularly valuable for its emphasis on consent is Michael Warner, "New English Sodom," *American Literature* 64 (March 1992): 19–47.

3. See Louis Hartz, *The Liberal Tradition in America: An Interpretation of American Political Thought since the Revolution* (New York: Harcourt, Brace, 1955). A pair of relevant studies are, on the Puritans, Theodore Dwight Bozeman, *To Live Ancient Lives: The Primitivist Dimension in Puritanism* (Chapel Hill: University of North Carolina Press, 1988); and, on early American culture generally, Jack P. Greene, *The Intellectual Construction of America: Exceptionalism and Identity from 1492 to 1800* (Chapel Hill: University of North Carolina Press, 1993). A good overview of the current state of early American studies is Philip F. Gura, "Early American Literature at the New Century," *William and Mary Quarterly* 57 (July 2000): 599–620.

4. Max Weber, *The Protestant Ethic and the Spirit of Capitalism*, trans. Talcott Parsons (New York: Scribner's, 1958), p. 121.

5. See John Demos, "Shame and Guilt in Early New England," in Carol Z. Stearns and Peter N. Stearns, eds., *Emotion and Social Change: Toward a New Psychohistory* (New York: Holmes and Maier, 1988), pp. 69–85; Roger Thompson, "'Holy Watchfulness' and Communal Conformism: The Functions of Defamation in Early New England Communities," *New England Quarterly* 56 (1983): 504–22; and David H. Flaherty, *Privacy in Colonial New England* (Charlottesville: University Press of Virginia, 1972). Flaherty argues that the Puritans were able to maintain a sphere of privacy, but in my opinion his evidence militates against his conclusions.

6. Nathaniel Hawthorne, *The Scarlet Letter* (Boston: Bedford Books, 1991), pp. 68, 74.

7. Augustine, *The Confessions*, trans. F. J. Sheed (New York: Sheed and Ward, 1942), pp. 198–202.

8. Bacon is quoted in Ramie Targoff, *Common Prayer: The Language of Public Devotion in Early Modern England* (Chicago: University of Chicago Press, 2001), p. 2.

9. This sample narrative is from Thomas Shepard's *The Parable of the Ten Virgins* (1660), quoted in Edmund S. Morgan, *Visible Saints: The History of a Puritan Idea* (Ithaca, N.Y.: Cornell University Press, 1963), p. 92. Anyone writing on this subject owes a debt to Morgan and to Patricia Caldwell, *The Puritan Conversion Narrative: The Beginnings of American Expression* (New York: Cambridge University Press, 1983).

10. See Max Weber's famous formulation from *The Protestant Ethic and the Spirit of Capitalism*, pp. 153–54.

11. The first quotation is from the Cambridge Platform (1648), in Williston Walker, *The Creeds and Platforms of Congregationalism* (Philadelphia, Pa.: Pilgrim Press, 1960), p. 223; the second is from Cotton's *The Way of Congregational Churches Cleared* (1648), in Caldwell, *The Puritan Conversion Narrative*, p. 51.

12. Quoted in Rodger M. Payne, *The Self and the Sacred: Conversion and Autobiography in Early American Protestantism* (Knoxville: University of Tennessee Press, 1998), pp. 28–29. Payne sees the conversion narratives as a discourse of American selfhood.

13. See Randall Balmer, *Mine Eyes Have Seen the Glory: A Journey into the Evangelical Subculture in America* (New York: Oxford University Press, 1989), pp. 204–6, passim. On the Promise Keepers, see Christine Leigh Heyrman, *Southern Cross: The Beginnings of the Bible Belt* (New York: Knopf, 1997), pp. 259–60. Another informative study is Virginia Lieson Brereton, *From Sin to Salvation: Stories of Women's Conversions, 1800 to the Present* (Bloomington: Indiana University Press, 1991). Balmer shows, by the way, that the concerns leading to the Half-Way Covenant still haunt evangelical parents today: how to pass on religious vitality from one generation to the next "within a tradition that defines itself by the conversion process" (p. 93).

14. See Heyrman, *Southern Cross*, and the various essays in Harry S. Stout and D. G. Hart, eds., *New Directions in American Religious History* (New York: Oxford University Press, 1997), especially the studies by Donald Mathews, Daniel Walker Howe, and Jon Butler.

15. See Hollinger's essay, "Jewish Intellectuals and the De-Christianization of American Public Culture in the Twentieth Century," in Stout and Hart, *New Directions in American Religious History*, p. 465. An excellent essay on Protestantism and presidential elections is George M. Marsden, "Afterword: Religion, Politics, and the Search for an American Consensus," in Mark A. Noll, ed., *Religion and American Politics: From the Colonial Period to the 1980s* (New York: Oxford University Press, 1990), pp. 380–90.

16. This is Blumenberg's argument in *The Legitimacy of the Modern Age.*

17. Norris's views come from his essay "A Plea for Romantic Fiction," which appears in his posthumous collection, *The Responsibilities of the Novelist* (1903; repr., New York: Hill and Wang, 1967), pp. 279–82.

18. Ralph Waldo Emerson, *The Conduct of Life* (1860; repr., New York: Home Library, n.d.), pp. 199, 196–97.

19. Edgar Allan Poe, "The Imp of the Perverse," in *The Complete Tales and Poems of Edgar Allan Poe* (New York: Modern Library, 1938), p. 284.

20. "The Decay of Lying" can be found in *The Artist as Critic: Critical Writings of Oscar Wilde*, ed. Richard Ellmann (1969; repr., Chicago: University of Chicago Press, 1982), pp. 290–320; quotations on pp. 304, 295.

21. For information on phrenology, I have relied on three works: Charles Colbert, *A Measure of Perfection: Phrenology and the Fine Arts in America* (Chapel Hill: University of North Carolina Press, 1997); John Davies, *Phrenology: Fad and Science* (New Haven, Conn.: Yale University Press, 1955); and Marc D. Falkoff, "Heads and Tales: American Letters in the Age of Phrenology" (Ph.D. diss., Brandeis University, 1997). I am particularly indebted to Falkoff's discussion of phrenology and psychoanalysis.

22. Herman Melville, *Moby-Dick*, ed. Charles Feidelson Jr. (New York: Macmillan, 1964), p. 82.

23. See Foucault's *History of Sexuality: Volume I: An Introduction*, trans. Robert Hurley (New York: Vintage, 1980). Peter Brooks, in his otherwise excellent *Troubling Confessions: Speaking Guilt in Law and Literature* (Chicago: University of Chicago Press, 2000), unfortunately relies on Foucault's analysis of the confes-

sional as the source of the West's "generalized transparency" (p. 9). This leads to the oddity of juxtaposing a medieval obligation, legislated by the Fourth Lateran Council of 1215, with court cases taken exclusively from the United States. In a review of *Troubling Confessions*, Terry Eagleton points out how much better public confessionalism describes the United States than the larger entity that is Western culture. See Eagleton's "Qui s'accuse, s'excuse," *London Review of Books* 22 (1 June 2000): 34–35.

Foucault's position might win support from Hawthorne, of all people. In *The Marble Faun* (1860), a novel written during his stay in Italy, Hawthorne has his heroine, the virginal Hilda, seek out an English-language confessional at St. Peter's Cathedral and confide her witness of a murder to the waiting priest. The confession is said to lift the burden from Hilda's spirit and to restore her to a feeling of purity. I examine Hawthorne's attraction to Catholicism in my reading of *The Scarlet Letter*.

24. In "Qui s'accuse, s'excuse," p. 34.

25. For an illustration, see Elisabeth Roudinesco and Michel Plon, *Dictionnaire de la Psychanlyse* (Paris: Fayard, 1997); also see the review of this work by G. W. Pigman III in *Psychoanalytic Books: A Quarterly Journal of Reviews* 10 (1999): 10–15. Pigman points to numerous patronizing misconceptions of American psychoanalysis.

26. Walker Percy, *The Moviegoer* (New York: Ivy Books, 1988), p. 199.

27. Walker Percy, *Love in the Ruins: The Adventures of a Bad Catholic at a Time Near the End of the World* (New York: Ivy Books, 1989), pp. 99–100, 340.

28. See Regis A. Duffy, "Penance," in Francis Schussler Fiorenza and John P. Galvin, eds., *Systematic Theology: Catholic Perspectives* (Minneapolis, Minn.: Fortress, 1991), 2:233–49.

29. My source for these matters is James M. O'Toole, "Decline and Fall: Toward a Social History of Confession," unpublished manuscript. I am grateful to Professor O'Toole for sharing his research with me.

30. Most of the information in this paragraph comes from Brooks, *Troubling Confessions*; see esp. pp. 84, 153.

31. The literature on this subject is vast. Two useful works are B. Guy Peters, *The Politics of Taxation: A Comparative Perspective* (Cambridge, Mass.: Basil Blackwell, 1991); and Gerald Carson, *The Golden Egg: The Personal Income Tax, Where It Came From, How It Grew* (Boston: Houghton Mifflin, 1977). Justice Jackson is quoted in Carson, *The Golden Egg*, p. 252.

32. Marryat is quoted in Jenny Franchot, *Roads to Rome: The Antebellum Protestant Encounter with Catholicism* (Berkeley: University of California Press, 1994), p. 137. On anti-Catholicism, see her book, esp. pp. 87–193. Interestingly, Freud made a connection between psychoanalysis and antimonasticism. He saw his method of treatment as "this-worldly" in that it combated mental illness's tendency to incapacitate the sufferer for daily existence. Psychotherapy enabled the patient to escape monastic disengagement by restoring him or her to health (including an active sexual life). See *Five Lectures on Psycho-Analysis*, trans. James Strachey (1909; repr., New York: Norton, 1961), p. 56.

33. William Penn, *Some Account of the Province of Pennsilvania* (1681), in Albert Cook Myers, ed., *Narratives of Early Pennsylvania, West New Jersey, and Delaware, 1630–1707* (New York: Scribner's, 1912), p. 202.

34. The quotation is from ibid., p. 208. See also Penn's *Letter from William Penn to the Committee of the Free Society of Traders* (1683), in Myers, *Narratives of*

Early Pennsylvania pp. 224. Two useful brief summaries of the Quaker project are John E. Pomfret, "The First Purchasers of Pennsylvania, 1681–1700," *Pennsylvania Magazine of History and Biography* 80 (April 1956): 137–63; and Hugh Brogan, *The Penguin History of the United States of America* (London: Penguin, 1985), pp. 93–97.

35. The quotation is from Brogan, *Penguin History of the United States,* p. 94.

36. Most of the information in this paragraph comes from Penn's *Certain Conditions and Concessions* (1681), in Samuel Hazard, ed., *Annals of Pennsylvania, from the Discovery of the Delaware* (Philadelphia, 1850), esp. pp. 518–19.

37. I take this formulation from Yaron Ezrahi, who uses it rather differently in his *The Descent of Icarus: Science and the Transformation of Contemporary Democracy* (Cambridge, Mass.: Harvard University Press, 1990).

38. Holme's plat and advertisement are the last three pages of the *Letter* (in Myers, *Narratives of Early Pennsylvania,* pp. 242–44; quotations on p. 243). Also see *Certain Conditions and Concessions,* p. 517.

39. On the American landscape, see the following works: John R. Stilgoe, *Common Landscape of America, 1580 to 1845* (New Haven, Conn.: Yale University Press, 1982); Hildegard Binder Johnson, *Order upon the Land: The U.S. Rectangular Land Survey and the Upper Mississippi Country* (New York: Oxford University Press, 1976); Johnson, "Towards a National Landscape," in Michael P. Conzen, ed., *The Making of the American Landscape* (Boston: Unwin Hyman, 1990), pp. 127–45; Denis Cosgrove, "The Measures of America," in James Corner and Alex S. MacLean, eds., *Taking Measures across the American Landscape* (New Haven, Conn.: Yale University Press, 1996), pp. 3–13; and Martin Bruckner, "Lessons in Geography: Maps, Spellers, and Other Grammars of Nationalism in the Early Republic," *American Quarterly* 51 (June 1999): 311–43.

40. As Peter S. Onuf aptly puts it, the land policy "would create value by producing knowledge." See Onuf's *Statehood and Union: A History of the Northwest Ordinance* (Bloomington: Indiana University Press, 1987), p. 41.

41. See Georg Simmel, "The Secret and the Secret Society," in Kurt H. Wolff, ed., *The Sociology of Georg Simmel* (Glencoe, Ill.: Free Press, 1950), pp. 305–76; and Jeremy Bentham, "Of Publicity," in *An Essay on Political Tactics,* vol. 2, *The Works of Jeremy Bentham,* ed. John Bowring (Edinburgh, 1843), pp. 310–17.

42. Turner's essay is reprinted in *Frontier and Section: Selected Essays of Frederick Jackson Turner,* ed. Ray Allen Billington (Englewood Cliffs, N.J.: Prentice-Hall, 1961), pp. 37–62. The quotation on democracy is from p. 58. Turner explicitly opposes his interpretation of the frontier's significance to the "slavery perspective." The pioneer experience made the nation, he insists, not slavery and the Civil War. Thus does he effectively erase blacks from the drama of American development.

43. Wolfgang Langewiesche, "The U.S.A. from the Air," *Harper's Magazine* 201 (October 1950): 176–98; quotations on pp. 188, 190. In addition to Langewiesche, Hildegard Binder Johnson is German born, and so is Martin Bruckner.

44. Ibid., pp. 188, 193.

45. See James C. Scott's *Seeing Like a State: How Certain Schemes to Improve the Human Condition Have Failed* (New Haven, Conn.: Yale University Press, 1998).

46. Holme, in *Letter from William Penn to the Committee of the Free Society of Traders,* p. 242.

47. Langewiesche, "The U.S.A. from the Air," p. 193.

48. Ibid.

49. For information on electronic warfare, see Geoffrey Perret, *A Country Made by War: From the Revolution to Vietnam—the Story of America's Rise to Power* (New York: Random House, 1989), esp. pp. 540–53.

50. See Spiro Kostof, *The City Shaped: Urban Patterns and Meanings through History* (Boston: Little, Brown, 1991), pp. 209–11; Wilbur Zelinsky, "The Imprint of Central Authority," in Conzen, *The Making of the American Landscape*, pp. 311–34; and Leonardo Benevolo, *History of Modern Architecture* (Cambridge, Mass.: MIT Press, 1971), 1:191–218.

51. Note the photographs of buildings designed by Louis Sullivan in Chicago, in Benevolo, *History of Modern Architecture*, 1:236–37. A striking example (on p. 237) is the Carson, Pirie and Scott building (1899).

52. See Jackson's study *Crabgrass Frontier: The Suburbanization of the United States* (New York: Oxford University Press, 1985); quotation on pp. 283–84.

53. The point about walls comes from ibid., p. 59. On the urban environment as disorder, see Robert H. Wiebe, *The Search for Order* (New York: Hill and Wang, 1967).

54. My account of the living room in this paragraph is much indebted to Karen Halttunen's "From Parlor to Living Room: Domestic Space, Interior Decoration, and the Culture of Personality," in Simon J. Bronner, ed., *Consuming Visions: Accumulation and Display of Goods in America, 1880–1920* (New York: Norton, 1989), pp. 157–89.

55. I am quoting from *The American Scene* (1907; repr., Bloomington: Indiana University Press, 1968), pp. 95, 101, 166–68.

56. Edith Wharton, *The Decoration of Houses* (1897; repr., New York: Norton, 1978), pp. 50, 111–12, 134.

57. Ibid., pp. 62–63, 90–91, 198.

58. Carl Jung, "Your Negroid and Indian Behavior," in Werner Sollors, ed., *Theories of Ethnicity: A Classical Reader* (London: Macmillan, 1996), p. 193.

59. For further development of the themes mentioned in this paragraph, see John A. Kouwenhoven, *The Beer Can by the Highway: Essays on What's "American" about America* (Garden City, N.Y.: Doubleday, 1961); Philip Fisher, *Still the New World: American Literature in a Culture of Creative Destruction* (Cambridge, Mass.: Harvard University Press, 1999); and David C. Mowery and Nathan Rosenberg, *Paths of Innovation: Technological Change in Twentieth-Century America* (New York: Cambridge University Press, 1998).

60. See Virilio's *War and Cinema: The Logistics of Perception*, trans. Patrick Camiller (London: Verso, 1989), pp. 26, passim.

61. See James R. Beniger, *The Control Revolution: Technological and Economic Origins of the Information Society* (Cambridge, Mass.: Harvard University Press, 1986).

62. The phrase, from *New Introductory Lectures on Psycho-Analysis*, is quoted by Philip Cushman in his *Constructing the Self, Constructing America* (Reading, Mass.: Addison-Wesley, 1995), p. 114. Cushman, a harsh critic of ego psychology, develops a parallel between the conquest of the wilderness and American "colonizing" of the psyche through various modes of the therapeutic.

63. Hartmann's treatise, written in German, was translated by David Rapaport (New York: International Universities Press, 1958). For a lucid (if perhaps overly

sympathetic) summary of ego psychology, see Rapaport's "A Historical Survey of Psychoanalytic Ego Psychology," which serves as the introduction to Erik H. Erikson, *Identity and the Life Cycle: Selected Papers* (New York: International Universities Press, 1959), pp. 5–17.

64. On this theme, see Jill Lepore, *The Name of War: King's Philip's War and the Origins of American Identity* (New York: Knopf, 1998). Lepore's book deals with the fate of the Algonquians in southern New England.

65. Jackson notes the role of the IRS in sponsoring suburbia in *Crabgrass Frontier*, pp. 293–96. An intriguing and relevant article on black exclusion is Catherine Jurca, "Tarzan, Lord of the Suburbs," *Modern Language Quarterly* 57 (September 1996): 479–504.

66. Jefferson's map can be found in Johnson, *Order upon the Land*, p. 41.

67. The quotations, from *Notes on the State of Virginia*, are in Jefferson, *Writings*, ed. Merrill D. Peterson (New York: Library of America, 1984), Query XIV, p. 272.

68. On Petty and the English debate over numerical facts, see Mary Poovey, *A History of the Modern Fact: Problems of Knowledge in the Sciences of Wealth and Society* (Chicago: University of Chicago Press, 1998), esp. pp. 93–143.

69. Robert A. Ferguson, "The American Enlightenment, 1750–1820," in Sacvan Bercovitch, ed., *The Cambridge History of American Literature* (New York: Cambridge University Press, 1994), 1:484. My subsequent discussion of the Declaration and the Constitution owes a debt to Ferguson's excellent treatment of "The Literature of Public Documents," pp. 470–95.

70. Among the many writers on the Declaration, I would single out Pauline Maier, *American Scripture: Making the Declaration of Independence* (New York: Vintage, 1998); Jay Fliegelman, *Declaring Independence: Jefferson, Natural Language, and the Culture of Performance* (Stanford, Calif.: Stanford University Press, 1993); Garry Wills, *Inventing America: Jefferson's Declaration of Independence* (Garden City, N.Y.: Doubleday, 1978); and the still valuable study by Carl Becker, *The Declaration of Independence: A Study in the History of Political Ideas* (1922; repr., New York: Knopf, 1964). On American political allegiances and how they differ from those held elsewhere, see Jonathan Freedland, *Bring Home the Revolution: The Case for a British Republic* (London: Fourth Estate, 1998); and Seymour Martin Lipset, *American Exceptionalism: A Double-Edged Sword* (New York: Norton, 1996). Also see Gordon S. Wood, *The Radicalism of the American Revolution* (New York: Knopf, 1991) on the spread of the Declaration's principles in the post-Revolutionary era. I am using the copy of the Declaration reprinted in the Library of America edition of Jefferson's *Writings*, pp. 19–24. This includes Jefferson's initial wording, as well as the final version adopted by the Continental Congress.

71. "To Lafayette," letter of 16 June 1792, in *Writings*, pp. 990–91.

72. In actuality, the balance of power between the king and the British Parliament was changing at this time, and there was some ambiguity about which of the two parties was sovereign. But the point is that "assent" implies an agreement among a superior and a subordinate, not among equals.

73. Quotations are from *Gateway to Citizenship*, a publication of the United States Immigration and Naturalization Service (Washington, D.C., 1943; revised, 1962), pp. 8, 12, 18.

74. On the public sphere, see Jürgen Habermas, *The Structural Transformation of the Public Sphere: An Inquiry into a Category of Bourgeois Society*, trans. Thomas

Burger, with the assistance of Frederick Lawrence (Cambridge, Mass.: MIT Press, 1989); and Michael Warner, *The Letters of the Republic: Publication and the Public Sphere in Eighteenth-Century America* (Cambridge, Mass.: Harvard University Press, 1990).

75. See Richard D. Brown, *The Strength of a People: The Idea of an Informed Citizenry in America, 1650–1870* (Chapel Hill: University of North Carolina Press, 1996).

76. And, again, land distribution underwrote the spread of knowledge. The Morrill Act of 1862 provided millions of acres for the support of higher education.

77. Quotations are from the Mentor Books paperback edition of *The Federalist Papers* (New York: New American Library, 1961); page numbers are given in the text. Useful studies of the essays by Hamilton, Madison, and Jay include Albert Furtwangler, *The Authority of Publius: A Reading of the Federalist Papers* (Ithaca, N.Y.: Cornell University Press, 1984); and James W. Ceaser, "Fame and *The Federalist*," in Peter McNamara, ed., *The Noblest Minds: Fame, Honor, and the American Founding* (Lanham, Md.: Rowman and Littlefield, 1999), pp. 187–206.

78. See Shklar's posthumous collection of essays, *Redeeming American Political Thought*, ed. Stanley Hoffmann and Dennis F. Thompson (Chicago: University of Chicago Press, 1998), esp. the first piece, "Alexander Hamilton and the Language of Political Science," pp. 3–13.

79. See Richard R. John, *Spreading the News: The American Postal System from Franklin to Morse* (Cambridge, Mass.: Harvard University Press, 1995). The figures on the number of postal offices appear on p. 5.

80. The quotation, from one Erastus Root (1796), appears in Patricia Cline Cohen, *A Calculating People: The Spread of Numeracy in Early America* (Chicago: University of Chicago Press, 1982), p. 129.

81. The material in this paragraph comes from Theodore M. Porter, *Trust in Numbers: The Pursuit of Objectivity in Science and Public Life* (Princeton, N.J.: Princeton University Press, 1995), although Porter draws different conclusions than I do.

82. L. Moholy-Nagy, *Vision in Motion* (1947; repr., Chicago: Paul Theobald, 1965), p. 328.

83. Ernest Hemingway, *A Farewell to Arms* (1929; repr., New York: Scribner's, 1957), p. 191. I examine Hemingway's style more fully in my treatment of *The Sun Also Rises*.

84. See Mitchel Y. Abolafia, *Making Markets: Opportunism and Restraint on Wall Street* (Cambridge, Mass.: Harvard University Press, 1996), chap. 3, pp. 64–79. (The chapter is titled "Taming the Market.")

85. See Paul Boyer, *When Time Shall Be No More: Prophecy Belief in Modern American Culture* (Cambridge, Mass.: Harvard University Press, 1992), p. 305. Boyer's book is a trove of fascinating material. Also still worthwhile is Ernest Lee Tuveson, *Redeemer Nation: The Idea of America's Millennial Role* (Chicago: University of Chicago Press, 1968).

86. Hal Lindsey, with C. C. Carlson, *The Late Great Planet Earth* (Grand Rapids, Mich.: Zondervan, 1970), p. vii.

87. The dates are from Boyer, *When Time Shall Be No More*, pp. 68, 81, 138.

88. Nicholas Lemann, *The Big Test: The Secret History of the American Meritocracy* (New York: Farrar, Straus and Giroux, 1999), p. 18.

89. The quotation is from another pioneer intelligence tester, James M. Cattell, and is cited in Leila Zenderland, *Measuring Minds: Henry Herbert Goddard and the Origins of American Intelligence Testing* (Cambridge: Cambridge University Press, 1998), p. 292. I have relied on this study for information about Goddard.

90. I am referring to the heredity-environment debates reanimated by the 1994 study of Richard Herrnstein and Charles Murray, *The Bell Curve*. On the controversy in general, see Leon Kamin, *The Science and Politics of I.Q.* (Potomac, Md.: Erlbaum, 1974).

91. McCarthy quoted in Stephen J. Whitfield, *The Culture of the Cold War*, 2d ed. (Baltimore, Md.: Johns Hopkins University Press, 1996), p. 37. For information on McCarthy, I have used this book and Michael Paul Rogin, *The Intellectuals and McCarthy: The Radical Spectre* (Cambridge, Mass.: MIT Press, 1967).

92. Philip Roth, *I Married a Communist* (Boston: Houghton Mifflin, 1998), p. 96.

93. On American women's involvement in politics, see Theda Skocpol, *Protecting Soldiers and Mothers: The Political Origins of Social Policy in the United States* (Cambridge, Mass.: Harvard University Press, 1992); and Paula Baker, "The Domestication of Politics: Women and American Political Society, 1780–1920," *American Historical Review* 89 (June 1984): 620–47. For a theoretical overview, see Jean Bethke Elshtain, *Public Man, Private Woman: Women in Social and Political Thought* (Princeton, N.J.: Princeton University Press, 1981).

94. See Alexander Keyssar, *The Right to Vote: The Contested History of Democracy in the United States* (New York: Basic Books, 2000). Keyssar points out that some property requirements were restored in the late nineteenth century, though 60 to 70 percent of white adult males could vote.

95. Alexis de Tocqueville, *Democracy in America*, ed. Phillips Bradley (New York: Vintage, 1945), 1:253; Grund is quoted in Lawrence H. Fuchs, *The American Kaleidoscope: Race, Ethnicity, and the Civic Culture* (1990; repr., Hanover, N. H.: Wesleyan University Press, 1995), pp. 24–25. Fuchs is very balanced on civic culture. See Skocpol, *Protecting Soldiers and Mothers*, on the minimal state.

96. See Baker, "The Domestication of Politics"; and Seth Koven and Sonya Michel, "Womanly Duties: Maternalist Politics and the Origins of Welfare States in France, Germany, Great Britain, and the United States," *American Historical Review* 95 (October 1990): 1076–108.

97. See Fuchs, *The American Kaleidoscope*; Walker quoted on p. 151; Du Bois quoted on p. 78. An exception among American blacks was Frederick Douglass, who championed the Constitution, not the Declaration, as an antislavery document. "This Fourth of July is *yours*, not *mine*," he told whites in his speech "The Meaning of July Fourth for the Negro" (1852). See Philip S. Foner, *The Life and Writings of Frederick Douglass*, vol. 2, *Pre–Civil War Decade, 1850–1860* (New York: International Publishers, 1950), pp. 181–204; quotation on p. 189.

98. The women's movement was complicit in this process and came to fruition partly by denigrating African-Americans and immigrants. Rogers M. Smith calls the post-Reconstruction backlash "The Gilded Age of Ascriptive Americanism." See *Civic Ideals: Conflicting Visions of Citizenship in U.S. History* (New Haven, Conn.: Yale University Press, 1997), pp. 347–409. Smith's book, with which I often find myself in disagreement, is an invaluable source of information.

99. The point is made by Keyssar, *The Right to Vote*, pp. xxiii–xxiv.

100. See Fliegelman's *Declaring Independence*.

101. This is basically the thesis of Warner, *The Letters of the Republic,* pp. 118–50.

102. Samuel Johnson, *Taxation No Tyranny,* in *Political Writings,* ed. Donald J. Greene (New Haven, Conn.: Yale University Press, 1977), pp. 454, 411.

Chapter 2

1. Gustave de Beaumont, *Marie; or, Slavery in the United States* (1835; repr., Baltimore, Md.: Johns Hopkins University Press, 1999). Page numbers refer to this text.

2. Alexis de Tocqueville, *Democracy in America,* ed. Phillips Bradley (New York: Vintage, 1945), 1:273.

3. Ibid. 273–74.

4. See Georges Duhamel, *America the Menace: Scenes from the Life of the Future,* trans. Charles Miner Thompson (1931; repr., New York: Arno, 1974), p. 133. On French anti-ocularcentrism, the essential work is Martin Jay, *Downcast Eyes: The Denigration of Vision in Twentieth-Century French Thought* (Berkeley: University of California Press, 1993). On French criticism of America, see Jean-Phillipe Mathy, *Extrême Occident: French Intellectuals and America* (Chicago: University of Chicago Press, 1993).

5. Tocqueville, *Democracy in America,* 1: 343–44, 438–39.

6. Ibid., 373, 389–90.

7. Beaumont is writing of Maryland and the North, not the South, where slavery did produce racial proximity.

8. Tocqueville, *Democracy in America,* 1:373.

9. On the "pathogen" of black Americans, see Clarence Walker, *Deromanticizing Black History: Critical Essays and Reappraisals* (Knoxville: University of Tennessee Press, 1991), pp. 9–10, passim.

10. A good recent summary is Louis Menand, *The Metaphysical Club: A Story of Ideas in America* (New York: Farrar, Straus and Giroux, 2001), pp. 97–112. Tocqueville also discusses segregation in detail. See *Democracy in America,* 1:370–439.

Chapter 3

1. I am not claiming that legibility is the goal of *all* forms of popular culture, although I confess to skepticism about findings of brain-numbing complexity or "resistance" in works of mass entertainment. For a study that makes the case for "epistemological flexibility" in antebellum exhibitions, see James W. Cook, *The Art of Deception: Playing with Fraud in the Age of Barnum* (Cambridge, Mass: Harvard University Press, 2001).

2. Studies of the Western are legion. A good recent example is Lee Clark Mitchell, *Westerns: Making the Man in Fiction and Film* (Chicago: University of Chicago Press, 1996).

3. Quotations from the Oxford paperback edition of *The Pathfinder; or the Inland Sea* (Oxford: Oxford University Press, 1992); page numbers are given in the text.

4. D. H. Lawrence, *Studies in Classic American Literature* (1923; repr., New York: Viking, 1968), p. 55.

5. Quotations from the Signet Classic edition of *The Last of the Mohicans: A Narrative of 1757* (New York: Signet Classic, 1980); page numbers are given in the text.

6. Quotations from *The Deerslayer* (New York: Washington Square Press, 1961); page numbers in the text refer to this edition.

7. Twain's essay is reprinted in George Perkins, ed., *The Theory of the American Novel* (New York: Rinehart Editions, 1970), pp. 116–29; quotations on pp. 128, 119, 123–24.

8. Ibid., p. 121.

9. Not that Western novels did not continue to have a popular following, as shown by the success of Zane Grey and (in our own time) Louis L'Amour.

10. Doris Sommer, *Foundational Fictions: The National Romances of Latin America* (Berkeley: University of California Press, 1991), p. 59. Jane Tompkins similarly writes of Cooper's "obsessive preoccupation with systems of classification" in *Sensational Designs: The Cultural Work of American Fiction, 1790–1860* (New York: Oxford University Press, 1985), pp. 94–121; (quotation on p. 105).

11. Lawrence, *Studies*, p. 62.

12. Quotations from Poe's stories refer to *The Complete Tales and Poems of Edgar Allan Poe* (New York: Modern Library, 1938); page numbers are given in the text.

13. See David M. Henkin, *City Reading: Written Words and Public Spaces in Antebellum New York* (New York: Columbia University Press, 1998), p. 177.

14. The phrase an "allegory of psychoanalysis" is Shoshana Felman's, from her *Jacques Lacan and the Adventure of Insight: Psychoanalysis in Contemporary Culture* (Cambridge, Mass.: Harvard University Press, 1987), p. 11. On Dupin's method of analysis, the reader should consult the essays in Umberto Eco and Thomas A. Sebeok, eds., *The Sign of Three: Dupin, Holmes, Peirce* (Bloomington: Indiana University Press, 1983), esp. Nancy Harrowitz's "The Body of the Detective Model: Charles S. Peirce and Edgar Allan Poe," pp. 179–97.

15. I first heard this idea proposed by Takayuki Tatsumi, in a lecture on "Murders in the Rue Morgue" that he delivered in 1991 at the Sapporo Seminar in American Studies, now sadly defunct. The paper has since been published as "Literacy, Literality, Literature: The Rise of Cultural Aristocracy in 'The Murders in the Rue Morgue,'" *Journal of American and Canadian Studies* 12 (1994): 1–23. See also the relevant discussion of P. T. Barnum's man-monkey exhibit known as "What Is It?" in Cook, *The Arts of Deception*, pp. 118–62. This curiosity was presumed to be a cross between an African and an ape.

16. Thomas Jefferson, *Notes on the State of Virginia* (1784–85), in *Writings*, ed. Merrill D. Peterson (New York: Library of America, 1984), p. 265.

17. Page numbers refer to *The Psychopathology of Everyday Life*, trans. James Strachey (repr., New York: Norton, 1989).

18. For more on the fin de siècle perception of Jews, see the following works by Sander L. Gilman: *The Jew's Body* (New York: Routledge, 1991), and *The Case of Sigmund Freud: Medicine and Identity at the Fin de Siècle* (Baltimore, Md.: Johns Hopkins University Press, 1993).

19. Two valuable treatments of detective fiction and photography are Ronald R. Thomas, *Detective Fiction and the Rise of Forensic Science* (Cambridge: Cambridge University Press, 1999); and Tom Gunning, "Tracing the Individual Body: Photography, Detectives, and Early Cinema," in Leo Charney and Vanessa R. Schwartz, eds., *Cinema and the Invention of Modern Life* (Berkeley: University of California Press, 1995), pp. 15–45.

20. The quotation is from Bazin's essay "The Evolution of the Language of Cinema," in his *What Is Cinema?* trans. Hugh Gray (Berkeley: University of California Press, 1967), 1:27.

21. See Jacques Lacan, "Seminar on 'The Purloined Letter,'" trans. Jeffrey Mehlman, in John P. Muller and William J. Richardson, eds., *The Purloined Poe: Lacan, Derrida and Psychoanalytic Reading* (Baltimore, Md.: Johns Hopkins University Press, 1988), pp. 28–54.

22. Lacan's distortion of Freud's understanding of the unconscious as a cauldron of drives, not words, has been noted by Daniel Bougnoux, "Lacan, Sure— and Then What?" in Todd Dufresne, ed., *Returns of the "French Freud": Freud, Lacan, and Beyond* (New York: Routledge, 1997), pp. 91–106.

23. My discussion of Poe and Freud here has benefited from Shawn Rosenheim, "Detective Fiction, Psychoanalysis, and the Analytic Sublime," in Shawn Rosenheim and Stephen Rachman, eds., *The American Face of Edgar Allan Poe* (Baltimore, Md.: Johns Hopkins University Press, 1995), pp. 153–78.

24. On these matters, see Richard H. Brodhead, *Cultures of Letters: Scenes of Reading and Writing in Nineteenth-Century America* (Chicago: University of Chicago Press, 1993), pp. 48–68; and Lauren Berlant, "The Female Woman: Fanny Fern and the Form of Sentiment," *American Literary History* 3 (fall 1991): 429–54.

25. The quoted phrase is Fern's subtitle. Quotations are from *Ruth Hall and Other Writings*, ed. Joyce W. Warren (1855; repr., New Brunswick, N.J.: Rutgers University Press, 1986); page numbers are given in the text.

26. For a somewhat similar argument about the eighteenth-century English novel, see Nancy Armstrong, *Desire and Domestic Fiction: A Political History of the Novel* (New York: Oxford University Press, 1987).

Chapter 4

1. Scholarship on these historical changes is voluminous. Readers might consult, on the Puritans, John Demos, "Shame and Guilt in Early New England," in Carol Z. Stearns and Peter N. Stearns, eds., *Emotion and Social Change: Toward a New Psychohistory* (New York: Holmes and Maier, 1988), pp. 69–85; on the mid–nineteenth century, T. Walter Herbert, *Dearest Beloved: The Hawthornes and the Making of the Middle-Class Family* (Cambridge, Mass.: Harvard University Press, 1993); and on the fin de siècle, Robert H. Wiebe, *The Search for Order* (New York: Hill and Wang, 1967).

2. Quotations are from the Bedford Books edition of *The Scarlet Letter* (Boston, 1991); page numbers are given in the text.

3. See Richard R. John, *Spreading the News: The American Postal System from Franklin to Morse* (Cambridge, Mass.: Harvard University Press, 1995), pp. 31, 41.

4. I have contributed to what I now consider a misreading in my *American Romanticism and the Marketplace* (Chicago: University of Chicago Press, 1985), pp. 92–94.

5. For an excellent treatment of privacy in Hawthorne, with special reference to *The House of the Seven Gables*, see Milette Shamir, "Hawthorne's Romance and the Right to Privacy," *American Quarterly* 49 (December 1997): 746–79.

6. The secondary literature on Melville and *Moby-Dick* is immense. Works that have influenced my reading include, on epistemology, Richard H. Brodhead, *Hawthorne, Melville, and the Novel* (Chicago: University of Chicago Press, 1976), pp. 134–62; and Paul Brodtkorb Jr., *Ishmael's White World: A Phenomenological*

Reading of Moby-Dick (New Haven, Conn.: Yale University Press, 1965); and on the political theme, F. O. Matthiessen, *American Renaissance: Art and Expression in the Age of Emerson and Whitman* (New York: Oxford University Press, 1941), pp. 396–466; Alan Heimert, "*Moby-Dick* and American Political Symbolism," *American Quarterly* 15 (winter 1963): 498–534; Michael Paul Rogin, *Subversive Genealogy: The Politics and Art of Herman Melville* (New York: Knopf, 1983); and Donald E. Pease, *Visionary Compacts: American Renaissance Writings in Cultural Context* (Madison: University of Wisconsin Press, 1987), pp. 235–75. On writing in Melville's work, see Elizabeth Renker, *Strike through the Mask: Herman Melville and the Scene of Writing* (Baltimore, Md.: Johns Hopkins University Press, 1996).

7. Page numbers refer to Herman Melville, *Moby-Dick; or, The Whale*, ed. Charles Feidelson Jr. (1851; repr., New York: Macmillan, 1964).

8. "Address to the Young Men's Lyceum of Springfield," reprinted in Abraham Lincoln, *Selected Speeches, Messages, and Letters*, ed. T. Harry Williams (New York: Rinehart Editions, 1957), pp. 5–14; quotation on p. 6. Subsequent citations to the "Address," with page numbers, are from this edition.

9. Rogin, *Subversive Genealogy*, p. 222.

10. Edmund Wilson, *Patriotic Gore: Studies in the Literature of the Civil War* (New York: Oxford University Press, 1966), pp. 106–15.

11. Quotations are from *Walden* (1854; repr., Princeton, N.J.: Princeton University Press, 1973); subsequent page numbers are given in the text.

12. "Resistance to Civil Government" (Thoreau's original title for his 1849 essay) in *Reform Papers*, ed. Wendell Glick (Princeton, N.J.: Princeton University Press, 1973), p. 87.

13. But see the reading by Walter Benn Michaels, "*Walden*'s False Bottoms," *Glyph* 1 (1977): 132–49. The reader should also consult Sharon Cameron, *Writing Nature: Henry Thoreau's Journal* (Chicago: University of Chicago Press, 1985); Lawrence Buell, *The Environmental Imagination: Thoreau, Nature Writing, and the Formation of American Culture* (Cambridge, Mass.: Harvard University Press, 1995); and Milette Shamir, "The Cult of Privacy: Domestic Space and Gender in Antebellum Fiction" (Ph.D. diss., Brandeis University, 1996), pp. 127–93.

14. On Thoreau's revisions, see J. Lyndon Shanley, *The Making of Walden; with the Text of the First Version* (Chicago: University of Chicago Press, 1957).

15. Alexis de Tocqueville, *Democracy in America*, ed. Phillips Bradley (New York: Vintage, 1945), 2: 104.

16. Cameron, *Writing Nature*, p. 13; see also Leo Stoller, *After Walden: Thoreau's Changing Views on Economic Man* (Stanford, Calif.: Stanford University Press, 1957).

17. Henry James, *The American* (repr., New York: Penguin Classics, 1986); subsequent page numbers are given in the text.

18. I trust it will be evident that the France of *The American* is a fictional construct and not an accurate picture of French society, which of course has its own strain of legibility and rationalism.

19. The argument has been made by Kenneth W. Warren in *Black and White Strangers: Race and American Literary Realism* (Chicago: University of Chicago Press, 1993), pp. 18–47. Warren's position has been disputed by Gert Buelens, "Possessing the American Scene: Race and Vulgarity, Seduction and Judgment," in Gert Buelens, ed., *Enacting History in Henry James: Narrative, Power, and Ethics* (New York: Cambridge University Press, 1997), pp. 166–92; and Ross

Posnock, *Color and Culture: Black Writers and the Making of the Modern Intellectual* (Cambridge, Mass.: Harvard University Press, 1998), pp. 228–30. On *The American*, see also John Carlos Rowe, "The Politics of Innocence in Henry James's *The American*," in Martha Banta, ed., *New Essays on "The American"* (New York: Cambridge University Press, 1987), pp. 69–97; Rowe, *The Other Henry James* (Durham, N.C.: Duke University Press, 1998), pp. 56–74; Richard Poirier, *The Comic Sense of Henry James: A Study of the Early Novels* (New York: Oxford University Press, 1967), pp. 44–94; Edwin Sill Fussell, *The Catholic Side of Henry James* (New York: Cambridge University Press, 1993), pp. 80–86; and Mark Seltzer, *Bodies and Machines* (New York: Routledge, 1992), pp. 49–59, 63–83.

20. Poirier, *The Comic Sense of Henry James*, p. 84.

21. The scene is interestingly discussed by Seltzer in *Bodies and Machines*, pp. 66–69.

22. Henry James, *The American Scene* (repr., Bloomington: Indiana University Press, 1968), p. 419.

23. Louis Menand, *The Metaphysical Club: A Story of Ideas in America* (New York: Farrar, Straus and Giroux, 2001), p. 146.

24. "Preface" to *The American*, vol. 2 of the *New York Edition of the Novels and Tales of Henry James* (New York: Scribner's, 1907), p. xx.

Chapter 5

1. The phrase is from Robert H. Wiebe's *The Search for Order: 1877–1920* (New York: Hill and Wang, 1967), p. 81.

2. Samuel Warren and Louis D. Brandeis, "The Right to Privacy," *Harvard Law Review* 4 (December 1890): 193–220; quotations on pp. 196, 211.

3. Vachel Lindsay, *The Art of the Moving Picture*, rev. ed. (1922; repr., New York: Modern Library, 2000), p. 124.

4. Ibid., pp. 47–48; Richard Wright, "Psychiatry Comes to Harlem," *Free World* 12 (September 1946): 49–51. On the psychoanalytic tendency to equate black people with the unconscious, see Joel Pfister, "On Conceptualizing the Cultural History of Emotional and Psychological Life in America," in Joel Pfister and Nancy Schnog, eds., *Inventing the Psychological: Toward a Cultural History of Emotional Life in America* (New Haven, Conn.: Yale University Press, 1997), pp. 17–59; and Pfister, *Staging Depth: Eugene O'Neill and the Politics of Psychological Discourse* (Chapel Hill: University of North Carolina Press, 1995).

5. On Freud's dislike of the United States, see Peter Gay, *Freud: A Life for Our Time* (New York: Norton, 1988), p. 56. Stephen Heath notes Freud's suspicion of the moving pictures in "Cinema and Psychoanalysis," in Janet Bergstrom, ed., *Endless Night: Cinema and Psychoanalysis, Parallel Histories* (Berkeley: University of California Press, 1999), pp. 25–56.

6. Quoted in Martin Jay, *The Dialectical Imagination: A History of the Frankfurt School and the Institute of Social Research, 1923–1950* (Boston: Little, Brown, 1973), p. 173.

7. Partisans of this point of view are legion. A good example is Mitchell Stephens, *The Rise of the Image and the Fall of the Word* (New York: Oxford University Press, 1998).

8. The best treatments of image/text heterogeneity are by W. J. T. Mitchell; see his *Iconology: Image, Text, Ideology* (Chicago: University of Chicago Press, 1986)

and *Picture Theory: Essays on Verbal and Visual Representation* (Chicago: University of Chicago Press, 1994).

9. Ernest Jones, *Years of Maturity 1901–1919* (New York: Basic Books, 1953), p. 57. This is the second of Jones's three-volume *The Life and Work of Sigmund Freud.*

10. Hugo Munsterberg, *Psychotherapy* (London: T. Fisher Unwin, 1909), p. 125. For information on Munsterberg, I have consulted Matthew Hale Jr., *Human Science and Social Order: Hugo Munsterberg and the Origins of Applied Psychology* (Philadephia, Pa: Temple University Press, 1980), and Phyllis Keller, *States of Belonging: German-American Intellectuals and the First World War* (Cambridge, Mass.: Harvard University Press, 1979), esp. pp. 5–118. An excellent discussion of Munsterberg on the movies, which I discovered after drafting my own treatment, appears in Friedrich A. Kittler, *Gramaphone, Film, Typewriter*, trans. Geoffrey Winthrop-Young and Michael Wutz (Stanford, Calif.: Stanford University Press, 1999), pp. 160–72.

11. See, for an example, his study titled *The Americans*, trans. Edwin B. Holt (New York: McClure, Phillips, 1904).

12. Lindsay, *Art of the Moving Picture*, p. 133.

13. Hugo Munsterberg, *The Photoplay: A Psychological Study* (New York: D. Appleton, 1916), p. 183; subsequent page numbers are given in the text.

14. Hans Blumenberg, *The Legitimacy of the Modern Age*, trans. Robert M. Wallace (Cambridge, Mass.: MIT Press, 1983), p. 364. "Knowledge drive" is Ludwig Feuerbach's phrase.

15. In Walter Benjamin, *Illuminations*, trans. Harry Zohn, with an introduction by Hannah Arendt (New York: Schocken Books, 1969), p. 233.

16. Siegfried Kracauer, *Theory of Film: The Redemption of Physical Reality* (1960; repr., Princeton, N.J.: Princeton University Press, 1997), p. 299, for the quotation; pp. 50–52, on science and cinema.

17. For examples of these positions, see Jean-Louis Baudry, "The Apparatus: Metapsychological Approaches to the Impression of Reality in Cinema" (1975), in Gerald Mast, Marshall Cohen, and Leo Braudy, eds., *Film Theory and Criticism: Introductory Readings*, 4th ed. (New York: Oxford University Press, 1992), pp. 690–707; and Christian Metz, *The Imaginary Signifier: Psychoanalysis and the Cinema*, trans. Celia Britton et al. (Bloomington: Indiana University Press, 1982).

18. From "A Course of Treatment" (1932), in Sergei Eisenstein, *Film Form: Essays in Film Theory*, trans. Jay Leyda (San Diego: Harcourt Brace, 1949), pp. 103, 105. Also see Béla Balázs, *Theory of the Film: Character and Growth of a New Art*, trans. Edith Bone (New York: Roy Publishers, 1953), esp. pp. 118–38.

19. Quoted in Bert Cardullo, Harry Geduld, Ronald Gottesman, and Leigh Woods, eds., *Playing to the Camera: Film Actors Discuss Their Craft* (New Haven, Conn.: Yale University Press, 1998), p. 196. On the theatrical origins of filmic restraint, see Michael R. Booth, *Theatre in the Victorian Age* (Cambridge: Cambridge University Press, 1991), and Randall Knoper, *Acting Naturally: Mark Twain and the Culture of Performance* (Berkeley: University of California Press, 1995), pp. 55–95.

20. Quoted in *Playing to the Camera*, p. 307. I have previously discussed some of these issues in *Differences in the Dark: American Movies and English Theater* (New York: Columbia University Press, 1998), pp. 62–64.

21. Lindsay, *Art of the Moving Picture*, pp. III–12, 139.

22. Ibid., pp. 166–67.

23. The quotations are in Eric Caplan, *Mind Games: American Culture and the Birth of Psychotherapy* (Berkeley: University of California Press, 1998), p. 122; see pp. 117–48 on the Emmanuel Movement's importance.

24. The first quotation appears in Nathan G. Hale Jr., *Freud and the Americans: The Beginnings of Psychoanalysis in the United States, 1876–1917* (New York: Oxford University Press, 1971), p. 226. The second comes from *Five Lectures*, trans. James Strachey (1909; repr., New York: Norton, 1961), p. 56. Another passage "in the American grain" comes from the fourth lecture. Freud sets the tone for his New World dissemination by casting himself as a facilitator of sexual apocalypse:

> People are in general not candid over sexual matters. They do not show their sexuality freely, but to conceal it they wear a heavy overcoat woven of a tissue of lies, as though the weather were bad in the world of sexuality. Nor are they mistaken. It is a fact that sun and wind are not favorable to sexual activity in this civilized world of ours; none of us can reveal his eroticism freely to others. But when your patients discover that they can feel quite easy about it while they are under your treatment, they discard this veil of lies, and only then are you in a position to form a judgment on this debatable question. (*Five Lectures*, p. 43)

It will be noticed that though the emphasis here is on revelation, the act of disclosure occurs within the security of the physician's chambers.

25. *Five Lectures*, pp. 39–41.

26. "Recommendations to Physicians Practising Psycho-Analysis" (1912), in *The Standard Edition of the Complete Psychological Works of Sigmund Freud*, trans. James Strachey (London: Hogarth Press, 1958), 12:115.

27. Sigmund Freud, *The Interpretation of Dreams*, trans. James Strachey (1899; repr., New York: Avon, 1965), p. 574. Freud's accent on the visual declined over time, and in later pieces, most famously in the "Note on the Mystic Writing Pad" (1925), linguistic metaphors more or less supplanted optical ones as the signifiers of the psychic mechanism. The shift to a trope of writing has been noted by Jacques Derrida, among others (see "Freud and the Scene of Writing," in his *Writing and Difference*, trans. Alan Bass [Chicago: University of Chicago Press, 1978], pp. 196–231).

28. "On Beginning the Treatment" (1913), in *Standard Works*, 12:138.

29. Ibid., p. 134.

30. Walter Benjamin, "The Work of Art in the Age of Mechanical Production," in *Illuminations*, p. 235.

31. *The Selected Writings of Ralph Waldo Emerson*, ed. Brooks Atkinson (New York: Modern Library, 1950), p. 49.

32. Ibid., pp. 72, 48.

33. Paula Morantz Cohen proposes an argument like this one in her *Silent Film and the Triumph of the American Myth* (New York: Oxford University Press, 2001).

34. *Five Lectures*, p. 12.

35. Frank Norris, "The Mechanics of Fiction," in *The Responsibilities of the Novelist* (1903; repr., New York: Hill and Wang, 1967), p. 254.

36. For relevant readings of Norris's novel, see Walter Benn Michaels, *The Gold Standard and the Logic of Naturalism: American Fiction at the Turn of the Century* (Berkeley: University of California Press, 1987), pp. 137–80; and Mark Seltzer,

Bodies and Machines (New York: Routledge, 1992), pp. 25–44. On desire and Freudianism, see Lawrence Birken, *Consuming Desire: Sexual Science and the Emergence of a Culture of Abundance, 1817–1914* (Ithaca, N.Y.: Cornell University Press, 1988). On the historical background, a good study is Nell Irvin Painter, *Standing at Armageddon: The United States, 1877–1919* (New York: Norton, 1987).

37. Quotation from the Signet Classic reprint of *McTeague* (New York: New American Library, 1981), p. 37; subsequent page numbers are given in the text.

Chapter 6

1. See the excellent study by William Michael Morgan, "Public Engagements: Humanitarianism and Complicity in U.S. Literary Realism" (Ph.D. diss., Brandeis University, 2000), pp. 162–208. Morgan's manuscript, from which I have learned a great deal about Wharton's novel, is to be published by the University Press of New England. Wharton's scorn for Wilson is an undercurrent in Alan Price, *The End of the Age of Innocence: Edith Wharton and the First World War* (New York: St. Martin's, 1996).

2. Woodrow Wilson, *The New Freedom* (Garden City, N.Y.: Doubleday, Page, 1913), p. 132.

3. Wilson, the onetime paladin of transparency, favored adding a censorship clause to the Espionage Act. For more on these matters, see Daniel Patrick Moynihan, *Secrecy: The American Experience* (New Haven, Conn.: Yale University Press, 1998), pp. 81–115.

4. Edith Wharton, *Summer* (repr., New York: Bantam Books, 1993), p. 20; subsequent page numbers are given in the text.

5. See Susman's essay "'Personality' and the Making of Twentieth-Century Culture," in John H. Higham and Paul K. Conkin, eds., *New Directions in American Intellectual History* (Baltimore, Md.: Johns Hopkins University Press, 1979), pp. 212–26. *A Backward Glance* (1934) is the title of Wharton's autobiography.

6. Edith Wharton and Ogden Codman Jr., *The Decoration of Houses* (1897; repr., New York: Norton, 1978), p. 198.

7. Wharton and Freud did agree about Woodrow Wilson; they both despised him. See the remarkably vituperative psychobiography Freud collaborated on with William C. Bullitt, *Thomas Woodrow Wilson, Twenty-eighth President of the United States: A Psychological Study* (Boston: Houghton Mifflin, 1967).

8. F. Scott Fitzgerald, *The Great Gatsby* (1925; repr., New York: Scribner's, 1961). Subsequent page numbers are given in the text.

9. I emphatically do not mean as an "inverted Western," which is what Richard Lehan calls the novel in *"The Great Gatsby": The Limits of Wonder* (Boston: Twayne, 1990), p. 46.

10. The clearest case of spillage is the photographer Mr. McKee, who lives in the same building on 158th Street where Tom installs his mistress, Myrtle Wilson. McKee's photographs, like his dreams of success, are blurred and banal in comparison to Gatsby's grander (and more cinematic) ambitions. On photographic images in the novel, see Lawrence Jay Dessner, "Photography and *The Great Gatsby*" (1979), in Scott Donaldson, ed., *Critical Essays on F. Scott Fitzgerald's "The Great Gatsby"* (Boston: G. K. Hall, 1984), pp. 175–86. Philip Fisher is suggestive on the cinematic in Fitzgerald in his *Still the New World: American Literature in a Culture of Creative Destruction* (Cambridge, Mass: Harvard University. Press, 1999), pp. 265–67.

11. Fitzgerald's exact phrase was a "novel of selected incidents." Quoted in Thomas A. Pendleton, *I'm Sorry about the Clock: Chronology, Composition, and Narrative Technique in "The Great Gatsby"* (Selinsgrove, Pa.: Susquehanna University Press, 1993), p. 17.

12. Besides Pendleton, see R. W. Stallman, "*Gatsby* and the Hole in Time" (1955), in Harold Bloom, ed., *Gatsby* (New York: Chelsea House, 1991), pp. 55–63.

13. A point emphasized by Walter Benn Michaels in *Our America: Nativism, Modernism, and Pluralism* (Durham, N.C.: Duke University Press, 1995), pp. 23–28.

14. The reviews are quoted in Lehan, *The Great Gatsby*, pp. 16–17.

15. Pendleton cites Fitzgerald's letter in *I'm Sorry about the Clock*, p. 17.

16. Ernest Hemingway, *The Sun Also Rises* (1926; repr., New York: Scribner's, n.d.), p. 4; subsequent page references are given in the text.

17. On modernism and masculinity (as a rebellion against the Victorian "matriarch"), see Ann Douglas, *Terrible Honesty: Mongrel Manhattan in the 1920s* (New York: Farrar, Straus and Giroux, 1995). Valuable observations about Hemingway are scattered throughout Douglas's book. Other studies to which my own reading is indebted include Stanley Corkin, *Realism and the Birth of the Modern United States: Cinema, Literature, and Culture* (Athens: University of Georgia Press, 1996), pp. 161–91; the pieces collected in Linda Wagner-Martin, ed., *New Essays on "The Sun Also Rises"* (New York: Cambridge University Press, 1985); Eugene Kanjo, "Hemingway's Cinematic Style," in Charles M. Oliver, ed., *A Moving Picture Feast: The Filmgoer's Hemingway* (New York: Praeger, 1989), pp. 3–11; and two still impressive classics of Hemingway criticism, Mark Spilka, "The Death of Love in *The Sun Also Rises*," in Robert P. Weeks, ed., *Hemingway: A Collection of Critical Essays* (Englewood Cliffs, N.J.: Prentice-Hall, 1962), pp. 127–38; and Philip Young, *Ernest Hemingway: A Reconsideration* (University Park: Pennsylvania State University Press, 1966).

18. For a sympathetic discussion of Hemingway's Catholicism, see H. R. Stoneback, "In the Nominal Country of the Bogus: Hemingway's Catholicism and the Biographies," in Frank Scafella, ed., *Hemingway: Essays of Reassessment* (New York: Oxford University Press, 1991), pp. 105–40.

19. Young, *Ernest Hemingway: A Reconsideration*, esp. pp. 165–67; Young's reading has been widely challenged. For an example, see Robert D. Young, "Hemingway's Suicide in His Works," *Hemingway Review* 4 (spring 1985): 24–30.

20. A "nigger drummer" at a Paris club has the right idea. He sings and shouts, grinning at Brett, and Hemingway transcribes his words as an inaudible ellipsis: "'. . . . . .' the drummer sang softly" (p. 64).

Chapter 7

1. Frederick Douglass, *Narrative of the Life of Frederick Douglass, an American Slave* (1845; repr., New York: Penguin, 1986), p. 144; subsequent page numbers are given in the text. Relevant readings of the *Narrative* include William L. Andrews, *To Tell a Free Story: The First Century of Afro-American Autobiography, 1760–1865* (Urbana: University of Illinois Press, 1986), pp. 123–38; Houston A. Baker Jr., *Blues, Ideology, and Afro-American Literature: A Vernacular Theory* (Chicago: University of Chicago Press, 1984), pp. 39–55; John Burt, "Learning to Write: The Narrative of Frederick Douglass," *Western Humanities Review* 42 (winter 1988): 330–44; and Henry Louis Gates Jr., *Figures in Black: Words, Signs, and the "Racial"*

Self (New York: Oxford University Press, 1987), pp. 80–124. A perspective comparable to Douglass's from the early twentieth century is W. E. B. Du Bois's description of black American life as transpiring "behind the Veil" (in *The Souls of Black Folk* [1903]).

2. On Douglass's change of mind about the Constitution, see William S. McFeely, *Frederick Douglass* (New York: Norton, 1991), pp. 168–69, 204–7.

3. Mark Twain, *The Tragedy of Pudd'nhead Wilson* (1894; repr., New York: Signet Classic, 1964), p. 165; subsequent page numbers are given in the text. Two treatments of Twain's novel that I have found especially useful are Susan Gillman, *Dark Twins: Imposture and Identity in Mark Twain's America* (Chicago: University of Chicago Press, 1989), pp. 53–95; and Ronald R. Thomas, *Detective Fiction and the Rise of Forensic Science* (Cambridge: Cambridge University Press, 1999), pp. 240–56.

4. On this topic generally, see Matthew Frye Jacobson, *Whiteness of a Different Color: European Immigrants and the Alchemy of Race* (Cambridge, Mass.: Harvard University Press, 1998).

5. For a pertinent study on white-black relations, see Eric Lott, *Love and Theft: Blackface Minstrelsy and the American Working Class* (New York: Oxford University Press, 1993).

6. Sigmund Freud, "The Unconscious," in *On Metapsychology: The Theory of Psychoanalysis*, vol. 11 of *The Penguin Freud Library*, trans. James Strachey (London: Penguin, 1984), p. 195.

7. Ralph Ellison, *Invisible Man* (1952; repr., New York: Vintage, 1995), p. 3; subsequent page numbers are given in the text. Among the many excellent studies of Ellison's novel, see Baker, *Blues, Ideology, and Afro-American Literature*, pp. 172–99; Caffilene Allen, "The World as Possibility: The Significance of Freud's *Totem and Taboo* in Ellison's *Invisible Man*," *Literature and Psychology* 41 (1995): 1–18; and James F. Callahan, "Frequencies of Eloquence: The Performance and Composition of *Invisible Man*," in Robert O'Meally, ed., *New Essays on "Invisible Man"* (New York: Cambridge University Press, 1988), pp. 55–94.

8. A good short overview of this subject is Mary Dudziak, "Desegregation as a Cold War Imperative," in Richard Delgado, ed., *Critical Race Theory: The Cutting Edge* (Philadelphia, Pa.: Temple University Press, 1995), pp. 110–21.

9. A perceptive discussion of this episode, relevant to my own reading, is in Alan Nadel, *Invisible Criticism: Ralph Ellison and the American Canon* (Iowa City: University of Iowa Press, 1988), pp. 105–15.

10. Most critics interpret the epilogue's "principle" as an unambiguous reference to the Constitution. For an example, see Julia Eichelberger, *Prophets of Recognition: Ideology and the Individual in Novels by Ralph Ellison, Toni Morrison, Saul Bellow, and Eudora Welty* (Baton Rouge: Louisiana State University Press, 1999), pp. 39, 53.

11. Frantz Fanon, *Black Skin, White Masks*, trans. Charles Lam Markmann (New York: Grove, 1967), pp. 182, 192, 194.

12. Ibid., pp. 111–12.

13. Ibid., p. 116.

14. But see p. 221, where Fanon distinguishes between the Negro in France and the American Negro, to the advantage of the latter. "In the United States," he writes, "the Negro battles and is battled. There are laws that, little by little, are invalidated under the Constitution."

15. Ibid., pp. 181–3, 115, 157–60.

16. Philip Roth, *The Human Stain* (Boston: Houghton Mifflin, 2000), p. 37; subsequent page numbers are given in the text. A fine reading of Roth's novel is Ross Posnock, "Purity and Danger: On Philip Roth," *Raritan* 21 (fall 2001): 85–101.

17. Philip Roth, *The Facts: A Novelist's Autobiography* (New York: Vintage, 1997), pp. 184, 164. In *The Human Stain*, Zuckerman offers a similar reflection: "Writing personally is exposing and concealing at the same time" (p. 345).

18. See C. Vann Woodward, *Tom Watson: Agrarian Rebel* (New York: Oxford University Press, 1938); and Alexander Keyssar, *The Right to Vote: The Contested History of Democracy in the United States* (New York: Basic Books, 2000), p. 107.

19. Harriet Beecher Stowe, *Uncle Tom's Cabin* (1852; repr., New York: Bantam, 1981), pp. 227–29; Subsequent page numbers are given in the text.

20. On the entanglement of slavery with capitalism, with reference to Stowe's novel, see Walter Benn Michaels, *The Gold Standard and the Logic of Naturalism: American Literature at the Turn of the Century* (Berkeley: University of California Press, 1987), pp. 101–5.

21. The exception might be Tom Loker, who renounces slave catching after a bout of illness among the Quakers. But Loker undergoes a spiritualizing fever that transmutes him from brute to "weary child" (p. 200).

Equivocal Epilogue

1. George Orwell, *1984* (1949; repr., New York: Plume/Harcourt Brace, 1961), p. 122; subsequent page numbers are given in the text.

2. Henry James, *The American Scene* (1907; repr., Bloomington: Indiana University Press, 1968), p. 167.

3. See David Burnham, *The Rise of the Computer State* (New York: Random House, 1983), for an alarmist account.

4. B. F. Skinner, *Walden Two* (1948; repr., Englewood Cliffs, N.J.: Prentice-Hall, 1976), p. 93; subsequent page numbers are given in the text.

5. See Daniel W. Bjork, *B. F. Skinner: A Life* (New York: Basic Books, 1993), p. 152.

6. Henry David Thoreau, *Walden* (Princeton, N.J.: Princeton University Press, 1973), p. 325.

INDEX

abolition, 50
acting techniques, 117
African-Americans. *See* blacks
American, The (James), 79–80,
    100–107, 136
American Scene, The (James), 106
"American Scholar, The" (Emerson),
    121
Anthony, Susan B., 41
anti-Federalism, 46–47
anti-Semitism, 69, 112
apes, 67–68, 69
Arbella (ship), 5, 8, 19
architecture, 28–29
Argentina, 17
aristocracy, 19–20, 41, 52–57, 100–105
Aristotle, 41
Army Engineers (U.S.), 38
art, 104–5
artistic sincerity, 29
Art of the Moving Picture, The
    (Lindsay), 109, 118
ascriptive rank, 33
Austria, 16

Back Bay (Boston), 27
Back to the Future (movie), 122
Bacon, Francis, 10
Balmer, Randall, 11

"Bartleby, the Scrivener: A Story of
    Wall Street" (Melville), 182
Baudry, Jean-Louis, 53, 116
Bazin, André, 70
Beaumont, Gustave de, 52, 54–57, 80,
    100, 179
Beecher, Lyman, 180
"Benito Cereno" (Melville), 182
Benjamin, Walter, 115, 120
Bentham, Jeremy, 25
Bible, 8, 39, 50, 121
Binet, Alfred, 40
Birth of a Nation, The (movie), 109
blacks, 32, 112
    Beaumont on, 54–56
    in *Birth of a Nation,* 109
    in Europe, 173
    and intelligence tests, 40
    and July Fourth, 43
    slavery, 41, 43, 54, 68, 106, 160–63,
        172, 179, 182
    as subhuman, 68, 69
    and suburbia, 31
    texts by or about, 159–82
    Tocqueville on, 53–55
    Wright on, 110
Black Skin, White Masks (Fanon), 173
Blithedale Romance, The (Hawthorne),
    80